Mick was a huge influence – D

From beginning to end it's me, me, me, ——— —.— ——
narcissistic – Stephen Fry

I was going to give him a game but he wouldn't take his make-
up off – Allan Clarke

He's not one of mine – God

One found it enthralling – The Queen

I wouldn't have allowed that man in my party – Nelson
Mandela

Christ, son of God, or important prophet? After reading this
I'm no longer sure – The Pope

This lad knows nothing about dealing with green fly – Percy
Thrower

Jees, what y'thinking about? Just buy it; it's not a house or a
boat or anything. You'll get change from a tenner – Mad Mick
McCann from the banks of Bann

Coming out as a Bowie fan in Leeds, Yorkshire, England

Mick McCann

The memoirs of a Punk Romantic

First published by Armley Press 2006

Copy Editor: John Lake

Layout and Research: Ian Dobson

Cover Design: John Wheelhouse & Mick McCann

Proofreaders: Alan Dawson and Sarah Howells and thanks to Sarah
for encouraging me to focus and write the book.

For 28 years of sterling service, the grand order of the 'one-man
emotional and intellectual support network' hair-band of merit goes to
Dosher.

The conversation with John on the day of the Zorro and Co.,
wet/dry/wet/dry shirt fiasco is dedicated to Fermin – I wish I had been
your friend.

Contact: <armleypress@hotmail.co.uk>
<apunkromantic@hotmail.co.uk>

Armley Press, Hollywell House, Hollywell Lane,
Armley, Leeds, LS12 3HP

Dedicated to all I love and all I have loved,
especially my dead dad.

(Thanks to my children for carrying on a remarkable genetic line.)

My best friend, No.1 Soul Mate and love of my life,
Thanks Vic the Wonder Kid

Who are you and who am I?
Who have you been and who will you be?
Yesterday and tomorrow are different,
And so were you and so will you be.
Anon
(Trad. Irish folk song, C17)

Funded by The Pat Lindley Foundation For Friend Empowerment

1

'Right hand down, RIGHT HAND DOWN.' My brother shrieks, then looks at me and raises his eyes as if there is no danger. I am not stupid, I am looking from the 100-foot drop (or is it a 1000? Don't know, no idea) to the wheels of the ambulance. I can see that they are not fully attached to terra firma. Small stones bounce down the gorge, gaining pace and highlighting the threat, as the edge of tyres hover in space and the driver wipes sweat from his eye. One slip, one moment of misjudgement, loose ground or madness and we are dead, no question about it. I'd said it was a bad idea, but the older ones were carried away with the romance of it all. Even though the film has not been released yet, they have been possessed by the spirit of Indiana Jones.

This place is dangerous – not just this immediate place, this country. The British consulate had said it was safe, I'm sure they are wrong. You can smell the tension in the air, every town or village we pass through has political slogans writ large on walls. Not like British posturing but slogans that signal intent to pull out a machine gun and waste anyone who deviates from the sentiment by even the finest nuance. I don't care about the politics of the place – I am not even slightly interested, I like picking out the swear words scattered amongst the words on the walls but that's where my attention ends. The others have been discussing who are the Communists and who are the Fascists but I just turned up the hi-fi and daydreamed. Who gives a fuck?

People are not friendly, they stare angrily at the black ambulance with semi-naked women painted on the side, pumping out loud, alien music from an over powerful tape machine that had been installed for maximum-volume, surround sound. It is so hot that the sides are constantly down, making the vehicle more of an open van with a roof, a sound system on wheels in which I recline like Julius Caesar on the way to a crucifixion. I am so hot that young girls swoon as it passes, a vision of erotic godliness, just enough of this earth to make sex the vaguest of possibilities. Too gorgeous for their heads to contain as they fall to the ground flicking away small pebbles with tips of hair.

Strangely, as soon as adults find out we are British their disposition takes a huge shift, offering us bread, water and occasional daughters (or sons) to be deflowered. Must be something political; I don't care, my country's history is nothing to do with me. I do like friendly people.

It's the third day in the mountains and we are miles from anywhere now, the last village was about half an hour back and only had three and a half houses. We appear to have got through the most dangerous part of the dirt track and are speeding along at at least ten miles an hour. I made a mental note of where the road became wider than the ambulance and on the return journey that is where I will get out and walk, it's not like I can drive anyway, and I'm not going to die with the driver. It was their call, tossers.

Around a corner and 'Wow, I knew we should have come here', it's amazing. Snuggled at the base of mountains and hills is a large and beautiful lake, all shades of blue. We've been through some fairly remote places but this really is wilderness, not even the locals come here. Nobody comes here. Wildlife jumps and scats at the low-gear growl of the ambulance. I'm dying for a shit, there is supposed to be a toilet here and as it's a couple of days since I shat indoors, I am holding out for the cool touch of wood or porcelain. There it is, 'Kenny, can you pull up by't bog? I need a crap.'

I push open the wooden door, fist full of bog roll, the rusty hinges pop fragments and grind. Dropping onto the seat, pulling down my shorts and kicking the door shut in one movement, 'Look at that. WHAT THE FUCK?' I marvel at the irony of it, at last a statement I can understand, that means something, scrawled large in black marker pen the legend:

The Squinting Cat Pub, Leeds, Yorkshire, England.

I laugh out loud, I have been surrounded by the slogans of people who recently rose up against 50 years of brutal fascism, suffered huge poverty with all the associated suffering. Bollocks, I've learnt information from hearing the older kids talk, must try to clear it from my brain. The locals paint their ideology and hopes on the wall. People from my village respond by baring their soul via the name and address of the local pub. That is who they are, their entire identity, or at least the crucial element, is patronage to a particular drinking den. These are my people, I may even know someone who knows the person who shared this philosophical gem, though I won't know the person, not unless it's a dad of a mate. People from The Squinting Cat Pub are not known for their adventuring; how on earth did one make it here? Probably on the run.

Fuck, I just can't get away from the rednecks, they're stalking me, the bastards. I'm safe anyway, I haven't brought my make-up with

8

me, I forgot it, along with everything else I need. I'll tell you what, though, I've got every Bowie album ever made on tape, that's all I need, everything else is just bollocks. Who needs swimming trunks, a towel, soap or a toothbrush anyway?

Sorry, let me introduce myself, my name's Mick. I was born 18 years after the end of the 2nd World War, five years before the first man on the moon or 172 years after the birth of Michael Faraday, as I prefer to think of it.

So when did my catharsis begin? When did I metamorphose and make the first dangerous step outside the house in full make-up and silver, spiky hair? It was in Leeds, Yorkshire, England sometime during 1977/78. But when did my catharsis begin? I suppose it was in the womb. I don't really subscribe to the sudden, social change theory. The Pistols and The Damned didn't come out of a vacuum in '76/'77, *The Stooges* by The Stooges came out in '69 and, in my world, is the first Punk album and Johnny Rotten knew that. My coming out probably seemed abrupt, but it developed over time, all things came to bear.

Grandmother's experience of being a sudden, homeless, single mother of three in the unforgiving '40s. My mother riding to school, through the snow on a huge white Shire horse seems romantic but it will have affected her, and subsequently me, differently to my kids riding to school in a fifteen-year-old Mini Metro with a heater and a tape player that sometimes work. I'm scarring my children in a twenty-first-century kind of way, the shame of the eleven year old if he's seen by his mates. When they spot us, they sing 'Chitty-Chitty Bang Bang', loudly; I'm a bad father who had a good mother.

I hate to think of the reaction my mum and grandma must have got in the '40s. Gran went to her brother for help. He loaned her money to get a house and charged the same interest that a bank would have, had they loaned money to penniless, homeless women with three kids and no job, which they didn't. It mattered not what kind of income a woman had, they were not responsible or intelligent enough to have something as complex as a mortgage. It was a man's world back then as my grandfather, who I never met, proved.

'Michael, Michael it's your song, you love this one, listen.'
We all live in a yellow submarine, a yellow submarine, a yellow submarine

9

We all live in a yellow submarine, a yellow submarine, a yellow submarine.
Yes, I liked it but even then, aged four, I wanted more: it was a nursery rhyme that I sang loud but it left a space. This wasn't my music.

When I was a little older I was given a box record player to mess about with. It was light blue and cream, covered in some sort of mock-leatherette, matt, veined, vinyl material. A solid box with a speaker in the lid, a volume and treble control. This state-of-the-art machine was made by Fidelity or maybe PYE. It was loud. It was brilliant. There was a metal pole, bang in the middle of the turntable. You lined the hole in the record up with the pole and, dropped the record, which, in turn, tumbled onto the turntable. On the side of the turntable hovered an L-shaped arm which had only one function. You put the arm across, the record played once. You left the arm off, it played for ever. There was a small break in between each play for the arm with the stylus on to return home and then journey back to the beginning of the song. Once back over the top of the record it would clunk down and start the exciting, slightly undulating, pre-song hiss.

It was this deck that powered the first song that I controlled. The song that stirred my early childhood rebellion was 'Dynamite' by Cliff Richard. I played it over and over again. I don't know how old I was but if I left the L-shaped arm off, it repeated. It may have lasted a week, maybe a year, time moves differently when you're little. How embarrassing is that? The man who makes Andrew Lloyd Webber look like an anarchist began by chance my rock and roll rebellion.

Probably as a consequence of endless, single-track Cliff Richard one of my older siblings introduced a feature which blew my mind. Stacking singles. Not only could this box of tricks play a record for ever without you needing to move *and* allow you to alter the treble but its crowning glory: it was a record stacking monster. I could line up lots of singles, all at the same time.

The technological wizardry of the box meant that by using the arm, that previously only had one function, you could place multiple singles on the pole, hovering over the deck. I was a six-year-old teenager, I could multi-stack. They would play one after another, forming a pile of singles on the deck. If the stack of records on the turntable got too high the stylus would rise and fall like the big dipper, making the songs jump, and a three minute record would last 30 seconds. Alternatively, the pile of singles would make the song speed up as the needle went down the warp and slow down as it climbed the other side. There was a completely ridiculous, small lever: switch it to 33 RPM and it made the records crap. Other than the 'make records crap' feature, this little box was a design masterpiece.

I later discovered a single that 'the make records crap' feature couldn't ruin. By this time I understood that 'the make records crap' feature was dual-function. When combined with the small records it was a design disaster but when used in conjunction with big records it had a second function. The second function was marvellous, a 'stop big records from sounding like Pinky and Perky' function. How cool was that? Mindst you, I still thought the first function was a design mistake, other than for one record. The 33 switch with 'A Thin Line Between Love and Hate' by The Pretenders is a maudlin sensation. A glorious, slow song anyway but slow it down further and it makes Leonard Cohen sound like a happy, vibrato Thrash Metal band.

2

The first crisis in my life, the first time I fully realised that the world was not fair, that I hated life and that I was going to run away from home and live an independent life in the woods at Temple Newsam was aged nine. 1973 and Mr David Bowie was playing in Leeds, at the Rollarena, my older brother was going and so was I; I had to. Except, apparently, I was too young, the tickets were sold out, even my brother didn't think I was old enough and no one would tell me how to get to the Rollarena. Thirty years later I still hate my mother and live beneath the park keeper's hut on the Temple Newsam estate.

Seeing David Bowie at Leeds Rollarena meant everything to me. Had I known how to use Yellow Pages, an A to Z and a compass I would have gone, I would have got in and I would have sung a duet with David and nobody would have stopped me.

I do not remember where the Bowie obsession started. I remember all my mates at junior school were into Slade, I was into Bowie, we argued and then played. I remember being very giddy, waiting for him on *Top Of The Pops* to perform 'Starman' and the 'video' to 'Drive In Saturday', a garden and a cine camera. My giddiness was comparable to waiting for the '75 European Cup Final between my beloved Leeds United and Bayern Munich, ultra-kid-Christmas, my-head-will-drop-off kind of excitement.

There's a thing. Apparently 'Bohemian Rhapsody' ('75) was the first pop video, so what, in '73 was the film that accompanied 'Drive In Saturday'? What is the video to 'Life on Mars', again '73, although the song is older, with Bowie, looking gorgeous in a washed out room, blue suit and blue eye shadow? Why are they not known as the first pop videos? There is also strong evidence that Bowie developed the first light bulb in 1902, which is ignored by science. Some of my friends are currently considering his influence on the early use of the wheel, although I think that's a bit fanciful, 2000 BC, I don't think his influence stretches back that far.

On the video thing, there are films for songs from the '60s and probably before – was it 'special effects'? Was it the format? And was 'Bohemian Rhapsody' the first song to contain special effects or use video tape? I doubt it, and smell a media myth. 'Drive In Saturday' from '73 with the film of the garden and cine camera actually contains the line, *Like the video films we saw.* Is it relevant? I don't know. Does it matter? I'd rather not say, it's personal.

I began painting Bowie obsessively around the age of 12, but he used to get annoyed and run away dripping. During art lessons at school I was in control of the class, because I loved art and 30 twelve year olds running around with full paint brushes is a dodgy studio to work in. I think the art teacher used to just sit at the front working and think '2M, McCann will take this lesson'. He'd set them a task then leave them to it, I'd paint Bowie, they'd run around having paint fights and I'd have to restore order.

'Right, sorry, attention please class! If a single drop of paint goes within a foot of my picture, the flicker will die, slowly.'

'Aw yeh, McCann who do you think you are?'

'Try it, just carry on doing what you're doing, if the paint hits my picture you're dead.'

The class would quieten to a mumbled, 'Who does he think he is? I could tek'im.' But the definite nature of the statement coupled with a determined stare persuaded the class that my pictures were to be avoided. The first time it happened the cock of the class looked up in a 'this pride is mine, are you trying to rut one of my lionesses?' kind of way and I returned an 'I will fight you if you like' look and he smiled and got on. What most kids, in those days, didn't understand is that lads who knew they were harder than you didn't like to beat you up. I learnt this at junior school when I had tried to fight the cock of the school over some injustice, he simply placed his hand on my head and my arms went around like a windmill, when he let go and I got the opportunity of a punch he grimaced and moved his arm quickly, I flew across the room and the teacher arrived. The second cock of the school didn't know if he could chin me, so we stood toe to toe punching each other in the face remorselessly for what felt like hours. It was horrible, it hurt and, as we both thought we'd lost the fight, we spent the next two weeks avoiding each other.

I should mention that where I was, in 1970s Leeds, fighting was what you did, it was normal. I don't think it was for most of the children at my primary school, but for me I grew up fighting, my mum hated it, always sat me down and said, 'You can't do that, it's wrong.'

I'd never hit anyone who didn't want to hit me; I'd never bully people, that was wrong. But sometimes you'd fight a stranger who wanted to fight, you didn't back down, no matter what. From a young age, we travelled around in ways that children today are stopped from doing, I'd tag on to my older brothers or sometimes just with friends to the woods, you'd go out in the morning and return when you returned as long as it was before tea. Seven-year-old kids used to walk home from school on their own and let themselves into their houses, children had a freedom they do not have today.

My eldest brother, Steve, hitch-hiked from Leeds to go camping in Wales with a mate aged eleven/twelve. All they had was a bottle of Irn Bru and a packet of Cuppa Soup. Their tent was a series of plastic bags stapled together. The point is that a couple of weeks later they returned home. At the age of eleven/twelve they could handle hitch-hiking from Leeds to Wales and camping for a couple of weeks.

It was in the woods that we built our masterpiece, under the nest of a Tawny Owl, squirrel, and then Tawny Owl again after we bricked the squirrel. We decided who operated on our territory. Years of dedication and experimentation led us to build the greatest of all dens, well no, not a den but a bunker, submerged under the ground, with mud steps. Had Hitler been tracked by the Russkies to Whitkirk, Leeds, Yorkshire, England he would have been safe in our den, 'cepting p'raps that I would have split on him. I think even within our strict non-splitting code I'd have been safe splitting on Hitler, he murdered people for God's sake, not like the up-standing, righteous nation that I popped out in. Anyway, the den; a 36 ton Iosef Stalin 1 tank over the top may have scattered the camouflage leaves but it wouldn't have dented our magnificent structure, we used corrugated iron and everything.

About the owl, don't let Willy tell you that it was a 'Kestrel Owl', there is no such thing, the stupid get. It was a Tawny Owl, and I know this for sure. Neither was it a Barn Owl, as all the other kids insisted, it was a Tawny Owl that lived high above our den, dozing through the day.

'Shuddup, there's no such thing as a Tawny Owl, y'dick, it's a Barn Owl.'

My membership of the YOC, and regular bird-watching trips did nothing to persuade the kids that not only do Tawny Owls exist but one was acting as look-out for our den.

We kept things there, posted look-outs as we approached it and set up little traps so that we would know if our secret had spread amongst other local kids. (The menu of a taverna in Kythira boasted, as one of its specialities, 'Roasted, local, wild kid'; I gave it a wide berth and instead plumped for a dish I'd never had before.)

Hedge hopping and apple scrumping, jumping into hedges from trees.

Swings were in. We had one that swung out over Hollyshaw Lane. It rose up just at the crucial time to skim over the top of cars. The 38, double-decker bus was a problem but once you've seen someone smash into the side of a bus on a swing, your timing improves.

A passing pensioner said to us, 'Don't you think that's a bit dangerous?'

'No, it goes over the cars.'

'Yeh, but the drivers don't know that.'

'Eh?'

'The driver could swerve to miss you and pile into a car coming the other way.'

'Ooh yeh, that's a fair point that, int'it?'

'It is, int'it, shall we move the swing?'

'We best 'ad.'

So we moved the swing to a better, higher point for the fluttering in the stomach but not as good for dodging the beams.

We always had fires, we were careful, no one got hurt, nothing burnt down, it was normal and it was safe. I'd slink into my house and down the cellar, silent as a cat. Plunge my arm, head and upper torso into a huge, thick, brown paper sack that stank of soil and secretly pull out a couple of spuds, watched by my mother. Back up to the woods for roast tatties, or burnt tatties as they usually were. They often tasted like shit but that didn't matter, it was the chucking them in the fire that counted, surviving in the wild, that was where the buzz was to be found.

The first time I got the bus on my own, me and Dom Brown went to Roundhay Park, aged seven or eight, it was packed; I stood up to let a man sit down, 'that's what you do, he's an adult, my legs are better than his.' The man sat me on his knee and chatted friendly like, there was nothing dodgy, he wasn't trying to grope me, he was telling me how his kids were just my age and how good they were. Dom Brown stuck his head through the bar in the seat behind us and started singing, 'Mick likes coffee, Mick likes Tea, Mick likes sitting on a black man's knee.' The guy and me weren't embarrassed, we just ignored him and chatted about stuff, Dom stopped singing. I'm sure there's some Claudette Colvin analogy there somewhere but I really can't be arsed.

We've lost something; that could never happen today, that was not a dangerous situation. The relationship between adults and children has changed, men always winked at me when I was a kid, I don't even look at children I don't know nowadays. Social paranoia is damaging our heads and our world.

With independence you had to think and learn. Me and Terry Waite used to go to Elland Road while we were still in junior school, ten new pence to get in. So one time I woke up looking at the ceiling of the Kop, we made a mistake, and learnt a lesson. I had the wind knocked out of me, couldn't breathe and passed out. It is no exaggeration to say that strangers probably saved my life. How lucky you are. A world without Mick – what an appalling thought.
'Tommy, Tommy, grab this little'un.'
'Bill, there's a little'un coming down.'
'Dave, Dave, cop this lad.'
It was surreal, coming round, calmly gazing at iron girders as I floated across the top of the crowd towards the exit. Terry was following me but he was fully conscious, laughing and whooping with excitement. We decided that the middle of the Kop behind a barrier was not a safe place to be; the weight of 500 grown men jumping on us was, at this moment, just beyond our capabilities. From that day, we returned to the police gantry at the back of the Kop, 12.30 every game we were there. I hated the violence, racism and the 'get yur tits out for the lads', which was prevalent – I didn't know why but it made my skin crawl.

I have a memory of a memory of an atmosphere. It's a certainty, carved in nuclei, in receptors and cells, it may be false but it's a certainty. Just because I'm absolutely positive that I have a memory of a memory of an atmosphere doesn't mean that the first memory of the atmosphere was real. It may have been suggested to me in all sorts of ways, but it is a vague and hazy picture, that smells, that sounds, that lives. I never could make out the image clearly, it was more of an atmosphere, a moment. I can date that snapshot very precisely, I was two-and-a-half. It is not like a clear memory of a breathless radio shouting out the movements of the ball across Celtic Park football pitch in 1969, so animated and overwrought that the radio must explode. I better not get too close, it is dangerous. I got close and it became a glorious and, at times, tragic love affair. That is a clear memory. A memory stuffed full of tension, the tension of my father explaining that he thought that Leeds and Celtic were the two best teams in Europe. Although it isn't the final, whoever wins this game is likely to win the European Cup. The game is so closely balanced that either team can win. Celtic won but lost in the final. This is not my memory of a memory of an atmosphere. I was five during the Leeds-Celtic European Cup semi-final; this was a memory of the atmosphere of the world cup in England in 1966. I have no proof and, as I have said, I was two-and-a-half so it may be false. This is my first memory and it is not quite a memory. There are no specifics, no detail, just a feeling in the air, an ambience. 'Appen my dad knelt down and said, 'Try to remember this, it will probably never happen again in your lifetime.' Perhaps there was just a fuss and a joy that a young consciousness immediately locked onto as unusual, a shift in the world. Babies/young children deal in atmospheres and can read them like no other age group.

When I was a baby, feeding, if I grabbed my mum's ears she giggled silently.

Something that didn't make my skin crawl, it got up and walked, was seeing my mother fall. The impact with ground juddered through my bones, marrow vibrating for minutes – Mum can get hurt. It was the moment when I realised that my mother was mortal, I was too young to know the phrase but not the meaning. I was watching her through a window, return home with bags of shopping, she missed the curb and crashed to the ground, her glasses flew off, blood, she'd hurt herself. Some strange genetic warning buzzed through my heart, I was very young and a survival alarm rang through my being, I need her to live. Not a selfish sentiment but natural human programming.
As a child, I was somehow good with numbers, letters and puzzles. Everything at junior school was just so easy, I often sat on my own at the front of the class doing stuff way ahead of the other kids and even that was piss-ball. I blew a massive potential, I just lost it, I don't know how it happened, school just held no interest for me at all. Maybe being a fat westerner with a love of the here and now, I grew up with no imperative. I'm not particularly smart now. I was later told, by a mother of a friend who taught at the school, that in an I.Q. test all the children took, I was shown to be a genius, easy. Not just scraped in by a couple of points but that I should have received a letter asking me to run Mensa which, at the age of nine, was unusual. Don't us Brits hate that? You could meet Eddie Gray in a darkened room and hear him say, 'Yeh I was a decent footballer.' And everyone in the room would be thinking I bet he wasn't that good....

17

'Did you hear him? That bloody Mozart bloke? I can knock out a good tune! Bet he's crap.'

It's obviously all bollocks anyway, different people have different gifts and my young hoop-jumping didn't produce anything. I always knew I was remarkable, that I would live a blessed life, no pain, plenty of gain, I was wrong. I missed out on having the highest score in the history of the school by one mark. I knew of the boy who had the extra mark, he was a lot older, did the Oxbridge thing and will now be eminent, where as I'm a professional failure. As a kid I was smart as fuck, in my head clarity ruled. As an adult I'm an under-achieving, woolly-headed buffoon.

As a youth I was good with words and ideas, given an even playing field I could take part in any philosophical debate. I never started from a point of view that was set in stone, it was always negotiable. If someone had a point of view that contradicted mine but seemed right, I'd say, 'Yeh, you're right.' I remember sitting on Manston Park aged twelve and converting a couple of American Jehovah's Witnesses to my dislike and distrust of any form of organised religion. They woke up that morning full of the love of God and went home full of questions. It's easy, organised religion may be good for your social life, may produce a feeling of community, it may allow you to face emotional trauma by ignoring it, give reassurance. Its effluence can be the creation of the 'other', justification for action without thought, removal of responsibility, social control, oppression, pigheaded righteousness, greed, hypocrisy, injustice, murder, genocide.

Given that God is good and 'all-knowing' why on earth would God give a flying fuck if millions of ants stand and sit and kneel and mumble nursery rhymes? One of the first thoughts to enter my young head when we started doing Jesus, was, 'What's going on with Judas, poor lad? What a set-up. God knows what's going to happen and his plan to give up his son to the world wouldn't have worked without the stitching up of Judas.' If I forgot my P.E. kit 'appen God's the kind of fella who would make me do maths while the netball team watch P.E.

The 1ˢᵗ Fact What I Know: Organised religion has no unique benefits and is fundamentally shite.

3

I'd spent long enough cribbing off others, grabbing bits of music off my older siblings, now was time for a rite of passage, a declaration of my distinct identity. I would drive my musical stake into the ground and make an independent musical decision, my first single. What a risk, but I had to stand tall and solid by whatever I decided. I saved pocket money and gave it to ar'kid so that he could choose me a single.

'What do you want me to get you?'

'Anything you want.'

'Yeh, but is there anything you've heard that you like?'

'Yeh, loads of stuff but I want something new.'

OK, so you've no idea what you want, you want me to choose a single for you, yeh?'

'Yeh.'

'What if you don't like it?'

'I will.'

'Judy Teen' by Cockney Rebel, that's what it says. Err. This is crap.

'Steve, that record is crap.'

'It's not, it's a belting single. I asked you what you fancied and you didn't know.'

'Yeh, but I thought you'd buy something good, this is crap.'

'Look I'll buy it off y' and give you y'money back, OK?'

'OK.'

'But don't ask me to buy you owt else.'

'Don't worry, I won't.'

Anyway a little while later he bought me 'Teenage Rampage' by The Sweet.

'We want Sweet.'

'We want Sweet.'

'We want Sweet.'

Ba Bow------Ba Bow------Ba Bow-Ba Bow.

'That's more like it, this is brilliant.'

'Hmm, thought you'd like it.'

So my first single was 'Judy Teen', shit, and then my other first single was 'Teenage Rampage' brilliant. How stupid I felt as I grew to love 'Judy Teen' and 'Teenage Rampage' slipped towards the back of my single collection.

Back to my obsession. There is not a moment that I can point to and say, 'That's when I discovered Mr David Bowie.' I don't even know at what stage my older siblings got into him. My sister reckons *Hunky Dory*, '71, but I will have heard it through the walls of the terrace house that we all grew up in. It was a large, Edwardian, terraced house, in a middlish-class area of what I now think of as the rougher side of Leeds. One of my school friends from Seacroft thought it was a mansion and looked down on me. Who I was changed when he saw my house, which confused me. I used to go into Seacroft, Gipton, and Halton Moor all the time and never looked down on anyone who wasn't low.

David lit a fire inside me that still burns – even now I think he's an artist; you know, like Mozart, Wagner, Charlie Parker or Kylie. I'm guessing but I don't think he has the technical/musical knowledge that they did, but he moved me in ways music rarely does. I defy anyone to listen to *Hunky Dory* or *The Rise and Fall of Ziggy Stardust and the Spiders from Mars* five times, loudly and not feel their soul start to vibrate. From there you move on through glorious albums. There are few things in life that are certain, here is one: if a person listens to 'Sweet Thing/Candidate/Sweet Thing Reprise', from the '74 album *Diamond Dogs*, once a day for a week they will be a different person, life will change. For me that is the pinnacle of popular music, everything was building to that moment. Things change, develop, but basically modern dance music will be pulling a lot of the same emotional and physical strings that Elvis pulled 45 years ago. 'Sweet Thing' plays on the strings of a whole different instrument. The closest to it is Jacques Brel, but it's darker, seedier, more oblique, arranged like Gershwin, with the emotional kick of a room full of pre-menstrual women trying to teach pubescent, teenage boys how to strip down the engine of a Ford Capri mark II.

For me, the awful irony of 'Sweet Thing' is that it is followed on the album by 'Rebel Rebel'. How sick is that? Definitely in the top five worst Bowie tracks recorded outside the '80s, along with 'Jean Genie'. Everyone in the world, over 20, will recognise the first four bars of 'Rebel Rebel'. Who, other than disciples, has heard 'Sweet Thing'? You couldn't sell soap powder with 'Sweet Thing', maybe social decay or a totalitarian state, but not soap powder.

4

The first thing you need to know about coming out as a Bowie fan in Leeds, Yorkshire, England 1977/78 is that you had to be able to growl, deep and primal. If that didn't work, cock-sure, cutting humour was your last line of defence.

It just hit me one day. Why don't I get one of our Kate's kimonos? I've got some greasepaint, I'll go down to the Arndale Centre and buy that silver hairspray. Belt; tight, black jeans; shoes are a problem but our Kate's black, knee-length boots will probably fit me and she doesn't wear them.

'Kate, make-up and that, what's it about then?'

'Would you knock before you come into my room? What?'

'Make-up, I want something to make a black line like that one under your eye, and long eyelashes.'

'What?'

'May I borrow some of your make-up, please?'

'What, for you?'

'Yes, I've got a look I want, kinda Bowie-ish.'

'What for?'

'I'm going to the youth club tonight and I've got a look I want. You know your boots?'

'Woah, slow down, you want to go to St Mary's in make-up?'

'Yes.'

'Mike, you've got to be kidding, you'll get killed. Which boots?'

'The ones that you used to wear that go to your knees.'

Kate roots in the bottom of her wardrobe.

'You mean these?'

'Yeh, those, will they fit me?'

'Will you slow down? You want to go to St Mary's in make-up and women's boots?'

'Yeh, and you never wear those kimonos, do you?'

'Mike, you'll get lynched. Do you understand what you're doing?'

'Kate, I think sometimes you forget just how hard I am.'

'You'll get killed by people my age. Men. You can't fight men.'

'Come on Kate, why would men chin me?'

'Because some of them are psychotic and they wouldn't be able to handle a boy dressed up like a woman, you'll be challenging their sexuality and they will kill you.'

'Kate that's their problem, I'm doing it. The boots, the kimono, the make-up talk to me.'

21

'Here, try them on. What about your friends? They won't talk to you, everybody will laugh and tease you.'

'Well they're not friends then, I'm doing it.'

'Do they fit? Let's have a look. They're not bad.'

'They're too big, my feet are moving around.'

'Big socks.'

'What?'

'Big socks, football socks will pad them out. Be careful with my kimonos. I might not wear them but I like them. Here, look, you can have this eye-liner, pull your eye down like this and draw a straight line underneath, if it smudges lick your finger and take it carefully along like this. You can use this mascara tonight but I like it and you're not using it all the time.'

'I'm going down to Boots anyway, I'll buy one. What is it?'

'You can't go into Boots and buy make-up.'

'Why not?'

'Yeh, I suppose. Well you can borrow mi'stuff if you promise me one thing, no two things: if anybody older starts, run, yeh? Don't try to fight, run, yeh?'

'Yes.'

'Promise?'

'Yes.'

'I mean it.'

'Yes, if they're older I'll run, I promise.'

'Do you want me to walk up with you?'

'Come on Kate, I'm thirteen, I can look after myself.'

'OK, promise number two. Pop in and see me before you go out, yeh?

'Yeh, I was going to anyway to make sure I've done it right.'

Somewhere between age eight and ten, I remember Kate sewing my oldest brother, Steve, into a shirt. It was pure white, shiny, satiny, skin-tight, no buttons and the arms billowed slightly at the bottom like a wizard's cape. Kate was sewing down the seam at the side. I think this had two effects on my young mind: number one, men could spend time doing unusual things with clothes and appearance, number two, it struck me just how creative and honest Kate was. She was a perfect consultant, if I'd have looked like a twat Kate would have said, 'Mike, it's not working.' I would listen.

Kate's was the only opinion in the world that could have arrested or slowed the pace of my coming out.

What was I doing in my coming out? I just had an urge, more than that, a compulsion. No choice. It was me and I was it. I had found myself, grown into myself. A boy born into a brain with, for the first 13 years, the wrong attitude to cosmetics and effeminate clothing. This was a natural, sub-conscious rite of passage, there was no build to the decision, no thought process, one second later and I was coming out, no matter what.

I had no coming-out contemporaries, so it wasn't being part of a movement or group, there didn't appear to be any bonding to be had. There was no plan or conceived pay-off or price to be paid. I wasn't looking for anything but, in retrospect, the only alternative youth culture to immerse myself in seemed to be a dirty denim, rocker type. *That* had absolutely no appeal to me. I liked bands like Led Zep, Deep Purple, Wishbone Ash, Free, Thin Lizzy, Pink Floyd etc. but it just seemed a bit tired. It just wasn't me to get into stripping down bikes and doing handstands, at 70 miles an hour, on the road to Garforth. It seemed so stereotypically boyish – I had no urge to write my name in toothpaste on the back of settees or shit in drawers.

I was listening to some Punk, loved the first Damned album, and that, with the recently released *Heroes*, was the album that I listened to most, the energy felt fresh and new. Although very resistant to the first Clash album, I had been battered, by constantly hearing it, into absolutely loving it.

So I was into 2 of the 3 Punk albums but didn't really recognise Punk as a movement and also didn't like the way it mirrored my experiences and surroundings, dirty, rough, and monosyllabic, I wanted to kick against 'the hard', I wanted to find another self. Although I didn't know it, I needed brutal surgery, to explore and define my space, piss on my garden wall, mark my territory. I needed to say, 'I am here, this is me and I am so me, so sure I'm me, that I can be me in relative social isolation.' I wanted to feel comfortable using multiple syllables no matter who I was speaking to.

It wasn't a need to make people stop and stare, that was a bi-product. There was no yearning to go into The Arndale Centre and shout, 'Look at me, here, me, at me.' People would obviously think it was attention-seeking, but it wasn't. When you seek attention you usually have an idea what sort of attention you will receive, laughter, approval, pity, empathy, anger etc. I had no thought or concern about people's reactions – until my sister brought it up, it never crossed my mind that there would be a reaction. It was a purely, fundamentally personal thing, between me and me, no God, no family, no friends.

23

Bowie had an influence but so did cheese-and-onion-crisp sandwiches, so did my grandmother or being slapped hard across the face by a mad nun, listening to men die during the night in hospital when I was eleven/twelve. So did growing up in a haunted house, crapping on a neighbour's staircase when I felt too old to crap on neighbour's staircases but not old enough to ask where the toilet was. So did passion, sadness, arrogance, loneliness, stability, empathy and precipice.

Not a shallow thing – 99% of people would judge it so, but they were wrong.

My coming out, to some extent, was to counter the constant whiff of violence, the background hum of testosterone. I had a gentler side, a calmer side, a creative side, a beautiful side, an inclusive side, an open outlook, an area of Mick that needed developing. It had always been there, it was just that I wanted that side of me in the ascendancy. I couldn't shake off the conditioning of the terrain of the first 13 years of life, but I could manipulate it. I had to mine the good-seam Michael. I'd always defended people getting bullied; no matter what the odds I'd stand. I'd stand against ten lads and say, 'Jump me now and I'll get you one by one.' It was some ingrained idea of fairness, Catholic guilt thing; I wouldn't be able to live with myself if I just stood back and watched, injustice really got my mad up. On the bus, first day of senior school, a fifth former tried to bully me, the fact that he was 16 and I was 11 really enraged me, he was touching six foot and I was scraping five. Any idea of survival was secondary to an overwhelming need to inflict as much pain on him as possible; he wouldn't get off the bus, he backed away, trying to grab at and fend away a whirlwind of kicks and punches. I couldn't get at him but the apology and associated humiliation helped.

At the time I felt like I didn't have prejudice, no isms or ists. Later, I decided that social conditioning meant that everyone had isms and ists, absolutely everyone. You just had to recognise them within and without whenever you encountered them. You had to accept them and try to change or exorcise them.

On the cusp of 'coming out' I had been emboldened when my friend, Richard McHale, and I, entered into the democratic process. We wrote to Ron Greenwood, the England football manager, advising him that Tony Currie was in the form of his life and was by far the best midfield player in the English league. We got a letter back on proper

FA headed paper that even looked like Ron had signed it, saying that Tony was indeed playing well and was being closely monitored. A couple of months later Tony was back in an England shirt and that was our decision not Ron's.

5

Money in my pocket and I'm off down the Arndale Centre.

'Mascara, eye-liner and silver hairspray. Silver hairspray, eye-liner and mascara. Silver hairspray, eye-liner and mascara.'

Walking, hardly noticed, past people on the way down Hollyshaw Lane, it is just another day. I am unaware that my life is about to take a bit of a twist, a detour. I am focussing on 'the look' and how to achieve the look not the ramifications of the look. I don't realise that I should be savouring this anonymity.

The Arndale, in Crossgates, may have been lined by glass-fronted shops but it was more than a shopping centre. A social club for young and old alike, a meeting place, a hub. I started hanging out there from nine or ten with mates, sipping cold drinks and flattening plates of chips in the Wimpy Bar. Often flashing the cash to pay as, due to my milk-round, I was rich within that socio-economic group. It was *the* place to hang out, it had no real competition. Not Seacroft Shopping Centre.

I only visited Seacroft shopping centre a couple of times – Jesus, it was grim. The kind of place you would try to leave as soon as you entered, to me it stank, it stank of bargains discoloured by desperation. Pushing open the door to the ground floor, it felt a bit unkempt, shop-fronts looked dirty and litter lay on the floor which pulled at your feet with a slight squelch. This was the posh bit. The cellar of the shopping centre had a medieval aura, you could imagine people chained to the walls in the dark corners or being stretched across racks. People so hard and world-weary that they don't even whimper. The floor needed straw putting down.

Part of my distaste for the place was the stench of the unfamiliar, it disorientated me, I didn't know it, there were few familiar faces and even the shop-fronts looked alien. A sadness hung in the air, a lack of trust or friendship, no one seemed to make eye contact. 'Appen that it was just me who didn't know anyone – but I did, I was nodding to the occasional kid and stopping for conversation with others. It was full of shops for poor people, people who had to shop there, captive, no need for enticement, no need for dreams. The industrial revolution starts here.

The Arndale Centre was clean and shiny, polished to within an inch of its veneer; it had bins. Upper-working-class, aspiring to middle-class. The floor of the central walkway glimmered into the shimmering floors of the shops, full of sparkling things that nobody needed. Obviously this is all perspective, someone stepping back from a 21st-century Leeds City Centre shopping experience would smell my young Seacroft Shopping Centre odour, or at least a time warp. At the time it felt like a cutting-edge, retail therapy palace. People worked there, not just in the shops but emptying bins and giving directions and information to shoppers. It had doors that slid open automatically. It had a Woolworths. This truly was the space age.

My first, unaccompanied-by-adults, sorties into the Arndale Centre were for parents' birthday or Christmas presents. The first shop to truly claim my patronage was the modelling shop. A long, thin shop stacked from wall to wall, interrupted by a central aisle, floor to ceiling with boxes of models, mainly Airfix and Revel. Racks of paints and glue. No pinks, purples or mauves, just proper male colours and occasional yellow for wing-tips. It had everything, the whole Airfix catalogue was there. Fighters, fighter bombers, bombers, transport planes, landing craft, destroyers, cruisers, pocket battleships, battleships, aircraft carriers, lorries, petrol tankers, tanks. British, American, Russian, German and Japanese. I don't remember the Italians or French. I went to war.

'Neeowwn, dugga-dugga-dugga. Cripes, there's a Hun on my tail. Fiddling fuselage, I'm hit. Phut-phut-phut. I have to bail before the fire gets to the petrol! Jumping juniper, where's my parachute? It must be here somewhere. No. Ah well, I'll just have to jump. Wait a minute, if I get this right I may be able to land on the wing of that plane. Aaaaah, aaaah! Dufffff. Phew, that was lucky. Now to knock out this Kraut and toss him from the plane. Learn to fly, fascist! Oh no, he thinks I'm a dirty German! Don't shoot me, I'm on your side. If only the Messerschmitt wasn't such an inferior plane I could get away from this Spitfire. Ccyyyck-ccyyck, calling all Allied pilots, ccyyyck-ccyyck I'm a Tommy, don't shoot, ccyyyck-ccyyck. Jees, that was lucky, he's run out of ammo. Oh no, I can't return home, they'll shoot me down. Good job I'm fluent in German and I've got my fake German passport, Baron Von Hitzleberger, occupation: German flying ace. Jumping hockey sticks! I should have written that bit in German! Hopefully they won't notice as I pass through German customs.'

The boxes varied in size, but basic shapes and dimensions carried across the range, or series, as us aficionados called them. The colouring of the boxes varied little, blue or stormy sky denoting aircraft, blue or stormy sea denoting ships; the main difference being some planes or tanks were put against a desert landscape. The camouflage again, pretty much went across the range, greens, browns, blues and greys. This unavoidably mushy presentation was effective. It refined the product, concentrated my young mind on the thing, the essence, there was little interfering with the focus on the weapon. With Airfix models, as with all art, it was the process that counted, the making. Once it was finished you could appreciate a job well done or recognise your mistakes but ultimately you were running back to the beginning of the process.

My Airfix collection went to well over a hundred, funded by saving pocket money and later by my milk-round. Dog-fights, hung with cotton and drawing pins, covering my bedroom ceiling. Sea battles arranged on shelves or cupboards. My dad saying goodnight by strafing me with a Junker or Messerschmitt and then tickling away any chance of me drifting to slumber within the next twenty minutes; being scolded down the stairs by my mum as she came to try to calm the eight-year-old storm.

The baddies, particularly the Germans, had the design edge, you only have to look at an SS uniform to see that; their weapons were simply cooler. Take the Spitfire, Mosquito and Hurricane out of the equation and the German weapons were simply more modern, stream lined and powerful.

Mindst you, this technological supremacy of 'the German war machine' may be one of these modern myths to cover the Allies' incompetence. Apparently, the French had an equivalent amount of weaponry and some of it was more advanced than the Germans'. Contrary to popular, racist, British myth-making the French will not have been, 'surrender monkeys', the average French fighting man was as brave as any; more, the Germans got lucky. Yes, lucky. If you don't play or watch footie you may not understand the full extent and influence of luck or chance upon the universe. It is *the* crucial element. We got lucky, we had the North Sea to save our asses.

There were no German troops in the Arndale Centre. It was an L-shaped, wide arcade, it was not huge but it was big enough. Every 50 yards was a thick, central pillar with seating areas that hugged the bottom. Plastic plants over hung, packed in above your head thick and dense – some say they saw Pygmies living in the undergrowth but we all knew that that was the magic mushrooms kicking in. Mindst you, the occasional poisoned dart in the side of the neck made us question our position.

There was an Eastern European woman who was always there – she'll be dead now. She was haunted by some earth-shattering tragedy and was teased relent-lent-lentlessly by the local kids. Kids with easy lives. Comfortable, safe kids who wouldn't understand the tragic if it came up and shot their mother. We, in Leeds, Yorkshire, England and beyond, think we have problems, struggles in life, we haven't, not usually. Historically and around the world, people have real troubles while we complicate our lives to pretend that we have; we haven't, not usually.

Anyway this woman was your archetypal 'bag lady' and every day she could be seen in the Arndale Centre, protesting to the ceiling, reliving old arguments. Stridently making her case and then, within a nanosecond, pleading, pleading with all she had to some unseen, by all but her, person of power. I always wanted to know who was at the other end of the conversation. For the kids of Crossgates, Leeds, Yorkshire, England, 1975 to '84 she was a laughing-stock, someone to prod and tease. She'd occasionally gesture towards her persecutors like someone wafting away a fly, but more often she was elsewhere.

Whenever she sat next to me I'd acknowledge her if she spoke at me, which she usually did. We'd have conversations, speaking about separate topics, in different languages. She was very persuasive and I usually listened, making all the right noises and gestures and in the right places like you do with teachers. If anyone I knew came along, I'd stop, not out of embarrassment but because they would see the daftness of the conversation, of the situation, and would have to laugh. Not laughing out of cruelty but at the lack of logic, the absurdity. Things we don't understand or that surprise us, due to a lack of order or convention, often make us laugh. A hang-gliding zebra is ridiculous, i.e. outside the normal; hence I feel that the sight of one may make me titter or at the very least, smile. Similarly a lamp post that says, 'Fuck off,' as people, not you, walk past.

We used to make a huge pile of leaves at the base of a lamp-post on Hollyshaw Lane in Whitkirk, Leeds, Yorkshire, England. Within this pile of leaves we'd place a young lad called Doofer, or rather he'd place himself, he was about seven and fearless. We'd watch from the woods over the road; as someone, anyone under 40, approached we'd whistle gently and he'd jump out screaming at the top of his voice. The sight of the people's reaction, witnessing the dawn of the monster of the leaves, running away or jumping out of their skin, still makes me laugh now, heartily. It was the funniest thing I have *ever* encountered, ever, funnier than a Morecombe and Wise show that made milk come down my nose for half an hour. The unexpected is funny but a reaction to the unexpected is funnier.

Anyway, I never once heard the Eastern European bag lady speak or react knowingly, to English. She never held eye contact for long, she was always scatting around. One day I was sat with her and we were happily babbling at each other, she looked right at me, in the eye, and laughed and laughed holding eye contact and shaking her head. It was so weird, who was I? What had I said? I'm almost certain that she wasn't reacting to me, perhaps the rhythm or intonation of my words, but not to words. We bonded, it was instantly lost as she broke off to chastise some invisible tormentor and we were back to our meaningless gibber. For a moment she looked at me with love in her eyes and it made me shiver.

6
(Make-up counter, Boots the chemists)

'Can I help you love?'

'No you're alright, thanks. Does this run?'

'No, look it says there. Is it for your girl friend or your sister?'

'No it's for me.'

The other woman on the counters' jaw drops and she stares right at me, I look straight back at her, she keeps looking – if she'd have been male this would be a fighting look. The woman serving me glances at her and she looks away sneering.

'It's not?'

'It is.'

'Are you in a show?'

'Yeh, kinda.'

'Well won't they do it for you?'

'Who?'

'Whoever's organised the show.'

'No, I'm doing it.'

'Alright love, let's have a look at you. Ooh, you've got good lashes. What look are you after?'

'I've got the look, I'm just after the mascara.'

'OK love, that'll be 21p please, have you got your foundation? Because if you buy this cream, the powder's free and it's perfect for your complexion.'

'What?'

'Listen love, is someone helping you with this?'

'No. Yeh, my sister.'

'OK, so you've got everything else?'

'Yeh, I've got an eye-liner and greasepaint.'

'Ooh, you don't want greasepaint.'

'I know, I've already got it.'

'No, I mean you don't want to use greasepaint, it's terrible for your skin.'

'OK, thanks.'

'Shall I take for the hair-spray as well?'

I nod, look up and, although she is helpful, wonder how she can advise people on make-up. I'm sure there is a face in there somewhere but I wouldn't like to bet where it is, she is three layers beyond features. A blanded-out face like the models in the magazines, plain, all the features are the right distances apart and in proportion, balanced but with no character, a boring face. Models always had that initial 'she's attractive' but after looking at a pretty face for twenty seconds there are few surprises. Apparently 'well proportioned' faces trigger a subconscious judgement that the person is genetically solid and healthy. What a load of bullshit, like pretty people never get hereditary cancer. I'd had pretty girls chasing me for a while, but their faces didn't seem to move much. I'd shag them anyway but then what? I'd recently split up with the girl who shared my virginity and her face was jam-packed with her personality and we talked about everything and nothing, she was great and I treated her like shit.

I lost my virginity aged 13. I didn't have sex with the first to offer, it just wasn't right. It was with my first love, we'd been together as boyfriend and girlfriend for a while and she was a soul mate, I suppose – even though I haven't seen her for years, she still is. It didn't feel 'seedy' to me, as we loved each other. It was first love, first love more real than death and as sweet as a yawn. You never again touch the intensity and purity of first love. Even at the time, due to age, I knew it had to be a doomed love, which distilled and condensed it. Your first love is like a family member, you haven't learnt the romantic rules of survival, homeopathic distances, and the person is fully into your soul, all consuming. My split with her coincided loosely with my 'coming out' and even though I instigated it, it broke my young heart into pieces. She was the only girlfriend that I didn't warn about my propensity for skirt-chasing. The pain in her eyes is permanently etched onto my soul like a fallen comrade.

In quiet moments, alone in my room I would play sad songs and wallow, sobbing with abandon.

My death lies there between your thighs,
Your cool fingers will close my eyes.

No one before me had ever experienced this heroic, fated pain. I had been deceived by the deities, a historic betrayal, 'How could God do this to us? Why can't I have a normal attractiveness to girls rather than this mesmeric aura? Why won't girls leave me alone? They are only after one thing; their love is not pure as ours was.' Raising my face to the sky, 'Father, how can you allow them to use me so?'

My mind would recount over and over again the first kiss, that left my lips buzzing for days, and I could suck out every droplet of misery. I wanted to experience heart break to the full, I wished I was the victim, so that I could be Romeo tragic. The fact that I had shagged around behind her back and dumped her was ignored, I didn't want it to spoil my epic agony. Despair, much more fun than guilt.

If you go away, on this summer's day,
Then you might as well take the sun away.

As I named this first love as a soul mate, I'd like to include a précis of an article that I've just had published in, 'The Royal Journal of Life: Before and After Death.' Which has revolutionised current thinking on SMC – I'm a man of countless talents.

The Soul Mate Convention.

The convention for the status of Soul Mate is, apparently, that we only have one. I have asked experts in the afterlife, such as Genghis Khan and Walt Disney, and this is agreed. We have one soul mate. Now this is a shallow, unconsidered, non-functioning opinion. For this single-soul-mate perception I have a couple of questions:

Do we only have one soul mate throughout our life? Can't you have one at twelve, another at 22, another at 37, etc.?

What if you make a bad soul mate decision early in life, can you appeal?

Has a soul mate got anything to do with the afterlife, with eternity?

Is the concept 'soul mate' just for the 'here and now'?

So is it my religious up bringing that gives the concept 'soul' a meaning that is more than the physical? (For me, the soul is not restrained by physics, there are no time/space constraints on the soul as there are on the body.)

How do you choose your soul mate?

What if the person you've chosen chooses someone else? What then?

When you are in heaven can you have weekend breaks or holidays? I mean we all need to get away sometimes, don't we?

Taking it that 'soul mate' isn't simply an immediate concept, I have some further questions on the Soul Mate Convention but strangely these questions appear not to be presented in the form of a list, spooky.

We spend eternity with one person, how puritanical is that? **The 2nd Fact What I Know: Eternity is a Long Time.** Can we only be spiritually and emotionally attached to one person? We need to sort this out and come to a consensus before we die. We don't want to spend eternity bickering about what is and isn't allowed in our personal relationships, that would be simply wasteful and, although we may believe that we are in heaven, sounds like a precise description of purgatory to me.

Now I, being promiscuous, have got shed-loads of Soul Mates. I find the idea of spending eternity with one person a bit scary, they'd kill me, I'd drive them out of their mind and off a cliff. I'm alright in short bursts but not for ever.

Is the afterlife simply cerebral, consciousness-based, or are time, space and physicality at play? Do we spend eternity, it being a long time, in a sham mental stupor, an illusion? How sad.

Anyway listen God and good buddies, when I'm dead I want to hang out with all my soul mates, not just one.

7

Back home I have everything, silver hairspray, belt with a big, silver buckle, tight, black jeans, kimono, Kate's black knee-length boots, greasepaint, eyeliner, mascara. I decide that the greasepaint is the place to start, I pull the cellophane back and peel the gold metallic paper, it is rock-hard. I run my finger over the end of it and pull it across my cheek, there is a faint and slightly pathetic, white line. Pulling the end up, I draw the stick across the same line, there is one huge, thick smudge at the beginning of my line and nothing else. I try to smudge it in with my fingers but it hardly moves. I look closely in the mirror at the large, hard, dollop of white butter perched on the side of my face. 'I'm doing this and I'm doing it tonight, not tomorrow, not next week, tonight.' There's a churning and the confusion of my heart sinking while also speeding away, my head feels hot but not hot enough to melt the ugly iceberg attached to the side of my face. I plunge the greasepaint down my trousers and rest it between my inner thigh and right testicle. I walk, John Wayne-like, over to the turntable and remove Bowie's dark, urban, instrumental piece 'Sense of Doubt' from the deck – you know the tune, you do, in your subconscious you know the tune. Think of the music that plays in your head when you imagine a car slowly moving through Cold War East Berlin, filming the bleak cityscape and hopelessness, that's it, that's 'Sense of Doubt'.

'David, I love you, but you're not doing this to me now.'

I pull *Machine Head*, Deep Purple, from the white, paper sleeve, place the needle to 'Lazy', sitting back at my mirror, the huge, gothic organ is what I need, swelling and rising, it is a man thing, a man moment, I need to be strong and butch to do this. What a track, the pinnacle of rock 'n' roll in all its maleness. Pure testosterone injected through my eardrums – no moment before or after that could compare. What the black blues players in the 'teens, '20s and '30s started, this track finished.

I pull the greasepaint from my crotch, head going like a nodding dog on the back shelf of a car, heart pumping positive, and draw the stick across my face. That's it, it smoothes across my face like a fine margarine on a bridge-roll crisp butty. Face completely even-white in minutes. I don't fancy the 'stick the small pencil in the eye' routine but it is easy, first time, both eyes perfect black line. The mascara, likewise, easy. How do women manage to take so long over make-up and such a fuss? I would answer that question later. God, I look really weird. Big, white mask. The silver hair, again, easy – although it gets all over my hands, it also thickens my wispy top of head spike so that it spikes at better angles and to the side, it looks much bigger. The silver works with the white, but it isn't quite right, my face isn't quite right. I wrap around the black be-dragoned kimono and tighten the big buckled belt around it, pull the boots over the tight black kegs, fiddle for a while to get the ballooning out of the knee area and knock on Kate's door.

'Come i-in.......Bloody hell.'

'What?'

'What's that? You didn't say anything about greasepaint. Is that mine? You cheeky little bugger.'

'Is it too much? There's no subtlety to it.'

'No it'll work well with the lights in there. It's just a bit of a shock, it's really weird, but it works. You need....'

'What?'

'Here. Come here. Shut your eyes.'

I feel her fingers rub repeatedly over my eyelids and above, but below my brows. I open my eyes, I can't see what she's done.

'No wait a minute, sit still.'

After patting a little, browny-pink pad on my cheeks, she pulls out a big brush.

'Bloody hell I'm going to have to wash this.'

Circling it around in a plastic container she brushes it across my cheekbones.

'Don't use the greasepaint again, talk to me tomorrow.'

'Does it look stupid?'

'No, honestly, it looks really good, come have a look.'

She's finished. There are shadows above my eyes and my cheeks have sunk into my face. I am staring at a stranger, a rather striking and attractive stranger.

'Ooh, I know what you need.'

She pulls Mum's long, white, fur coat from her wardrobe.

'I can't wear that, it's Mum's.'

'She doesn't use it, she gave it to me but I wouldn't be seen dead in it. Try it on.'

'Yes, that works.'

'Listen, remember the promise? Run.'

'Yes.'

Returning to my room, I am still growling slightly from the Deep Purple and Iggy that I'd been listening to earlier. I don't want to leave the house growling – that is not what it is about, I have to be cheeky, confident but gentle, not aggressive, not tense. I have to exude calm confidence or I will get beaten. I need to chill out, but retain the buzz, 'On the Street Where you Live', Nat King Cole strokes my head as I stare at the freak in the mirror. Deep breath, here we go, I know I have to do it, so let's go.

Passing the toilet, I clump down the stairs past the front-room door, which is ajar – there is my dad, slumped, feet stretched out on to a buffet.

'You're not leaving the house dressed like that.'

'See y'.'

'You're not leaving the house dressed like that.'

'Yeh, see y'later.'

My mum comes running out of the room, crisis in her eyes, which makes me sad, she gasps, 'I think you look lovely, love, I'll see you later.'

I hated upsetting my dad, he was a good man, I didn't want to make him ashamed, I didn't want to make my parents argue, but I had to do it. He watched me walk by. That was the mark of a man, a real man, he dealt out physical violence at school, it was his job, that's what he did. He did not hit his own kids, that's what he didn't do, ever. And here is his little lad, taking a huge social risk, a risk that could label his family the ultimate freak show. They were already mavericks, he certainly was, but what if his mates from The Station tap-room saw his son like that? Well they will, he's going out, and if they don't, they will certainly hear about his son going around like a complete puff. Metaphorically, he stepped aside, he could have picked me up under his arm and carried me to bed but he stepped aside. From a background of being marched to church by a stick to allowing your young, teenage son to leave the house dressed like a woman and not standing in the way. That man made a huge leap in consciousness; he was social change in action. I later discovered that boys following me into the same risks, were severely beaten by fathers, severely beaten. It didn't stop them, just sometimes they got battered, the urge to come out and play was just too strong. But now I had to shake the upset out of my head because I was out, I could feel the air moving through my face, I was definitely out.

It was a warm, sticky, evening, clear sky but with a waft in the air. A gentle sway with little effect. I was right inside myself, not nervous but breathing out loud, or was it that I was so aware, so attuned, that my hearing was sub-aqua heightened? I couldn't tell. A certain amount of tension and a purpose in my stride like I was on my way to a fight where I would sweep away the opponent with quick, hard hands delivered before he was properly set. I had this wrong, I needed the other fighting mind-set where you step back and watch every sinew twitch, keep out of range, move in and move out. The technique you need for someone bigger and stronger, the state of mind that allows you to see them in slow motion where speed and agility does the damage but a couple of mis-timings and you're lost, battered by physics. Cautiously determined.

Turning my first corner on the way to St Mary's youth club, a man stops and stares, his face is a mixture of anger and repulsion as if I'd just shat on his grandmother, I hadn't just shat on his grandmother – that was the previous week. I stare back and walk on. A few yards on I bump into a couple of schoolmates heading in the opposite direction.

'Fuckin'ell, Mick. What y'doing?'

'I'm on my way to the youthy.'

'Are you going like that? It looks mental, it's brilliant, you're a nutter. Fucking hell.'

'Yeh.'

'See y'.'

'See y'.'

They know me quite well, we'd shared schools since we were four/five. I think they put it down to me being a bit zany, mental, daring. We now go to a Catholic grammar school about five miles away from where we live, so other than kids from my junior school and in the immediate surroundings of our street, I don't know that many of my local peer group.

On the way up Hollyshaw Lane there are a couple of punks coming down. They are older and punks are a bit scary. These two look mean and aggressive, bad timing really, there aren't that many around, so trust me to bump into a couple at such a defining and vulnerable moment. I am already getting butterflies, starting to feel a bit 'what on earth am I doing walking around Leeds in girly clothes, over the top make-up and silver spiky hair, couldn't I just leave it in my bedroom?'. My nattering head chastised me, 'It's your body, your area, your right to do what the fuck you like. Anyway you didn't have a decision, this is who you are, it may change, but right now this is you and you are it, and anyone who doesn't like it can fuck right off.' They are on top of me now, I tighten my lips and stare right out front, no path-gazing for me, it's always better to know when the punch is coming. They move towards me, my brain tightens.

'Fuckin'ell, you look mental.'
'What?'
'You look fucking brilliant.'
'Ur right, ta.'
'Fuckin'ell, you've got some bollocks.'
'What?' I stare down at my crotch.
'Going out like that. You've got bollocks.'
'Uhm.'
'What are you? Are you a sort of punk?'
'No not really.'
'Have you heard any punk?'
'Yeh, I really like The Clash and I've got The Damned album.'
'D'y'? It's brilliunt, int it, the Clash album?'
'Yeh, I love 'Janie Jones'.'
'What?'
'The track off the Clash album. But I prefer the Damned, it's heavier.'
'Yeh, so what are you? What are you into?'
'Bowie.'
'Ahh, Bowie, "Aladdinsane" is a belting album, int it. Anyway see you later, love. You've got some bollocks, come see me if you get any trouble.'
'Yeh, I'll be alright, see y'.'
'I'm serious, any hassle, come'n find me.'
'Cheers. Yeh, I'll be alright.'

This encounter gave me a small buzz – I had been accepted, included into something. I felt, strangely, part of a group, part of a movement, almost stronger, although I wasn't really part of Punk. Or was I? I loved the music I'd heard and, in a weird way, weren't they 'coming out' in a similar way to me? Well they were coming out in an opposite way but they were still coming out or had been through coming out, they had a context, an explanation.

'Listen, Mam, I'm a punk and nothing you say is going to change that.'

My context and explanation were a bit more difficult, there weren't men in effeminate clothes being banned from shopping centres or castigated on TV.

Through the double-doors and funnel to a table where a guy is taking money, I can sense people nudging each other in the queue, or should I say, I can sense people in the queue nudging each other? The man at the table looks up, stares a bit but doesn't react, good lad. I slide into the youthy and head for the side. A friend comes over.

'What y' doing? You look like a complete puff. Mick go home now before anyone sees y'.'

'What! No. It's none of your business.'

'Mick y' look like a queer twat, go home and take it off.'

'Err, no.'

'Come on Mick, what y' doing?'

The friend, bigger than me, is pulling me to the door, I'd had a fight with him in the past and he boxed the pants off me, although he said it was a draw, so I pretended it was too. I regain my balance and yank my arm away from his grip. Go home now? I am more likely to circumnavigate the world's oceans in a shopping trolley. I stand away from him as another friend begs me to go home. Go home now? I am more likely to traverse the north face of the Eiger on a chopper. My resolve has been drained and the intensity of it all is making my bottom lip shake. God, why do they care? It just doesn't matter that much, it's not that important. All my positive energy, all my cocky confidence, gone.

'You're not coming near me looking like that.'

'Er, fuck you' is the only response I can muster.

I think it is an honest response and kinda sums up how I feel towards them, also I like the fact that it is precise. Yes, 'Fuck you.' No grey area there. Another friend comes over and says, 'Take n'notice, they're tossers, you don't look that bad. Y'shuda gobbed 'im. Stupid get.'

I've only been in here a couple of minutes, and there is certainly a bit of a fuss, people who I don't really know are speaking to me or nodding, in a respectful manner, friendly like. I haven't been to St Mary's many times, I've been a few times on a Tuesday when it's table tennis, etc., but Friday night is the big night, the Disco. I start being led all over the place by girls introducing me to more girls, girls whose friend fancies me and her friend's friend and her other friend.

'I've already met her, she introduced me to you.'

I escape and try to become peripheral, but eyes are constant, flitting away as I look around or just staring and smiling. I like girls rather a lot, so this female attention is quite enough compensation. They are all over me, like a Durex on a dick. I am going to do something else, something just as potentially embarrassing and risky. For a change, I am going to take it just a little too far.

Although I'd tried not to think about it, like a boxer before a fight ignoring possible defeat, part of my mind was independent of the logical side. It hadn't escaped my imagination that there was at least a 50% chance that I could be laughed at by 250 to 300 kids. Prior to

40

doing it, that was what I had to resign myself to. Could I stand tall and slink off into a corner, looking like I didn't give a shit, while 275 kids laughed and pointed? In my coming out, and everything around it, there was a very real possibility that I could become a social pariah and freak laughing-stock, poked and prodded by all manner of children and young adults. As a by-product, it would have been opposite to what I wanted.

I wanted to gentle up myself, my interaction with my surroundings, wash a little colour into my monochrome world and, paradoxically, would end up biting the fingers that poked. Bringing more aggression and violence into my world, more growling and spitting. Fighting more than ever with all sorts of new comers, realising that I wasn't as hard as I thought I was. My size, my weight, I'd win, right? Always had. As I would come across very hard people rather than just 'handy', I'd start to lose fights, my confidence would wane and fear increase. Hiding fear is a crucial trick for a young, vulnerable teenager, my cock sure outlook would evaporate. It could be that every time I left the house I would encounter violence. My friends and family were very supportive but how could I know whom I might alienate and lose? Although everyone needs friends and even radiators need love, I thought, 'Fuck it. What will be, will be. I *have* to do this.'

If they play Bowie at the youthy it is usually something like 'Jean Genie' or 'Rebel Rebel' just before or after rock music, sometimes 'Fame', 'Sound and Vision', 'Golden Years' or 'Young Americans' is sandwiched in the disco. I've taken the album *Heroes* up with me and given it to the DJ asking him to play the title track; I want the full version not the single. The DJ is mid-20s and a John Travolta-influenced individual. For large sections of the evening people dance in synchronised lines, similar to line-dancing, maybe it actually is line-dancing, doing the same moves, a hundred kids single-clapping at the same time. It all seems a bit sad but who am I to judge? Perhaps they feel the power of the group, the warm fuzz of belonging. Do I belong? I'm not really into dancing at the youthy, or maybe I am too embarrassed to do so. In my bedroom I had practised a few moves to 'Heroes', moving with rhythm and in time, not exactly dancing. I don't really have any reference points, just a couple of snippets of Bowie miming that I'd seen on television. Telly was a live experience in those days, no videos or DVDs, three channels with little chance of a 'current' programme being repeated.

The opening bars of 'Heroes' fill the youthy, the floor clears, I walk into the middle, heart pounding, and start to walk on the spot, like moonwalking but going nowhere. A circle of people surrounds me, as I go on the circle deepens into a smudge of faces and I expect them to start shouting, 'Fight, fight, fight, fight', I'm half waiting for the kicks. I sway and move, interpreting the words with my hands and body, crouching like a sumo wrestler and pulling my elbows in towards my chest and rising, straightening and moving to one side or the other, putting in the odd, half-remembered move or gesture that I thought I'd seen in the little snippets of film of Bowie.

'Heroes' is symbolic of my doomed first love and every gesture, every move, is genuine and heartfelt, maybe even slightly raw. I mean it. 'Heroes' banging out loud simply moves me on an elemental level, it digs in and pulls out a physiological reaction, like wading through nettles in short pants.

The DJ kindly lets the song play all the way to the fade at the end and I walk on the spot out of the song. The song ends and I walk for real, the crowd in front of me parts to a deafening silence and they start clapping, cheering and whistling, strangers saying, 'Fucking brilliant,' as I walk past. How bizarre? These people are weird.

This wasn't how I'd imagined it. In my head I'd be doing it in a quiet corner; that was ridiculous and a bit silly. How could I expect, looking how I was looking, to do something very unusual that none of them had seen before, quietly in a corner? Also it wasn't the kind of thing that you could do quietly in the corner. The second 'Heroes' came on I realised that if I was going to do it, I had to stride, valiantly, into the centre of the dance floor, cocky and confident, and take whatever flak was coming. I tried not to give people's possible response that much thought, it was a bit scary, I'd concentrated on the mime as a distraction and the nerves, adrenaline and fear carried me through.

The reaction of the kids was really surprising and confusing, I wasn't naturally built to suit this kind of caper. My Nemesis was. I was stocky and fairly squat, Marc was a bit taller and thinner, certainly more graceful in a Bowiesque kinda way. Marc Golden was a Bowie fan, of my age group, from Seacroft, had a better name and came out a little while after me. He probably came out independently, as I had, although, being from Seacroft, was more likely to come across Bowie-influenced individuals, not in a biblical sense, obviously. As soon as I heard of him I liked him, although anyone who mentioned him did it in a competitive context – I wasn't competing with anyone.

When I finally saw him mime, some time later, I thought he was better at it than me, it was a big thing, but I would have quite happily told him so, had we not been sworn enemies. Sworn by everyone but me. The chuntering teenagers kept feeding us unpleasant, misinformation about the other.

'He said you are......', 'When he sees you he's going to.....', 'If you go anywhere near him he's gonna.....', 'He said your mother shagged an ostrich.'

'What's wrong with shagging ostriches? Do they not have wants and desires?'

I didn't listen to the prattling,

Sorry, nothing to do with anything but I've just had an idea for a cover version: 'Mozart's Requiem - The Happy Mix.' What y'think? It's the interbreeding grandparents what did it, not me.

I had absolutely no problem with Marc, why should I? He was the only person coming from anywhere near where I was. We had too much in common for me to dislike him, I was much more traditionally attractive than him but he had a more interesting face. The first time I saw him I smiled, nodded said, 'Alright,' and, given the chance, would have said, 'Looking good, Marc, almost as sexy as me.' But he took the nod, smile and hello as sarcasm, looked straight ahead and walked, 'Pity, but I'll keep doing it.' Marc was obviously unsure about the prattling teenagers, about truth and fiction. He looked really good, he was like a darker, leaner version of me, I preferred dark, I was always intrigued by my opposite. I was more 'Ziggy' he was more 'Diamond Dogs'.

Although heavily warned against it, before I knew Marc or any of his mates, I go to John Smeaton youthy; this is, dead-centre, Marc's patch. My presence is enough to convince Marc's entourage that I am pissing on his doorstep. To make it worse and with no forethought, they play a Bowie track and I mime, equivalent to pissing on his doorstep and patting his father's bottom as I leave the garden. There is no malice on my part, I am not conscious of fondling his father. The lad who, my radar detects, is going to attack me is a bit older and supposed to be REALLY hard but he dun't worry me, quite fancy him, it will do my reputation no harm at all. His friend however, though taller is closer to my fighting weight, I don't fancy at all. The one that is supposed to be REALLY hard is built like a brick shithouse and slightly taller than me, all bravado and head strong, he will come at me in a blaze of aggression, easy. His mate is menacing, cold and calculating, he has 'I'm an experienced street fighter' tattooed across his forehead, and I have 'I want to fight the shit-house' emblazoned in my stare, I avoid all eye contact with the street fighter. The shit-house may chin me, but at least I will understand the game and have half a chance. The other I just don't fancy, at all, not a bit, not even a small bit of a bit. It is touch and go who will attack first, but it doesn't come. I get the feeling, which was later confirmed, that Marc has dissuaded the lads from jumping me, which is good as I'd gone on my own, it is their patch and, unless they fought fair, which they wouldn't have, I'd have got battered.

Later, when I knew Marc a little better, we were never close enough, I stopped one of my mates from bricking him while he was on stage; like you do.

Unlike me, Marc did have a hard working-class background, his father never stood aside and let him leave the house, the bruises were the testimony. After leaving school he worked down the pit, was made redundant after the miners' strike, and drifted into a fairly serious habit which, the last time I saw him, he had broken. The only thing I know for sure about Marc is that from that moment to this, no matter what the circumstances, he will have looked good. Fact. Marc had a gift for wearing clothes, put him in anything, he'd carry it off, he'd wear it well. **The 2nd Fact What I Know: Marc Golden wore clothes well.**

I'd just like to say at this point that I realise that I've had two **2nd Facts What I Know**. Why is this a problem? Why would you have preferred the second **2nd Fact What I Know** to have been **the 3rd**? There is no **3rd Fact What I Know**, just two **2nd Facts What I Know**. So the world has been plunged into chaos – live with it. This is my world and *you* are the voyeur, I make the important decisions around here not you, you are passive and trapped. You have one choice, read or don't; even then, when you've put me down, I'll still be here babbling. You can't control everything, y'despotic get, loosen out and let go.

8

There's an often short but glorious period of time, somewhere between 13 and early 20s, when we control our destiny, the world. The future is our domain, we own it and that knowledge gives us confidence. You could say that, tomorrow belongs to us, but I wouldn't because that would be too like a Nazi scene from some '70s musical. The length of this ownership of life is indeterminate, it may be a week, it may span a decade, only in blessed lives does it stretch much further. In this place, most, if not all, things are possible. I have only recently accepted, and it wasn't easy, that at 42 I am actually very unlikely to play for Leeds United; that's extended adolescence for you.

At some random point in this time of confidence what we do or don't, say or didn't say becomes relevant. Before we arrived in this new terrain we simply were, we had no serious impact on our world around us, it was just there. Shit on a neighbour's staircase, someone would clean it up saying, 'I'm sure it was an accident.' Although we felt guilt and responsibility acutely, our actions didn't seem to scar the landscape. As we slip, moist, out of our cocoon, into this place of power, we shake out our colours knowing that this is our field, the nectar is ours, we can scat and flutter, take time to allow the sun to warm our wings. We cannot see the random squat in the flower, we have a million flowers, we may never see the random. The paper, square pyramid that children yesterday stuck their small fingers into, picking out a colour or a destiny that was always ridiculous, is now an unseen, small-scale threat. This is the most popular section of life and this can be the most defining.

There can be a serene composure about and around the butterflies, a different perspective flitting above the pasture – nothing is as important. They are suffering big-time pressures but can appear calm, controlled, analytical to the point of needing a punch. Complex things can appear simple and simple things they show to have dimensions. Controlling situations by removing themselves from boring or difficult conversations with a silly comment, 'Career? Flying Concorde looks cool, but maybe I'll just win The Lottery.' Giggle, look away, end of monotonous conversation. Sometimes they think they are ten or twelve and then realise they are half way through their driving test, they sit in limbo not sure when or how to leave the 'safe to shit on a neighbours stairs' place. Ah well. 'Che sera, sera', is a dangerous and lazy stand-point and can deflect responsibility but it is one of the few facts I know. Is it, in fact, a 'truism'? (Theoreticians a simple yes/no will do, no detail please, I'm flowing.) **The 3rd Fact What I Know: What will be will be.** (Ha. I lied; there is a 3rd Fact What I Know). The butterflies can experience with an intensity that gets slowly diluted by experience, sudden rushes or a constant pulse of heightened emotion. Nobody has the acute emotional receptors and awareness of a teenager.

In the haze of our awakening the sun obscures chance, luck, destiny, bad moves. In our heads the destiny is ours to mould, the only anxiety is can we be arsed moulding it? The residual memory of shitting on a staircase without responsibility comes into play, along with a constant background hum of people who seem static, trapped in a spider's web, whispering, 'This is the most important time of your life, don't you want to visit the spider with me?' The sad thing is that this is a crucial time, the web bouncers are right. Consequences count but they can be difficult to see. Randomness is invisible in this place – a birth, a death, an accident, a misunderstanding, a misplaced word, an inspirational teacher, getting noticed by a bully, being born a fourth child, a first child. You can meet someone, by chance, who points to flowers in the field that you would have never seen, the fragrance of which could stay with you for life; a few minutes later, and they have left the room before you enter it. Someone has a huge talent, a keenly defined sense of humour or a passion and you nod and walk by. Make decisions, skip school, sniff that glue, steal from that window, beat that boy, forget that Durex, and reduce the pasture, burn a whole acre of grassland, reduce possibilities to simple prescriptions.

At some, seemingly random, point (and just as we earlier in life slipped from childhood into the wider world of experience and increased anger as we shit on a neighbour's staircase) we step through that gate and out of the field of butterflies, and we are fucked. Perspective is defined from outside, priorities are quite clear but difficult to obtain, we are sucked into adulthood where the question 'But what do we really need?' does not exist. I need to connect with my kids and just miss, are they stepping into the paddock I left years ago and does this geographical distance nail down an emotional distance? Is it necessary? Do they need to detach so that we can let go? We need time, we haven't got it, we need to maintain important relationships that float away into the mist. We need our old composure but how can the pressure allow that, and what is the pressure? Is it a fair exchange? Did we make a decision? Which one was it? Did we choose? Did you chuck a boyfriend and then by comparison to all the next ones, realise that he was witty, intelligent, considerate, good with sex, and then see him ten years later with three kids shouting, 'And his tackle worked.' His last book only sold three million so you were probably right to dump him, who'd have wanted an easy life with the nicest man you ever met, who, by the way, completely doted on you? Where are you now? How did you get there? Do you like it here? Who do you wish were with you? Shall you stay there, or do you want to go elsewhere? Can you make that decision? Do you remember the sun on your wings? My passions are on the wane and I am a lesser man for it. I have stifled my creativity and I am no longer myself, just the least interesting part of myself. How did I allow that to happen? People are all that counts, in the immortal words of Miss Dynamite, 'We leave this world alone, so who gives a fuck about the things you own?' There are people who I genuinely love. Lots of people. I like people but I do not feel close enough to them. I feel very open and often they seem very closed, I'm sure they feel the same. May I state at this point, I am not open to physical shows of affection, this is my space so keep the fuck out. Don't try that 'pretending to kiss my cheek with your lips perpendicular to my ear' routine or I'll drop you faster than a cat who's just spotted the flea powder, y'cunt. Only Greek fishermen and very select friends, are safe kissing my cheek, and that is a solid, stone fact. Respect and consideration of others is what counts. Somehow it is hard to say the simple thing, 'I like/love you. These are all your good points.' We get distracted by the drab routine, the functioning of life and forget the crucial essence of life, those around us, whom we love.

Why did I not have physical contact with my father? I did when I was younger, where did it go? When did it stop? Why was he questioning his relationship with his kids on his deathbed? He was a great dad, with me a very modern dad of his time. He was positive and supportive, how could he be questioning himself so fundamentally at this defining moment? I listed his good points, tried to reassure him but he remained uncertain. **The 17th Fact What I Know: My Dad was a Good Dad.**

When I was a lad, in Whitkirk, Leeds, Yorkshire, England, my dad was the only adult who started water-fights in the street. Including all kids and any adults who were daft enough to walk past him when he had a squeezy bottle in his hand. I don't remember any other adults joining in.

Fact of Life No. 1: When men die people say, 'Ooh he was a character.'
Fact of Life No. 2: People exaggerate at funerals.
Fact of Life No. 3: The dead person usually wasn't a 'character'.
Fact of Life No. 4: My dad was 'a character'.
Fact of Life No. 5: At my dad's funeral nobody needed to say, 'Ooh he was a character.'

My parents used to live opposite the no.165 bus stop going to Castleford. The bus only came, at best, every 30 minutes, you miss it, you got no option, you're waiting. As you waited for the bus there was no shelter and nowhere you could shelter in the safe knowledge that you would catch the bus, should it come. In rain or cold, if my dad noticed someone arrive at the bus stop just after the bus, he would put on the kettle, put a little bowl of sugar on a tray, make a tea or a coffee; apparently, with years of experience, he could spot a coffee drinker.

'You can't trust coffee drinkers.'

He'd then take these across the busy road and say, 'How many sugars?'

When I could, I used to watch the people's reactions, they were priceless and I never saw anyone who was anything but genuinely grateful. One time when it was bouncing it down, he lent them a brolly. If they tried to engage him in conversation he'd say, 'Can't stand and chat, it's freezing.'

'What shall I do with the cup?'

'Either leave it on the wall, or take it with you, I've got loads.'

He had a garage full of cups and mugs, his stock for the market store, and they always got the seconds. If there were a few people, he'd take a few cups of tea or coffee, if someone else arrived while he was passing over the beverage he'd take their order.

It was funny watching the reactions as people passed a group at the bus stop, sipping from china cups.

On the A64 to Scarborough, we are towing a caravan. The traffic is stationary and has been for some time. Dad pulls over into the lay-by, sets up the kitchen – big pans full of water – pulls out a stack of paper cups and he's off. He's seen a coach load of pensioners on a day-trip to the coast, they're a bit miserable gazing at a queue of vehicles super-glued to the tarmac. Dad enters the coach with his big pot of tea, 'How many sugars, love?' in his Australian accent. He delivers tea to the coach, messing about, telling jokes in accents from around

48

the UK. He gets them laughing and singing songs, then he's off to decamp, lest the traffic frees itself.

Age eleven, sitting in the Wimpy Bar, Crossgates, with my mates, I hear a faint whistle and lower my head. The whistling gets closer and I think about going to the toilet.

'Mick look, it's your dad.' I was too slow.

'He's brilliant, he's a nutter, he doesn't give a shit.'

Coming around the corner, with a plank of wood over his shoulder, whistling at the top of his lips interspersed with nodding and 'Good afternoon' to anyone who looked, which was everyone. What was he whistling? Go on guess, walking through a crowded shopping centre, plank of wood over his shoulder, 'Hi-Ho Hi-Ho, It's Off to Fucking Work We Go.'

My dad was generally full of the joy of life but also had dark moods. I miss him.

He could talk to my mates, they liked him, and he'd somehow mastered the art of communicating with kids without it being strained or difficult. It was strange how it took me years to accept his extrovertedness, I simple found it hugely embarrassing until one day I thought it was a gift. It also made me not quite care what people thought. His first ever new car was a Lada and being excited, while also being aware of the stigma, anyone who entered the house got a guided tour of his Lada. It was a comic routine that he honed and tightened with each tour, until the last few people to see the show were genuinely guffawing as they finished.

We weren't close to our extended family, neither emotionally nor geographically. Dad came from Widnes and my mother came from a village near Wakefield and we rarely visited these places. As I wasn't party to much interaction, I only know what I was told, so other than very sparse memories I only have reports. I can remember two visits to Widnes, one daytime going from aunts and uncles to aunts and uncles and at each house the aunt would absolutely insist that the children had eggs and chips. An hour between visits meant that we managed the first few no problem, but by the time we got to the fifth, the adults had to step in.

'No you're OK Gertrude, really, they've already eaten at Rita's, Theresa's, Phyllis's and Nelly's.'

Ooh, I don't know, thought I. What is it with kids and food?

I was young but received huge plates of eggs and chips – the only variation was what with? It was from the list of fried mushroom, bread, tomatoes or beans, sometimes all four, sometimes just one of the four. Eight eggs in a five-hour period – I didn't shit again until my 27th birthday, a glorious moment, shit black as coal. My uncle Zephyr had a Zephyr car, which made me giggle, I couldn't work out if he was named after the car or the car was named after him.

The other time I went over to Widnes, again I was young, I'd guess about nine. We went to a wedding or a big anniversary. All these people kept coming over and being really gushing, cuddling and hugging, 'I haven't seen you since you were this high.' I recognised not one of them. Later on in the evening a young man came over and said, 'Fancy a club?'

'I won't be allowed to go.'

'I've checked with your mum and dad and you can.'

He was right, I checked and I could go. Standing outside the function hall, the taxi arrives.

'Taxi for McCann.'

Jesus, how did he know my name?

'How did you know my name?'

'I booked the taxi in my name.'

'Eh?'

'It's my surname as well.'

'Ah, so we are related.'

'Yeh, I'm your cousin.'

The club was out of Widnes and felt like the middle of nowhere. I had a brilliant time, I was so fussed over by the women, they made me feel really special.

'Oooh, can you bring him back in ten years' time?'

I just had a really good time, my cousin was popular and very funny, he looked after me. God knows how he got me into the club but there was a pay-off for him because once the women had finished cooing over me they moved onto him.

My dad came from a big Irish Catholic family, I used to think there were 13 of them but it's more likely to be between seven and nine. As a child he used to ride around on the back of a big St Bernards dog in the chip shop his mother ran. Apparently his father was quite a severe man and had been married before he met my grandmother but his first wife and three children died of TB. That could explain some of his severity, how that must scar you, watching your family die one by one. He was quite a successful man, a foreman at a chemical factory and quite well off. My grandmother was in service and got a job as my grandfather's housekeeper, she became pregnant to him and they married. From a young age Dad was sent away to a Catholic seminary to train for the priesthood, age ten or eleven he returned for a weekend, walked into the front room and there, laid out, dead on the table, was his father.

Generations of kids leaving St Benedict's school, in the '60s and '70s, thought that Mr McCann had a gas-powered TV, and unfeasibly receptive nostrils and ears. In his youth he played rugby league to a reasonable standard, while playing for Widnes second or third team his finger got trodden on and dislocated, they reset it, then and there, on the pitch but not properly, after much trying of other things it was amputated. He'd often say, 'I only ever had two days off work in my life, one to have my finger amputated and the second to bury my first daughter.'

Dad would hide the amputated finger from the kids at school and then while speaking to them he'd start fiddling with his ear and then suddenly poke his finger right into his ear past the knuckle and twist it as if he was trying to get something out. He'd then repeat it, getting his finger up his nose past the knuckle, he'd carry on speaking and turning slightly so that the class could see that he hadn't simply bent his finger, and then pretended that he didn't understand what the fuss was about.

They tried again and again to fix my dad's finger but he finally had to go into hospital to have it amputated in the late '50s. While there, entertaining the troops, or clients as we like to call them in the 21st century, with songs, jokes and general messing around he was spotted by a music-hall impresario. He saw my dad's gift of communication in a light-hearted manner that all but family loved and offered him a season at some seaside resort, down south. My mother was pregnant with her second child, the first dying in awful circumstances a couple of years earlier, he was therefore reluctant to leave her for a couple of months and declined the offer. My parents had no doubt at all that the guy was genuine. My father's reticence led the guy to keep upping his offer until he was apparently being offered seriously good money but the contract was short and the timing really bad, my dad was also contracted to a teaching job with a reliable income. He occasionally mentioned this situation and I could see in his eyes that he knew he'd missed a potentially life-changing opportunity. There is no doubt that, when dealing with people, he could have rivalled Bruce Forsyth or Jimmy Tarbuck, not Tommy Cooper or Eric Morecambe but certainly Brucie or Tarbie.

My mother came from a long line of farmers and farm labourers based around Wakefield. She has an early memory of travelling through Wakefield in awe of the fireworks only to find out later that she'd been journeying through an air raid. My grandmother and grandfather were cousins, sorry, **cousins,** as in first cousins, doesn't that explain a few things? Grandma's parents gave them ten pounds as a wedding gift with which they bought a milk-round and worked their way up to buying a farm, apparently Grandma did most of the running of the farm. My mum used to play hide and seek on the farm with the school inspector – she wanted schooling, but her father wouldn't allow it as he didn't think that she needed a formal education to be a farmer's wife. This led my mother to regard education above all other things; her energy levels had dropped a tad by the time I entered high school. One day my grandmother returned to the farm with the three kids after a short holiday in Scarborough, and all their belongings were on the front lawn – she had nowhere to go, no job, no access to money, nothing. Men could do this in the '40s, 'Eeh, them were the days.' My granddad was a shameless profiteer during the war, burying sides of meat in a container in a field to sell on the black market. He made a lot of money but that all went to his 'fancy woman' along with everything of any worth that my grandma owned, or didn't, as men owned all in them days. 'Eeh, them were the days.' Alternatively, he may just have been doing a bit of wheeler-dealing on the black market to provide for his family, these kinds of stories are prone to exaggeration. Standing by the well with the government inspector who's getting towards the end of his cigarette; Granddad praying he doesn't throw it down the well – it may not react too nicely with the cans of petrol stashed down there.

My mother spent most of her teenage years close to Dewsbury and as I've signalled her father's attitude, which I'm sure was a shared experience and introduced a three-quarter-rural upbringing, I'd like to add something. While my mother was in her late teens her best friend was Jean Oates, they used to go out dancing, and no I don't think that's a euphemism. Anyway she became the first ever female RAC mechanic bike rider. So think on, leave your Northern, country-bumpkin, timid-womenfolk prejudices at the door, freak face.

I remember repeatedly asking, 'Are we nearly there yet, Dad?' I am a young child, that's what we do, dads drive, mums hand over the occasional boiled sweets and look at sisters with concern. My sister used to throw up in cars, that's what Kate did. Distraction was the best policy for Mum and Dad.

'Altogether now...,
Well you'll never get to heaven, in a biscuit tin,
Cos a biscuit tin won't fit you in.
Well you'll never get to heaven, in a biscuit tin,
Cos a biscuit tin won't fit you in.
I don't wanna smell my lord no more.'
'So I've got a what? So she's your mum? You've got a mum?'

The journey undulated up and down fairly grim, unfriendly, semi-industrial scapes and I tried to come to terms with the concept of my mum's mum. She was weird, old, spoke too quickly, I could only pick out sporadic words, no linkage, no flow, a dialect I could hardly understand. She seemed to talk non-stop and she definitely didn't breathe. She had spent her whole life in Netherton, a small place outside Wakefield. My dad was helpful, attentive but, like me, he wanted to be elsewhere. The others knew her, greeted her with familiarity, knew where things were and looked at me like I should know, but this place was completely new. The cooker stretched right across a wall and was big and black. I didn't know that cookers could be black and this one heated the house as well. The house was small, the garden tidy, tiered and useless; every time I moved, I did it on a plant and Grandma didn't like that, but she liked me. She came out and down to my level, 'Play down there by the coal-sheds, but don't go near the green one.'

I used to visit my grandma as a boy, and I remember painting her cupboard when I got older. She never stayed at our house, she stopped, never would again, not since one night when she was babysitting, simultaneously looking at the young kids sleeping in bed and listening to them playing downstairs. The older kids were sleeping in the attic, she'd just checked, and they'd need to pass her to get downstairs. The poltergeists were at play, running up and down the hallway, laughing, the sound of children playing. It was simply accepted that the house was haunted, a fact of life, you just lived with it – not Grandma, she never stayed again, I remember her visiting years later and picking up on her unease. They used to get giddy when Mum and Dad were away and quiet when they were at home. The first time I stayed in the house on my own, aged eleven, I shouted down the stairs from the attic, 'It's me, you're not scaring me, will you keep the noise down? I'm trying to sleep.' My heart pounded but the noises stopped, I returned to the top of the stairs, 'Thank you.'

When I was older and after I'd come out as a Bowie-influenced individual, while visiting my grandma, she said, 'We did laugh when you used to play the fool with y' make-up.'

My loves, my passions, my definition of self, tied so permanently to her umbilical gene. Her battles through life, her changing society, her social stigmas and her strengths were a length of steel down my spine. 'The fool!' My working-class roots that enabled me to grasp my moments of the eternal, my bravery, my convictions, my freedoms, my art, my babe-magnetic sexual aura, reduced to the vaguely ridiculous. A potential ice-pick through the back of my soul's identity. My hide had thickened. Whereas in the past there would have been a scene, now I just blushed slightly and nodded. It did mean that I spent the next six months saying to anyone who'd listen, 'I may look like a woman but I've shagged loads of byrds, hundreds, maybe thousands and anyway, I'm not gay, I know that because I tried it and it didn't agree with me.'

To which the little old lady in the queue at the post office said, 'That's nice, love,' while her friend started telling me that she'd liked women all her life, men made her skin crawl, but there was no such thing as lesbians in 1915.

9

Growing up, in Leeds, Yorkshire, England, in the '70s, the world was completely off its trough, mental, mad, fucked-up. When I was ten or eleven I remember the three-day week, electricity and therefore lights, TVs, kettles, hot water, record players, electric blankets, not that I had such a thing, not working. Negotiating the house and playing cards via candlelight.

Social unrest, race-based riots or riotous pickets seemed a constant in the '70s. Images of bombs, insurrection and shootings filled our screens from across the Irish Sea. I was often called a 'Catholic cunt' by 'friends', and some kids at school displayed the tri-colour, with 'IRA' or guns drawn on the back of their ruck-sack. The football terraces, where I spent a lot of time, were full of hatred, racism, sexism and violence. I remember looking up at my dad with surprise as he walked past people beating each other senseless on the terraces; I thought he'd sort it out.

For the entirety of my childhood, the threat of nuclear war hung over us; it felt a very real possibility and we weren't fooled by the 'Protect and Survive' leaflets and television campaign. Death could come at any time, unannounced, unprepared for, and we knew it would be worse than anything we could imagine.

In the early '80s I became aware of one of my cousins from my mother's side, a male adult, who worked and looked after three children. At the time, this was extremely unusual, his wife had, 'run off to Greenham Common, leaving the kids'. Eeh, her name was mud, but the nuclear threat very real. We sometimes looked to the horizon and shuddered. We had the terrifying thought of an American president, the office having been degraded by Nixon, or an over-emotional Soviet with their fat fingers twitching over the little red button. Paranoia ruled.

Worse than this, worse then everything, the scariest thing of all, was the three-starred jumper. They may have been in the residual, but huge flares with big pockets on the side, three-starred jumpers and platform shoes were still around. Big-collared, bright-yellow shirts. I can honestly say that I never had a jumper with stars on it. My school mate did cross-country every week for a year in huge platform shoes. I don't think the teacher had even considered that he might not have had any other shoes. It was very funny, watching him clump through mud, sticking to his platforms, three feet off the ground.

The world seemed to be falling apart; to us kids in the '70s instability and madness were the norm. Money is one of the staples of life, I bet that since there were homo sapiens on this earth some form of tender existed, from nice pebbles or meat, to metal, to be traded. The decade started with people worrying about and then gazing at their coins with confusion, trying to work out what they were. It was belting for us kids, there was none of this '28 pennies make a shilling which is two-thirds of a crown, which is the fourth uncle of a guinea pig who once had a pound 40 times as big as his tanner'.

'A pound is a hundred pence, cool, that's all I need to know.'

Old ladies seemed to get it, but in shops other adults spent two hours paying for a newspaper, while the pensioners would shout, 'Oh bugger it! Just give him 7p you tosser, 3 tanners and he'll give you a ha'penny change.'

Similar to the introduction of the euro, with decimalisation the perception was that everything went up.

Even us, who recognised it and understood its perceived value, never knew what the money in our pocket was worth. Its worth would change between going to bed and getting up. If you imagine going to the shop to buy LMA Manager 2007, knowing that it costs £29.97, that is what it costs, but when you get there it suddenly costs £31.23. It's not just that shop that has put it up but the thing has gone up everywhere, it now costs £31.23. The perfect amount of money in your pants could suddenly become a halfpenny-short shopping disaster. Today, you shall not eat crisps.

Unaffordable crisps. You could not ignore politics in the '70s. Politics was almost exciting, big things seemed to be happening.

As I was coming into a consciousness of the world around me, it was totally unpredictable and chaotic, frenzied and foaming at the mouth. Britain had rabies, barking madly and chasing its tail – it was brilliant.

Britain was known as the 'sick old man of Europe', I'm sure I also remember it being called the dirty man of Europe. I grew up in the sick, dirty old man's underpants and somebody called the IMF were coming to change our underwear.

I recollect the word 'devaluation' but don't know if it was just a threat or a reality. I'm certain that there was a period in the '70s where people in full-time employment were only allowed to work for three days a week. A poet of national distinction, a wordsmith without compare, named it 'the three-day week'. Genius. It must have been awful for the workers, only working 24 hours a week, almost as down-trodden as some Germans in the 21st century.

It really did feel like you were at the edge of the end of the world, maybe today, maybe tomorrow, but the world was ending. We grew up with it, we thought it normal. There were times when everything stopped, trains, buses, hospitals, power, bin men. I can even remember bread shortages for God's sake, going to the supermarket with my mother and seeing a big gap where the bread should be.

My content analysis of '70s news programmes showed the most used words to be strikes, pickets, disputes, shortages, stoppages and cuts.

Women were not equal, they did not even pretend that women were equal. In the '50s and '60s, byrds were put back in their domestic box, but during the '70s they started escaping, we tried to round them up but they were too damn fast. I remember my mum getting part-time jobs, bringing home ice-lollies from the Treats factory, the economic anarchy making a second income more than useful. I can't say for sure that this went across society but I suspect it did. Many mums that I knew worked when they could and suddenly weren't there when you got home. They would get paid half or even a quarter of what a male doing the same job would get. They were not allowed things like mortgages independently; they had to get a proper person to sign for them, like a man.

This getting out to work may have been quite liberating but it certainly increased the female work-load. I suspect men's positioning was either to just ignore domestic duties or to make sure that they did them so badly that it was counter-productive. The old scams are the best. I grew up doing housework, vaccing, dusting, washing up, rubbing down the stair carpets with a damp cloth. I suspect my father as a boy never did. The '70s were hard for men, we don't like change and the pressure to put the bin out was awful.

My older sister Kate was a fairly radical feminist, so I grew up with that perspective as the norm and would often say, 'Ama feminist me, like ar'Kate'.

1976 was a boiling-hot summer, technically known as a heat wave. It brought stand pipes, people had to collect water from taps in the street, it din't bother us kids, less baths and just like camping.

The 1970s was the orange decade, the colour of the '70s was orange. Orange kitchens (Hygena QA), orange Choppers, orange three-wheeler, triangular cars. Kitchenalia, especially gadgets, were orange. Orange Tupperware lids. The game of the '70s was Monopoly. I think it came out in the '70s – or it could have been developed in 1934 by

Charles B. Darrow of Germantown, Pennsylvania, I'm really not sure Gilly, I couldn't say – and is the most popular board game of all time. Fuck you, chess. What was the colour of the best row of houses in Monopoly? If you said 'Purple' for Mayfair and Park Lane then you shouldn't be reading this, as you are clearly an opinionated, dumb shit who makes statements of fact around subjects that you know nothing about. The orange combo of Vine Street, Marlborough and Bow Street was the king combination of the Monopoly board. You land on orange when they're free and your chances of winning have increased drastically.

Soft furnishings in the '70s always contained orange, usually swirled in with other colours, yellows, browns and darker tones. We had a particularly tasteful carpet spun with orange twisting through very dark browns and purples. The thing is, at the time, it was tasteful, it's dead easy to look back and laugh and wonder how taste could have been so 'bad' – it wasn't bad just different. Our current liking for bland cream, light-brown and stone colours is very dull, but yes, it does look like an Ikea catalogue.

Orange did not exist in the 1960s, or before. Dutch football, you couldn't get much more '70s than Johan Cruyff, and the '70s was their decade, they may not have won anything but it was their decade. Green and purple were colours often associated with orange in a particularly tasteful way. Space Hoppers were '70s and always orange, it was the decade when pumpkins were replacing turnips at Halloween. The family of orange fruit; tangerines, nectarines etc. were discovered by Christopher Jamieson and expanded during the '70s. If you were a child in the '70s, what fruit was in the bottom of your Christmas sack? No – not an apple, that's wrong.

Jaffa cakes and Orange Club biscuits. Why is everybody over a certain age singing, *If you like a lot of chocolate on your biscuit, join our club?*

Irn Bru, so orange that it could clear a hang-over. Not Tizer, that was red or The Clangers, they were pink.

The most important orange happening of the '70s and the defining orange moment of the decade was the release of *Low*. The cover brought a new depth to our understanding of orange as an abstracted, tonal, mood colour. During the 1970s indicators on cars were always orange whereas now they're usually erm...well anyway, in the '70s they were orange. The '70s was the orange decade.

The release of *Low* by Mr David Bowie was not the defining orange moment of the 1970s, it is my obsession that forces me to make such an outlandish claim. With proper consideration I have to be truthful. I would love that it were *Low* that demanded the accolade of top orange phenomenon of the era. So with a slightly heavy heart and like a Catholic in a confessional I give the honour to the clear and unambiguous king of the '70s orange scene, Hot Wheels track. Hot Wheels track was the decisive orange happening of the '70s. At first they fiddled with other colours, but you can hear the designers and developers, 'How can they do this to us? It is against nature. Hot Wheels track cannot be red; it *is* orange that is what it *is*. That's its essence. Dogs bark, fish swim, flares get caught under your shoes and Hot Wheels track *is orange.*'

'What's that?'

'It's Hot Wheels track.'

'But it's, it's....'

'I know, I saw it in the shop and it was exciting and my mum said I could have it but then I got it home and realised what I'd done.'

'Buddi'ell!'

'I know, but I daren't tell her, I have to smile and play and pretend everything is alright but when she isn't around I don't go near it. Sometimes I wake in the middle of the night hoping that it was a nightmare, I turn my light on but the awful truth is always there. I have *red* Hot Wheels track.'

'Listen you can come and play with mine whenever y'like.'

'Oh thanks Mick, you don't know what that means to me. But how can I get that out of my bedroom?'

'You can't.'

'But it taunts me, it's always there reminding me of how stupid I was. It was so cool when I saw it in the shop but look at it. Look, really look, it's fucking red.'

'Aww, you swore.'

This design aberration nailed down in my young mind the most important binary opposite of my life; right and wrong. The clarity was overwhelming. Sometimes things are simple, they are logically worked through and have a pure state of right or wrong, good or bad. The madness of denying the soul of the track was mercifully brief and it rightfully takes the crown of the iconic orange symbol of the decade. The track was, from that moment forward, brought back into balance with the buzz of the universe and is **always** orange.

Then came Punk. It is very difficult to contextualise the effect of Punk. Before Punk Britain was a much more obviously class-ridden society, the royal family was revered, almost untouchable.

God save the Queen
The Fascist regime
She made you a moron
Potential H bomb

Within a few years the royal family were fair game and open to much more scrutiny. The effect was wider, Punk was an empowering movement basically saying, 'If you feel it's right, do it.' More people became more politically active on an individual level, people with a 'cause' or 'causes' became more common. On my coming out, I don't know what the effect was. It felt like I came out away from and independent of Punk but who knows how much and from where the attitude of 'fuck you, I am me' might have permeated my young head? The ideas of grasping the moment now, kicking against social norms, may have surrounded me, unrecognised. It is impossible to gauge how much Punk being in the media, sometimes on the street, eased the path of my coming out. I would need to speak to someone who came out slightly earlier, compare and contrast. Punks were usually friendly and accepting of me, which certainly helped me while I was out.

The crowning glory, the crucial and defining achievement of Punk, was to return the 'The' that the '70s Prog. Rockers/Rockers had dumped. Queen, Pink Floyd, Deep Purple. Led. Zep, Free, Wishbone Ash, King Crimson. All these bands, and more, had lost touch with their 'The'. The Damned, The Pistols, The Clash returned the 'The'. The simplicity, the lack of pretension, the how it is.

In my stomping ground, 1975 brought the first, little-publicised, attack by the Yorkshire Ripper. The woman, attacked on her doorstep, survived and it wasn't until the first murder that it came to our attention. His first fatal victim, Wilma McCann, as well as sharing my surname, was the auntie of a girl at school, a lovely lass who seemed embarrassed by her aunt's perceived profession, so found school difficult. She didn't realise that the majority of people at school were only concerned for her loss. For the next six years, through almost all of my slag years, women in Leeds lived in fear, their movements and freedoms curtailed.

The possibility of a sudden and brutal death stalked the night-time streets of their consciousness; female fear was all around me. Posters, supposedly, with the serial killer's handwriting on were all over

Leeds, a constant reminder. Women didn't go out of an evening, they certainly couldn't go out on their own, get a taxi on their own, the police wouldn't approach a lone woman as people were suspicious that it was a policeman. All white, medium-height men were a possible killer – question your husband's movements, what about people at work? In an Afghani way, boys and men ensured that any female going anywhere at night was accompanied; sometimes when my room was warm and cosy I'd say, 'Fuck it, you'll survive, we're just as likely to be killed by a hit and run and I don't want to die.' But I was alone in this and never quite saw it through.

When I was a lad, women in Leeds marched through the streets calling for a night-time curfew on all men.

Authority was very close to us in those days and I'm sure that if you were black it will have been even closer. Where we congregated was watched for 18 months by the police. People getting picked up on the way to and from our 'den', if they were new to the 'den' they always got stopped by the police. Although you'll wrongly think there was more to it, my best mate ended up in borstal for walking through the Arndale Centre dressed in a punky manner, he subsequently ate dog shit to prove his madness and scare the nutters in the borstal away.

When I was 15/16 I had a house party, and yes it will have been *wild*. Someone made a prank call to the emergency services, or a neighbour complained. It started without me and I arrived back at the house to two fire engines, three Black Mariahs, a handful of police cars, a couple of ambulances, and a few small vans with barking dogs. You would have thought the first to arrive might have put out a 'false alarm' call. No, the police wanted to come to the front door and threaten my 17/18-year-old brother; had he not been calmly assertive, or had we lived in a more working-class area, there would have been need for the emergency services. While 'marauding and rioting' in the Arndale Centre with fifty friends, we made the front page of *The Evening Post*, the fact that ten to 15 of us simply walked through wasn't of much interest to the journalist. I jousted with a few constables in the street, the one time I was caught 'bang to rights', the kindly officer said, 'Don't do it again. On your way.' In a friendly, Dixon of Dock Green kinda way. Even police officers are individuals.

Just because I have no police record at all, no warning, not even a parking ticket, doesn't mean I've never broken the law. A Tory leader may take 'class A' drugs in the safety of a university dorm and it's later accepted by all as the harmless dabbling of a young man, a working-class, young person does it on the street and is criminalised.

The '70s were a mad time, although I'm sure you can make that argument for any decade, the '70s were a tad chaotic, crazy, fucked-up. Just how fucked-up is shown by the unions, later, through the 'winter of discontent', leading Maggie Thatcher, by the nose, into 10 Downing Street and ensuring that the Tories stayed a while. It's strange, I remember the winter of discontent through television news, whereas the three-day week I remember through power cuts.

Some Thing That We Didn't Have In The '70s:

The term 'New Romantic.'
   We had the youth movement, in a pure street and individual form. Uncontaminated by misunderstanding music journalists, the media at large. Unbastardised by fat, lazy record companies whose only concern is maximum profit and being able to commercially package it so as to maximise its fluffy, national appeal. The movement was hard, northern and working-class, not really transplantable to leafy southern suburbs. This was a pure youth movement, not Man. United football club.

Other Things we didn't have in the '70s:

Mobile phones
Three substitutes
Food that cooked in three minutes
A liking of semi-skimmed milk
Cold calling
Children
Home computers
Adolph Hitler/the Third Reich
Radiohead
Electronic games other than TV blip tennis/squash
The '80s
Social paranoia
Jonny Howson
CCTV
Microwave ovens
'Everyone Says Hi!'

Music critics saying David's latest album is 'a return to form', just like they did for the last four, tossers
CD/DVD/Gameboy/Playstation/The X Box/Nintendo

Things we did have in the '70s:
The youth movement later labelled 'New Romantic'
Blakey segs
Ape-nis (half new pennies)
Dave Allen
An orange bias
Hip-hop
Jaws
The Volkswagen Golf
One substitute
Pink Monkey Birds
Thermos flasks
Friends who did somersaults off walls
The rise & fall of Marc Bolan
A propensity/inclination to ask strangers the time
General Pinochet
Johnny Giles
Tanners, the cutest of all coins
A Bouquet of Barbed Wire, although we weren't always allowed to watch it
A more interesting relationship with colour
Minnie Ripperton
Polystyrene tiles: in every home, they swept through Britain like laminate flooring

10

Who is it? And why I am so interested? She is not remarkable, not dazzling, she has not just come out as Barbarella, in Leeds, Yorkshire, England. There are no sexy, space-age costumes and a vague, sexual curiosity mixed with passive acceptance. A half-glimpsed, distant girl, slotting a key into a door, like a thousand other girls. Why was I standing and staring, I was just 14, hadn't quite come out but was so inundated with girls that I was only vaguely interested in them. I was completely fascinated, addicted to the whole, but the majority of the individuals, the parts of the whole, were simply there. I'd clock them and subconsciously log them but I didn't have to actually do anything because they would come to me. So why had I stopped and stared? Craned my neck? Why when the door shut behind her was I disappointed, felt like I'd missed something? She didn't scream sexuality and that was my main interest in females. She didn't have the legs of Joanna Lumley, or maybe she did, she was wearing jeans. But she certainly didn't have the leg-length enhancing, 'up the shirt while gently jogging without a hint of sweat' camera angle that Purdie had. There was no, 'That was good but I didn't quite get a flash of your white knickers as you jumped over the log. Let's go again.... Cut. Now can we try the full leg, slightly extended, from the front? And can you change those tights, there's a slight ladder.'

With this 'disappearing behind a door' girl, *you* wouldn't pick her out from a group of women – she wasn't Debbie Harry. *You* would not stop and stare – I would, just did. I shuddered, a strange positive shudder. Did I know her? No, I definitely didn't know her. I want to breed with her. Ah well, there aren't enough hours in the day to accommodate the demands of the current girls. The girls on their way out and in, the occasional girls, the intense girls, the girls that make me laugh or think, the girls who shine with a preened perfection and the girls who glow with a natural vitality, skin that radiates, re-energising under my touch, virile and alive.

I know who she is. I remember an orange Chopper bike, a mate and a jumble sale, a snippet of childhood. She was the girl with the jumble sale at her garden wall. An exciting jumble of kids' knick-knacks to be fiddled with, old stuff she'd had enough of, that made me want to run home for some change off mi mum. They made Tony want to grab them and peddle really fast. Tony's mum didn't like me, you can tell at that age, she was pleasant enough but there was something she just didn't like, I was polite, always loved manners, she just didn't like me.

Every day before school, eight or nine, we'd go to Marsden's, it was further than the other sweet shops but Tony always wanted to go there. I'd get a packet of chicken crisps and he'd come out with all manner of goodies. I was always jealous, he had enough to get whatever he wanted, he'd get loads of sweets and magazines and let me have any pictures of Bowie that were in. There were always pictures of Bowie in the pop magazines in 1972. Years later I realised why his mother didn't like me, she thought I was a spoilt, little, rich kid while she was struggling, bringing up two kids on her own, she didn't like the influence I was having on her child.

It was Tony's fault, he was my best mate. When he'd come home with all the magazines, pockets stuffed with sweet wrappers and half chewed Curly Wurlies he'd tell his mum that I bought him them all. I only bought the pop magazines to get the pictures of Bowie so, once I'd taken the pictures out, I gave the magazines to him. The truth was that I only had exactly enough to buy one bag of chicken crisps, not a quid and a bit's worth of chocolate, sweets and mags. She thought I was spoilt stupid. When I started my milk-round, I suddenly did have loads of money, which just confirmed all her fears. The truth was that Tony was an accomplished shoplifter – even me, his best mate, even I didn't have a clue.

I have only, knowingly, stolen anything once and it was at this, somewhere between the ages of seven and ten. It was a small toffee bar from our local sweet shop, I think I was just checking if I dare do it. It killed me. It wasn't right. I spent days on a rack, seeing injustice around the world and aligning myself with the baddies. God knows if it was the Catholicism. I think perhaps the Catholicism informed a more secular/social conscience of right and wrong. A couple of days later I returned to the shop and over-paid for something by exactly the amount of the item that I had whipped.

'You're change, love.'

I was at the door. 'I'm late, you're OK.'

The lady knew she had been the victim of some scam but couldn't fathom it.

At senior school one of my best mates was into burglary – we fell out over it, big time.

'But Mick, you're walking past an open window and there's two hundred quid sitting on the window ledge. You'd nick it.'

'No I wouldn't.'

65

'Yes you would.'

'No I wouldn't.'

'Two hundred quid, sitting there? You'd have it.'

'I wouldn't. In fact if I found a purse with money in, and an address, I'd either take it to the address, or to the police.'

'Would you fuck.'

'I would.'

'You're off your fucking head, you are, y'lying cunt.'

We almost came to blows and weren't friends anymore. His wasn't thieving out of need but motivated by greed. Ironically, a couple of months later I found a purse, with money in, in a phone box and kept it, the temptation and pay-off were too much. I didn't really, I found the woman who had lost it and returned it to her. She gave me very little reward, less than three percent of what was in the purse...tight cow.

'Tony, Tony, what y'doing?'

'What?'

'What y'doing?'

'I've nicked 'em.'

He had toy cars, some Clackers and a yo-yo and was pedalling furiously.

'You can't do that.'

'What?'

'You can't do that.'

'Whaaat?'

'Take 'em back.'

'Fuck off.'

'Take 'em back.'

'I can't take 'em back.'

'Why not.'

'I'll get caught y'tit.'

'Right give 'em here.'

'What?'

'Give 'em here, I'll take 'em back.'

'You can't take 'em back, you'll get caught y'tit.'

'Give 'em here. Give 'em here. I'll knack y'.'

He passed them over, swearing under his breath. When I got back to the jumble sale she was still there. She was pissed off, I gave them back, she scowled, I rode off. It was her, it was 'disappearing behind a door' girl. Did this childhood memory account for the fascination? At that young age, did she awaken a tingle of empathy? Perhaps in a former life she was a motor-racing champion and I worked in the pit or she was a particularly cruel prison guard and I was a prisoner, or vice versa. Maybe she was a farmer and I was a hen, the possibilities were endless. All I knew was that in my little world for some obscure, unfathomable reason, and being unknown to me, she was extraordinary. Like the favourite moustache/cardigan of someone waking from a coma, memories trashed. There was certainly a moment in time that stopped dead, a small road-block strewn across the lane of my mental connections. Anyway, not to worry, if it's meant to be, she'll come to me.

11

I'm not sure when I started the transition from youth club to Bowie/Roxy pubs and clubs, I had no interest in 'going to the pub' at all, only in going to places where they played my music. I know exactly when I first went into a pub to drink beer and, again, it's not something I would allow my kids today but the world and attitudes change. Christmas lunchtime, around my tenth birthday, literally a week either side of my tenth birthday. My dad and the milkman I worked for,

'Tim, your lad's a good little worker.'

'Yep, we're not afraid of a bit a hard graft, us lot.'

'He needs a Christmas bonus.'

'That's up to you, how much do you think?'

'Well, we haven't split all the tips up yet and there's more to come, he'll get at least fifteen quid off that.'

'Right, so not money. I know, let's take him for his first beer, he's working like a man so he should get a man's perks.'

'No Tim, you can't make me go to the pub and drink beer.'

'Come on, Dave.'

'Oh alright then, if I have to. What about you Mick, y'fancy it?'

'Yeh, alright.' Clearly, they're messing about.

'I'll have to park the van up somewhere where the missus won't see it.'

'OK, come on then.'

They sat me down, not in a corner, but in the middle of the tap-room. My dad went off and came back with three pints. I was expecting a small one or, more likely, a coke, but no, a pint. The glass wasn't a glass – it was a bucket and very full, I took my first drink by leaving it on the table and sipping from the side of the glass, both hands wrapped around it. It was lovely. I had already developed a taste for bitter as, since I was small, my dad had let me have at little sip of his every time he had a drink in front of the telly. This was different, this was a vintage Tetley's, colder and smoother than anything I had tasted, and it had more body than Giant Haystacks. Even now, when I hardly ever go to pubs, there is nothing on God's earth that can compare to a good pint of Tetley's. It is a religious experience, part of my heritage, there is nothing taken via the mouth that can excite my taste buds like that brown fluid, nothing. There is something taken via the mouth that can excite my penis more but not my taste buds. Anyway, we chatted in the pub and my initial nerves disappeared, after all it was their risk not mine. I didn't even think about trying to keep up with them, they were experienced and gifted in the art of downing Tetley's, but every time they got their second I got my next. I have no memory of how many I had other than it was more than one, I have no idea how I got home, I may have even walked.

'A'right, Tim's lad, 'ow y'doing? Yur a bit young to be out ont beer.'

'A'right, Tim's lad, start 'em young, that's the way.'

'A'right, Tim's lad, don't you be starting any trouble.'

'Tim's lad, yur a bit young to be out ont beer.'

Part of the excitement was that I was getting loads of attention from lots of strangers. A vague memory, the sort of unsolicited attention that only very young people get, starting its decline about age two. The centre of the whole universe starts to gradually become peripheral, strangers stop noticing kids around three unless they scream and kick and shout, 'Look at me.' Little 'uns miss the fuss. The barmaid just looked over every so often, whimsically shook her head and half smiled. There was no thought of questioning the moral or legal aspects of the situation, just a 'boys will be boys' resignation. She was hardly likely to question two of the pub's best customers. My dad didn't blow the household budget in a traditional Irish way, no, he had a market stall at Otley – on a Saturday and during school holidays he used to raise beer and additional money.

This sounds, at the very least, strange in the 21st century, taking a nine/ten year old to the pub for a beer, or a couple, but what you are missing is context and prejudice. As it's three working-class males in a pub, 1972/3, drinking beer during the day, the fact that one of them is so young makes me judge, tut and shake my head, 'Fuckin' rednecks.' But what I am missing is that we were being very sophisticated and continental. Were it Southern France and wine, I'd think it was alright. OK, I may quibble about the amount of alcohol that the boy drank, but the principle would be fine. In Leeds, Yorkshire, England 1972/73 taking a nine/ten year old to the pub for a few beers is, technically, child abuse.

I still haven't quite recovered from it, the wounds are raw, deep and permanent, I'm scarred. At a relatively young age, probably 12/13, my dad took me to the off-license and told the woman that sometimes he'd send me down for his beer, or other alcohol, so she should just serve me. She accepted this, passed the information on to the others who worked there and I had easy access to alcohol – my dad never sent me down to get his beer. Just like people who were beaten as a child, it didn't do me any harm, from a young age it gave me a mature attitude to alcohol, it was the heroin that I couldn't handle. Drinking is something that, for a long time, I haven't done to excess. While going through my teenage years I could always handle my drink, never got into any trouble through it and could aid those becalmed in the mist of drunken stupor, food expulsion via mouth or gripped by violent tendencies.

My second pub drinking visit and the start of going regularly happened around age 14/15. I was at Stevie Hulmes's (later known by the music press as 'Stevie Dead Vayne') house, we'd been messing around listening to music and writing songs. He suggested we go to The Staging Post for a lunch-time beer and to listen to music, etc.

'They won't serve me.' There was no way I looked 18, Stevie was taller, had a more worn face.

'I'll go to the bar, I know them, you'll be alright. Come on.' I realised that it wasn't a discussion, Stevie had decided that we were simply going and so what if I get chucked out? We went, Stevie got the beers in and we stayed for a few hours. It was fairly busy, plenty of attractive women but older. The music was my kind of stuff mixed with disco, so I was quite happy there. They played plenty of Roxy and Bowie album tracks which surprised me. Had there been crap music I would have lasted about half a pint.

I liked The Staging Post and started going regularly over the next few years. It was in a fairly hard part of Leeds but I only ever felt threatened there when someone wanted to beat shit out of me or one of my friends. There were always older people who didn't exactly look like me, but were coming from the same place, a maturer, effeminate look, make-up, etc., or Ferry suave, who were hard and would step in. It was here that I first became aware that although they looked very different, I wasn't absolutely and completely alone in my coming out. By the time I started going to The Staging Post I had refined and developed my look. I wore things like an electric-blue, wrap-around doctor's gown, made tubular, with a badge holding the bottom together just above the knee. Gold-lamé jacket with belt, a wrap-around black and shiny blouse top with long ties at the bottom that hung really well, a long, black cape with blood-red silk lining. These were usually worn with Lurex, skin-tight trousers or PVC pants and calf-length, black boots. I also had some knee-length, green-and-black, fabric boots, with really cool hooks going up the front, and although I had a plethora of long coats, my mother's white, fur coat had become a security blanket.

The trick was to develop your own 'look'. Yes I was influenced by Bowie but as a catalyst, not an image role model. It wasn't like I got photos of Bowie and tried to recreate a look or even took elements to create my syntagm; I didn't try to be David Bowie. Although, that was the essence of David – to be individual, to go off in a different direction from the norm.

My prize item of clothing, I have renamed. I have renamed it to avoid having to say, 'Plunged both hands into my muff.' This phrase is problematic for me as it reminds me of a prostitute friend and a biker with motorcycle gloves. The memory makes me pull strange faces and gurgle uncontrollably. Like this.

'BLLRRRRG-DDIIIIRRR-GRRR.'

So I try to avoid it.

My prize item of clothing, the thing to which I was most attached, although it's not strictly clothing, was my muffler. My muffler was brilliant – what an invention/design/idea. Whosoever first thought of a muffleresque device should be known by humankind in the same way as Newton, Da Vinci, Bowie or Einstein. The muffler, brown, tubular, furry, with cord that went around your head leaving the muffler over your stomach, was multi-functional. It kept your hands warm, its primary brief was a useful storage space when you wore tight clothing with little or no pocket possibilities, your hands were in and out, in again and out in seconds, unlike gloves. Lastly, and most importantly, it looked cool, a further layer of effeminalia. I wore a lot of jewellery, usually diamante dress jewellery or jet, earrings, brooches, necklaces, bracelets and bangles. If I needed something I couldn't find, I'd try to make my own, a black-leather choker with a large, green, glass jewel in the centre. Hair was usually either bleached spike or overlaid with flecks of colour.

Make-up was, by this time, full female make-up with which I had a gift – I was really good, with make-up. Talented. I approached my make-up like I approached my paintings, layering colours close in tonality up to the crucial killer colour. While still a teenager, I went out with an Avon Lady, and *she* used to come to *me* for make-up tips – sometimes when it wasn't going right, which happens to all of us, she'd just get me to do it for her. May I make a bold, arrogant and boastful statement? It is simply true, so it would be remiss of me to disclude it. I never went out with anyone who had the gift with make-up that I did. In fact, although I had sex with a mind-boggling amount of women, I never had sex with anyone who had my gift with make-up, except one. She was very short-sighted but boy could she handle blusher brushes. Other than this one, I was better at applying make-up than any woman I ever saw. What? It's true. You want me to lie? I did a lot of art, with a particular interest in tonality and shading. I was remarkable at applying make-up, better than you. It was a God-given gift. It wasn't me but God who spoke through my face, hands and make-up pallet. Saying, 'Fuck, this man is the best with make-up that I ever created and remarkably pretty. Are you sure he's one of mine?'

One other possible best at make-up rival was an extravagant fellow from the North East, but this was much later, early '80s in The Warehouse. This guy had perfect and varied make-up and a wonderful, flamboyant wardrobe. Even though I first came across him, not in the biblical sense, in the early '80s it was obvious that his skills had been honed over years. He was one of the few gay men who were still friendly with me when they realised that I was totally straight. We weren't best mates or owt but I always enjoyed seeing him, he was fun, but his gift was the scything one-liner removing the legs of anyone who even hinted at cattiness. He could see weaknesses and insecurity from 30 yards, and could nail them in five words. We never went head to head in aggressive verbal bitching, but I think it would have been too close to call. We'd go head to head in verbal banter but that was really a team game, passing quips, setting up open one-liners. He had a bullwhip of a tongue but never unleashed it on me – he'd often say things like, 'Aright Mick, y'whore, you're such a slut.' But this was honesty not bitchiness

His little brother and sister turned up a little later, the new generation. His little brother also had a gift. He wasn't very friendly to me, I think he was either slightly shy or competitive. I was asked not to woo his little sister, which I respected. She was very beautiful in a Celtic way, and she got over-friendly a few times but I declined because a friend had asked me to.

From the beginning, I didn't just wear 'girly' clothes, it depended on mood. Drainpipe, blue jeans that, as well as Bowie, I had written the names of Punk bands on, in bleach. These jeans would often go with my milk-round Major Domo boots, tucked into socks, that went a few inches higher than Doc Martins and, crucially, were black. I had various articles of more 'punky' clothes like a black dinner-jacket that had zips and chains held on with large safety-pins, with names of Punk bands and Bowie written on, in different colour paints, various army pants, some white army-style pants. My brother bought a parachute suit that he gave to me, from the Army and Navy store, which, along with jumble sales, was a great source of clothing. While wearing these more 'punky' clothes I'd often still retain make-up but quick, 'streety' make-up.

I also enjoyed ultra-tidy. An electric-blue, two-piece suit with red braces and tie, a white box-jacket made out of really cool, thick and earthy material, a black suit with short double-breasted jacket and baggyish trousers, similar length to *David Live*. This last suit I wore with very formal shirts, I'd got a couple from an antique shop, and a 'Wild West' gambler's necktie, kinda butterfly, figure-of-eight and thin. A few years later this style of suit became very popular with fringe 'New Romantics'.

Hats – I loved hats, there was nothing more exciting than a good hat. Hats were magical, they gave you poise, a poise that changed depending on the hat. Could I just say that people who take hats from other peoples heads, 'for a laugh', should have their genitalia removed using only a fork and spoon, nothing as sharp as a knife. I think that's 'a laugh'. In 1978 I sent this suggestion to the UN but received no response, neither did Amnesty International reply. Selfish tossers, they're all well and good at making a fuss when it comes to murder and torture but don't give a shit about freedom of head-wear – who defended my right to wear a hat, unimpeded? No one but me. Not many people messed with my hat a second time. The fork, spoon and genitalia combination really made their eyes smart. My favourite hats were a bippety-boppety hat and berets, worn separately, obviously.

The photo book by Steve Strange documenting the 'early' New Romantics, *The Book With No Name,* is stuffed full of good, honest folk from Leeds. The photos from this book are *at least* three years after I came out wearing make-up and girly clothes. I wasn't alone – when I came out I heard of other, older boys, who, also being very attractive, were doing a similar thing. God knows how long they had been out there. The Adelphi pub in Leeds had a Bowie/Roxy club upstairs at the same time as an NF meeting downstairs, which was nice. The skins really appreciated our sartorial elegance. They often commented on how nicely my make-up was applied, the sentence usually beginning in 'fucking' and ending in 'puff'.

I don't know when the Adelphi night was born but I started going in the late '70s, and had been aware of it for around a year. It was full of boys in make-up and girly clothes or make-up and an adapted 'Thin White Duke' look that was very New Romantic, four years earlier. The Precinct was another central Leeds place doing the same kind of things and attracting the same kind of people. The Staging Post in Whinmoor/Seacroft that I mentioned earlier, was another, not a Bowie club but played a lot of Bowie/Roxy Music, intermingling 'cool stuff' with pop and a definite presence of the girly boys. Amnesia, Leeds City Square, was a bit later but still before the general 'New Romantic' movement and stuffed full of Johnny Come Latelies. I don't really know what The Phono or Warehouse were doing at the time but they will have been linked.

The Adelphi and The Precinct had something of the street. The Precinct a Wild West saloon, the open street door meaning that some gunslinger may walk in at any time with an urge to slaughter a freak. A border-town bar, on the edge of the hard places, people passing through that you may never see again, on their way to freedom, escaping from the posse who'd been on their tail for weeks. Nicotine-stained mirrors, an odour of beer-drenched carpets and the glint of fragments of glass across the floor. Had there been sawdust down people would have certainly spat. Even the dance floor was a central platform, roped at regulation height, with the two corner entrances fulfilling the directive of the boxing ring, although the knuckles were bare.

There was certainly a smell of the street, but it was a relaxed atmosphere full of laughter and fast communication. People speaking too quickly with body and lips, gestures, facial expressions holding the essentials of life. Like the market on a Saturday afternoon.

The Adelphi was more family, more relaxed; people were familiar and regular, I was unaware of the style or Bowie-fan hierarchy. Some people modelled themselves on the glamorous; Bowie, Ferry, Monroe, Hepburn, Dietrich etc., and I'm sure there must have been some cultural capital in being the most Bowiesque creature in the club. As it was upstairs it was less conspicuous to the freak-hunters and more difficult for them to penetrate, the NF had to try to keep their noses clean or they may lose their downstairs meeting place.

In both places the music was king, mixing Bowie, Roxy, Iggy, Kraftwerk etc. Although neither place played out-and-out Punk there were post-Punk bands like Bauhaus, The Banshees, Magazine, Devo along with the inbetweenies – Simple Minds, Japan, The B 52s. The Precinct going more to the punky/alternative side, while in The Adelphi you were more likely to hear new, experimental music.

12
(Stepping off the school bus)

'McCann, have you got make-up on?'
'I don't think so.'
'Sir.'
'What?'
'I don't think so SIR.'
'You're alright sir, just call me McCann.'
'You've got a detention.'
'What fo'?'
'You know what for – have you got make-up on?'
'I don't think so sir. Sir, can y'give a detention for wearing make-up?'
'So you are wearing make-up?'
'I don't think so, sir.'
'Are you wearing make-up, McCann?'
'I didn't put any on this morning, sir.'
'Did you take it off last night?'
'I had a late night and I was straight up for mi milk-round.'
'Go take it off.'
'I'll be late for registration.'
'No you won't, you've got ten minutes. You look ridiculous.'
'No siiiirrrr, I look fabulous. I'm an artist. I have an urge to express miself. You know about artists sir, you know, like Van Gogh and all those composers. Sir, they were all a bit weird.'
'You're strange but you're no artist, McCann.'
'That's what they said to Van Gogh' (pause) 'sir.'
'McCann, every day I tell you about your uniform, every day. You'll get yourself suspended. Where's your tie?'
'It's in mi bag sir.'
'Well put it on.'
'Sir, I get too hot, I can't breathe.'
'Put it on.'
'I will.'
'Now.'
'Sir, I am wearing the uniform.'
'McCann, the school uniform does not include white ….shoes. What are they called?'
'Boppers sir, or Beetle Crushers.'
'Well why are you wearing them? They're for Teddy Boys.'

'No sir, these shoes were made for me, they're my shoes. They feel brilliant sir, they're really comfy.'

'You've written all over the side of them, The Damned, Stiff Little....'

'I know.'

'You should have black shoes McCann, you know that. What's that coat?'

'Do we have a school uniform coat, sir?'

'Well, it's certainly not green. What is that? Where did you get it?'

'Jumble sale, 10p, its real wool, really thick, feel it.'

'Is it an army coat? Those brass buttons look like a uniform.'

'So mi coats alright?'

'Not a school uniform, a different uniform.'

'I think it's a bus driver's coat; look, I took the sleeves up and shortened the bottom.'

'Sir.'

'What?'

'Shortened the bottom SIR.'

'Can you see? I stitched that miself, sir.'

'Go on McCann, you're going to be late. Ryan, get your tie on.'

'I can't sir, ar Shaun's nicked it.'

'GO!' Eighty kids go flying across the field, all but one of the runners watch them go. He is in the middle moving through kids. Two minutes later he is a solitary figure, disappearing into a dip in the field. The runners pick their way through the kids walking, punching arms, trying to wrestle each other to the ground, shouting, 'Slow down y'puffs, it in't a fucking race.' They are wrong, it is. It is a race for second place.

'Mick, stop being a swot and come downt' beck wi'us.'

They will hide in the woods and mix into the tail of the runners on the way back up. I need to run. It's like poking a gum that hurts slightly, a peculiar, perverse pleasure.

'Goughian, Monahan, Deery, GET MOVING!' The bearded chemistry teacher is barking at the back of the pack. He picks through the field, no breath, kids who are trying he encourages. He reaches me on the road, 'Come on, Michael. Dig.' I can't match his pace, he is a proper distance runner, stretched and lithe. Each stride approaching two of mine, I try to stride long. I try to keep up but have too much bulk and am at the extremities of my physical ability.

'Come on, just keep with me.'

I pick up the pace downhill, being carried by the incline.

'Dig deep.'
'Sir, this isn't my pace.'
'Come onnn!'
'This is it, sir, if I go any faster, I'll stop.'
I had and never would stop and walk during cross-country.
'Good pace. Keep it up, hold the pace.'
Eyebrows raised, face stretched, 'Sir.'
He glides away, skimming the earth.
I focus on a maroon shirt with a blue stripe. I gain and move past it. I focus on a maroon shirt with a red stripe. I gain and move past it. I move past another maroon shirt with a red stripe. I focus on a maroon shirt with a green stripe. I gain and move past it. A couple of yellows and I have no idea what combination of colours is out front. Into a section with a far horizon and I see one shirt, long off. The guy who disappeared down a dip is not of this race and invisible.

Impacts crunching through heels and thudding into my head, a steady beat drumming routine into my movement. Repetitive rhythm concentrating the brain on the throb of increased blood, extra oxygen and chemicals that give the world a surreal glow. The pulse only broken by pools of water and obstacles to be negotiated. Hot and moist while ground hardens and crackles underfoot, iced and glistening as it rises up before me. Millions of tiny muscle explosions pumping me forward. Noisy and visible breath heated by the lung where it arrives cold and sharp.

The guy out front thinks he's safe in second place but I will break him. The gap is diminishing yet large, the distance still sufficient. I am not going to slowly whittle away at his lead but devour it. When I can see the destination I can sprint for ever or at least 600 yards, flat out. The guy in first has long gone, I can not compete with him, he moves like a gazelle, there is no wastage. I am not built for this, my limbs are not long and my body carries too much bulk. I have an explosive physique with stamina. He is built for distance and lives at the top of a hill. When he runs he is a natural born marvel, he doesn't touch the ground.

I come over the brow of a hill on the school playing-fields, the school is in sight. The finishing-line is the eave of the changing room door, time has come to run. Kids watch from the window as I destroy space, anything to avoid physics. An older mate of one of my mates' brothers, comes around a corner.
'GOO ON MICK.'
More faces appear at the first-floor, chemistry-lab window.

'GO ON, YOU'VE GOT HIM.' He should be in lessons, he's blowing his cover.

The boy in second place can feel the breath of the cheetah behind him, he glances over his doomed shoulder. All his hard work is disappearing with each step, four miles of determination being publicly ripped to pieces, 80-odd kids behind count for nothing, he searches for energy but there is none left, his legs like lamp-posts start to stumble as his brain denies the lumps of concrete dragging him backwards.

The chemistry-lab windows slide open and kids start whistling and shouting, anything to avoid chemistry. They probably don't realise that the winner is already in the shower. I'm up to the shoulder of the lad.

'Alright Jaf.' He's a good lad, not a best mate but a mate.

'You bastard, Mick.'

'What?'

'Bastard.'

'Do you want to go in together?'

'What.'

'We'll go through the door together.'

'No, you beat me fair and square.'

'It doesn't matter, we'll go in together.'

'No you've won.'

'OK, see y'.' I run off waving to the crowd as he disappears towards the horizon. As I come up to the science block I take a detour and run up and down in front in fake celebration, leaping into and punching the air. Shaking my hands above my head.

'You haven't finished yet, y'tit.'

'What?' I pretend I can't hear him and see Jaf cornering the science block on the way to the changing-room door. I run along skipping and waving to the crowd.

'He's going to beat you, y'knob.'

'Eh?' I pretend I don't understand them.

This page is intentionally blank.

'YOU, BOY.'

Shit! It's Jake! His voice booms through my knees and makes them wobble; Jake smoked 472 fags a day, three at a time, and was scary. He was the deputy head and harder than the sheriff head. Older lads loved him and took his verbal batterings with glee, he sometimes let them speak.

'YOU, BOY, WHAT THE BLOODY 'ELL ARE YOU DOING?'

'Cross-country sir.'

NO YOU'RE NOT, WHAT Y'DOING?'

'A lap of honour, sir.'

He half-smirks, 'Get to the changing rooms, NOW.'

I run to the corner of the science block, clenched fist out front, where Jake couldn't see it, in mock celebration. Some other lads' heads are starting to mount the brow of the hill steaming, they're way back, no threat. Sat on the wall by the changing-room door is Jaf grinning, as I move towards the door he says, 'Woah, slow down! I thought we were going in together?'

'Whatever loser.' I quicken my pace.

'Bastard.'

'You get nothing for third in this life.'

How sweet or p'raps, even honourable, he waited for me so that we could go in together.

'Suckerrrrrr.'

As my foot hovers over the step of the gym I pull it back.

'Come on then.'

He is almost up to me as I jump through the door.

'Yye-e-ss!' He looks at me and laughs.

'Bastud!'

We go in chatting and he tells me that he's got some Eno I should listen to. I feign interest as I want to talk about Bowie, but Eno is an 'obscure' artist, and I am suitably impressed by his left-fieldedness. My obsession won't allow rivals, had it been a band I may have had more interest. He brought in a couple of albums the following day, I actually listened to it, didn't really get it but was intrigued enough to copy it. I occasionally listened to it but not enough, until Eno started working with David. The approval of *The Great One* brought me more often to the Eno. It took me a few more years to admit that the early Eno really was out there, more original, experimental and more of a signpost of certain things to come in popular music.

To be fair when I first heard Eno, Bowie was around the Plastic Soul/Thin White Duke stage and *Young Americans* was anything but safe for the time and place. A complete tangent from *Diamond Dogs* (single 'Rebel Rebel'), although '1984' was a directional clue, it was very risky. I suspect, although he probably wouldn't have stated it, that Dave wanted to avoid the Marc Bolan trap of giving the kids what they wanted and stagnating. Also, David was more songwriter and Eno more experimental artist, not that Eno hasn't written some belting songs or David experimented.

13

Kids today have no rebellion, like the society around them, they just have an urge to consume. As Poly Styrene warned in 1977 'Wo-oo-oh-oo-oh, in a consumer society,' and kids today consume and conform. Whether they're studying hard at school or stealing cars, as a group they don't surprise us. The myth or truth about Poly Styrene was that she was beautiful, used to be a model but made herself look as ugly as possible with the braces, bad make-up and clothes etc. Me, I wanted to look beautiful. X-Ray Spex were a Punk band – there were only ever four Punk bands, The Damned, The Pistols, The Clash and X-Ray Spex – the rest were something else. Penetration were wonderful but not a Punk band – not a bad thing – like the Banshees (for me, the first post-Punk band with Magazine the second) they had something else. A bit later Stiff Little Fingers became the fifth and last Punk band. There were lots of other heavy, fast, angry, aggressive bands, but they weren't Punk, not in my world. You have to understand that this is not true to anyone but me, no one I have ever spoken to, who was around at the time, agrees with me but I am right and they are wrong, easy.

There are two that I didn't listen to, The Slits and Slaughter and the Dogs, too busy with my Glen Miller and *The Threepenny Opera* at the time. I would not forgive Johnny Rotten for saying Iggy was an old fart in a suit, it was disrespectful; had *The Stooges* been released in '76 and not '69/'70 it would have been the first Punk album and both The Pistols and The Damned covered tracks from it. It influenced you, admit it y'tosser.

One of the most exciting moments of my life was in the drunken gambling scene from *Lock, Stock and Two Smoking Barrels*, in a cinema full of students, hearing 'Now I Wanna Be Your Dog' belt out and remove the young lady's head two seats in front. I wanted to scream, 'This is me, I am it.' Neither would I forgive Joe Strummer for the line from 'Clash City Rockers', 'Come on and show me say the bells of old Bowie.' May I point out that in '77 *Low* and *Heroes* were released, two of the most influential albums on the soundscape of the next two decades, popular music changed the second those albums entered the shops. But I suppose Joe was political with a capital P whereas Mr Bowie influenced the world on a much more subtle, lasting and personal level. I have no doubt Joe was sincere and politics was on the streets in those days. (I wrote this before Joe died, I've just listened to 'Complete Control' and have forgiven him everything, so Lord, you can let him into heaven now, forgive him his blasphemy. No really, it's OK, let him in.)

As I can't think of a really famous sociologist/philosopher, Poly Styrene was the Freud, Jung, Marx, of the Punk movement. The album *Germ-Free Adolescents* wasn't an early Punk album but it was a classic Punk album. Anyone questioning whether X-Ray Spex should be included as one of the four 'real' Punk bands should listen to 'Oh Bondage Up Yours', 'Identity', 'World Turned Day-Glo', 'Lets Submerge'. They contain the best 'Punk' vocals, the quintessential Punk vocals, the only vocals you would point at if someone wanted to form a Punk band with no knowledge of Punk, with Johnny Rotten next. What made Poly so remarkable in the Punk world was her intellectual vision, writing songs in '77/'78 about things that years later became cornerstone sociological subjects and theories – 'Identity', for God's sake. I think it unlikely that she will have read Marcus Hall, it's obviously possible, but I'd guess not. Obsessions with personal cleanliness and grooming, consumerism and retail therapy, advertising and marketing, processed food, genetic engineering etc. Obviously they were punky pop songs, not theses, but the subject matter is there. The Pistols and The Clash were much more in your face, political with a big P and I loved them for it.

Obviously the thing about there only ever being four Punk bands is ill-informed, opinionated, self-centred bullshit, so I'd like to apologise to the following:
The Adverts
The Buzzcocks
Sham 69
999
The Stranglers
Blondie
Generation X
The Angelic Upstarts
The Vibrators
Maybe the UK Subs
The Ramones
I am very sorry. Sorry that you weren't real Punk bands, y'twats, there were only four and you weren't it. Tough. Live with it.

My influence on The Ramones was not huge, it was not that important but it was definite and long-lasting. If The Ramones were a Punk band, which they pretty much were, not my type of Punk band but a

Punk band minus some of the trappings and attitudes, they were the first. Obviously there were only four Punk bands, four Punk bands and The Ramones who were kinda punky, almost Punk. I mean, how would you describe The Ramones? They were a Punk band in a not quite a Punk band kind of way. They played short, fast, quite heavy songs about punk rockers and sniffing glue, etc., wore drainpipe, ripped jeans and leather biker-jackets. So obviously you are going to associate them with Punk rock, so the Ramones were associated with Punk without quite being a definitive Punk band and yet, paradoxically, ticking a lot of the Punk-band boxes in a Punk band kinda way. So The Ramones were a Punk band and even though they were American, and Punk was a British/London movement with American influences, which came a couple of years after The Ramones, they were a Punk band, sort of. Could someone please tell me, were The Ramones a Punk band? A real, unadulterated, nailed-down Punk band? Of course they were, in their own Ramonesy way. They had long hair, which is a problem, I don't remember any guitar solos, but neither was there any snarl. The Ramones pretty much played three-chord rock 'n' roll, which Punk was getting away from. Anyway, as I said, my influence on The Ramones was not huge, not that important but it was definite and long-lasting.

My friend's older sister and her mate were going to see The Ramones. These two were unusual, everybody puts the happening of Punk as '76/'77 but in my part of Leeds you didn't see a lot of punks until '77/'78 – these two were certainly '76 punks. The legendary F-Club – the 1st Punk venue in Leeds – was full of punks in '76 but this was a clique and it was a small venue, they were not spread around the city like a year later. There was also the Junior F-Club for kids to go and see punk bands in the afternoon, how cool was that? I never went.

For some reason they really wanted me to go to The Ramones gig, they had a spare ticket and all my protestations were for nought, I was going.

Just inside the University one of them, who had disappeared, came running up to me and said, 'Come on.' Dragging me by the arm, she said excitedly, 'I've got us back stage.' It was easy, we just walked through to where The Ramones were warming and psyching up before the gig. The woman was very excited, it wasn't a big deal to me. Although I liked quite a few of their tracks, I wasn't really into The Ramones, to me they were just blokes in a band. They were very friendly and I ended up talking to who I later found out was the

84

singer. They all look the bloody same these Ramones. I just ignored what he was saying and said, 'So you into Bowie then?'

'Well, y'know, that "John I'm only Dancing", that's a good track.'

'Na, that's bollocks, you want to hear some proper Bowie.'

That was it, a non-stop list of recommendations, 'That album's this and this album is that.' Not a single mention of The Ramones, the poor guy is trying to prepare himself for the gig and he's faced with a babbling 14-year-old who had no need to breathe. He was polite and he went on stage to the shout of, '*Pin-Ups* – that's a good rock 'n' roll album,' ringing in his ears.

That was it, that was the end of it, until ten years later, flicking through a music paper which had a *Smash Hits*-esque question-and-answer session with Joey: Favourite colour - blue. Star sign - Taurus. Loves - cheesecake. Hates - Bowie fans. Yes! That was me, that was. I had scarred the man, traumatised him for life. Ten years later he still hadn't come to terms with the dwarf, gob-shite, Bowie fan who had stalked him in Leeds. My influence on The Ramones was not huge, it was not that important but it was definite and long-lasting.

Other than Bowie albums, I was only filled with a giddy excitement that forced me to leg off school to be there at opening time, first day of release, to buy two albums. The first was *Inflammable Materials* by Stiff Little Fingers, whom I'd previously seen live supporting, maybe, the Tom Robinson Band and the first Bauhaus album *In The Flat Field*. Now Bauhaus, like Japan, are another of those anachronistic bands, to me they were 'post-Punk' but make a list of things associated with 'Goths', the only youth movement, that I am aware of, to be directly attributed to Leeds '82/'83. I see a line through The Leeds Dandies and Punk, leading directly to Goth.

The Goth thing in Leeds is easy to see, by the time New Romantics were first starting to peer out of the front cover of *Smash Hits* this old Leeds movement had a Gothic offshoot. The roots of the Goth movement, the Bowiesque murmurings of Bauhaus, had been embraced in Leeds in the late '70s – as I said, I legged off school to get the album first day of release. It was the mix of The Leeds Dandies and darker Punk/post-Punk that led to the birth of Goth, or should I say the development of Goth, and may I say, just like Punk, the role of Iggy and The Stooges should not be ignored. In the early '80s Leeds/W. Yorks. bands such as The Sisters Of Mercy, The Southern Death Cult, The Skeletal Family (spot the Bowie song title) were setting down the Goth cornerstones for the only youth movement directly attributed to Leeds. New Romantics may have been walking around, clubbing and congregating in Leeds in '77/'78 but obviously that's a lie because we all know that *that* youth movement was '81/'82 – the London media know everything and, as they are dedicated to the truth, are always right.... tossers.

I'd like to point out that, although both these youth cultures were/are a joke to the music media, that gothy/metal/thrash, black fingernailed, cross/Satan type rock music is still one of, if not *the,* most popular music forms in the world.

Lists of things associated with 'Goths'/Bauhaus:
Black clothes
Black and dark make-up
Spiky hair
Horror-movie type stuff
Darkness
Heavy, guitar-based music
Closed curtains
Tattoos
A bit glamour, punky
Spiky buckles and general metal-work
Deep, male voices

'Bela Lugosi's Dead' was released '79, four/five years before the media started to pick up on Goth. At this point I will rest my case, other than to add that Bauhaus were hugely influenced by David.

13
(Shit, two chapter 13s – you've got no further – in fact, you've gone backwards)

I started a milk-round at the age of nine, obviously too young to be up on a morning at 5.15, carrying crates of milk, running from door to door, hurdling gates and fences, sneaking through gaps. I had a lot of freedom, maybe too much but then again I didn't get into thieving, dangerous drugs, pot-holing, and I never, knowingly, got a girl up the duff, which later convinced me through the laws of probability that I must be sterile. I did start to use two Durex at a time, an attempt to cheat probability, if three in 100 don't work then I was throwing out a fair amount of single-fettered sperm and multiple pregnancy seemed a certainty, so double-bagging reduced it from probable to simply possible. I had unbound personal freedom. The milk-round gave me financial freedom, I earnt what at the time was a lot of money. It was not a paper-round, it was a milk-round and ten to twenty times more lucrative. The milk-round also gave me space to think, athletic physical fitness, cleared my brain while the view of slumbering or stretching suburbia stained my outlook.

Winching my eyes open and gazing at the luminescent 'Westclock', the radioactive-clock people, with genuine, 100% radiation stalking through my childhood sanctuary from the age of seven.

'SHIT, it's 5 o'clock, I'm late.'

'What's going on? Must jump out of bed, milkman here anytime.'

'No don't make me, I'm tired and warm.'

Eyelids like paving slabs.

'GET UP.'

'No, he won't notice one less milk boy.'

I sigh, deep and desperate, at the rain battering my attic window. Outside the weather is unnatural, it's dark, it's cold, it's pissing it down and my body is suspended in a beautiful warm womb, so right, so natural, that I couldn't possibly move, no room. No birth, not today. Today is the day of the foetus.

'GET THE FUCK UP.'

'NO, I'll just wait for the milkman to throw stones at my window.'

Drifting through memories of him banging on a different bedroom window with a clothes prop. BANG, BANG, BANG.

I can hear it jolt through my skull. I prise my eyes open with a lump-hammer and five-inch masonry chisel, metaphorically obviously. One minute past five.

'Sweet Jesus, make it say three o'clock, please, I'll go to church and everything. Beautiful, generous God, two o'clock and I'll speak in Hebrew tongues.'

'Wait a minute, wait one, god-damn, glorious minute. Sweet Jesus. YES. YES. OH, LORD YES. Thank you Jesus. Glorious Jesu, The Holy Spirit and all the saints in heaven. Blessed Thursday. Blessed, Our Lady Of The Not Waking Boys Up Thursday. Erm, deity, you know that church stuff? I lied, I'm human, it's what we do. Your dodgy design – now get out of my bedroom, you omnipresent freak.

A moment better than sex and almost equivalent to Leeds United winning a major honour, waking when it's not your day for the milk-round. A moment in life to savour. You must have been woken by your alarm clock only to have that wonderful, 'It's Saturday' feeling, well multiply that life-affirming sensation by ten and you're halfway to Waking For The Milk-round When It's Not Your Day. Oh joyous seepage of euphoria. Ooh, snuggle, snuggle, snuggle. This *really* is religious, life changing. I consider jumping out of bed in the nuddy and running around my freezing-cold bedroom, with ice on the inside of the window, just to feel the benefit of my bed, but the thought is enough. I grin, I grin again and clasp my pillow to my chest, the only thing on God's earth that I truly love. Flipping my second pillow to the cold side I tease out every degree of chill, numbing my face with pre-sleep coma.

'I love you pillow, I love you warm bed.'

I slip back into the single-cell position adopted upon my conception, content through to my nucleus. The world is so cold and unfriendly, I am not part of it. It's a time for caves, leaves, fires, animal skins. Hibernation is a good idea.

Come, let us hibernate,
Let us celebrate together and
Welcome sleep into our hearts.
Sing together hymn number 32.

Glory To Waking For The Milk-round When It's Not Your Day.

Cold. Fuck Off.
Rain. Fuck Off.
Wind. Fuck Right Off.
Snow. Likewise.
AL LEY A A A LULA

This morning I will not force my weary ass from this bed but sink into comfort, drift into unconsciousness.

This morning I will not punch my frozen, sodden-gloved fingers through the snow slush in the top of the empties. Ha!

Warmth, pull tight around me.
Cold. Fuck Off.
Today you lose.
Rain. Fuck Off.
AL LEY A A A LULA
Soak Dave, through to his spongy skin.
Ha! Not me, not wet. Soak him. Sleep. Ooh, yes please. Ooh. Mmmm.

World. Fuck Off, I'm switching back to nothingness.
Clock tick away while I ignore you.
Hark, I hear no alarm.
Off-switch, silent guardian of my stupor.
Mind, forget the world for it is wet and shitty.
Not me, I am warm and delicious.
Yum, yum.
Night, night.

AL LEY A A A LULA Ha!

Walking away from a car crash.
Seeing your baby slide out of a fanny, or take its first step.
Passing your driving test.
Listening to a Bowie album when you're right in the mood.
Marrying your one, true love.
Your first orgasm.
Witnessing your father win an egg-and-spoon race.
A Tony Yeboah volley.
Watching *The Snowman* with your family on Christmas Eve.
Saying, 'Well Leeds *are* the champions.'
Let me introduce you to the **17th Fact What I Know: Waking For The Milk-Round When It's Not Your Day, is THE life moment.**

Moving through rows of houses, usually neat, old, new and in-between. Detached, semi-detached, terraced, bungalows detached and semi-detached, '30s, '50s, '60s, '70s, Edwardian, Victorian and Georgian, big, small, private and council. Private often had cars, council rarely. They always seemed like boxes to me, even the 'posher', more expensive houses seemed very average, very much a box in a row of boxes. To my youthful eye they all seemed slightly pathetic, *it* all seemed slightly pathetic. I didn't know of an alternative, I still don't and I've taken my place in the row but with a distant, haunting memory of something else, something I never quite fully perceived, a hint of an otherness that I never could comprehend. I'm not made for life in a caravan, spouting self-righteousness with a slightly naive, useful-to-the-extended-adolescent view of the world, be it deeply held.

In the 1970s the sunrise was dated and a bit old-fashioned. The moon and space were in.

The world has no need to breathe just before the sun comes up, a serenity that ghosts through your soul and stills your blood. Birdsong precedes the moment, flickering constantly and building in intensity until light rises from the ground. Light diffuse over white and grey blanket, the opposite sky, often as dramatic, mid- to deep-blue and black. Everything seems suddenly becalmed in a sea of anticipation, the birds must still be singing but not in your dimension, the awesome birth of the day is all you can contain. As the faint glow grows, it fills and paints the sky with colours anywhere between yellow and purple, or any combination of that spectrum. Blocks, or spears, of light stabbing the atmosphere that touches the earth, unlike any other light you will ever see. No matter how many times you see the sunrise it still had the ability to slap your face and say, 'Look up.' You stop, you stare and time stands still. Flat elongated shadows, rising and shortening as the sun comes up, splashing light on puddles glistening and spotlighting as you move by, micro-moments of blindness, being caught as you turn a corner by a wall of light.
    The first routine of lights moving through houses, subconscious semaphore, 'Get me out!' or 'I am content', the structure of lives, the women and men coughing up phlegm in the bathroom, crapping or pissing on cue. Running through the kitchen, slipping out of bed, so close that I can smell lives that I will never know, toothaches, headaches, cancers, heart attacks. Lives of hope, despair, achievement. Fascists, Communists, Liberals, Conservatives, Labourites, intellectuals and dumb shits. No memory of babies

crying, there were no babies in '73. Radios on, radios off, no morning TV in those days, not in the '70s. A certain night-dress or dressing-gown worn, certain rooms always lit, certain curtains always open or drawn, certain rooms noisy and certain rooms quiet. Certain empties always left out and certain empties being stock-piled inside, just, for no other reason than to wilfully piss me off. There was no such thing as certainty. I realise how condescending it was but I could not, nor did I try, to escape the fact that the rows of boxes seemed perfectly symbolic of and to contain the normal, the average, the prescribed, the ordinary. Routines of the ordinary, the structures of the ordinary, the beliefs and prejudices of the ordinary, the order of the ordinary, the bore of the ordinary. I was not ordinary, I was extraordinary I knew this to be the case, or slowly realised that this was the case. **The 5th Fact What I Know: I am extraordinary.**

All around me things were ordered, boxed, set, arranged, defined, things big and small, personal and social. Time usually dictated where I'd be, what period, what day, what lesson, at the swimming pool, at Elland Rd, on my way to a friend's, returning from a friend's, waking for the milk-round. Now I wanted to re-arrange, define, order. I wanted a control over the structure of my immediate surroundings. I had already started to tickle the surface by painting six-foot murals on my bedroom walls, this entailed staying up through the night and going straight out onto the milk-round or to school.

Smell of sodden trees and soil, rotting wood, punched in the face by sticky odour of flowers absent the previous day. Trumpet spitting rain from top lip, sprinkling rain tinkling on my skin and refreshing. The thwack of wet branch, sometimes a pleasant surprise, sometimes soaking areas that had been studiously guarded from the wet. With experience and knowledge the incidence of plant-borne soakings diminished, each trap subconsciously avoided, no thought, a kink in a run, a conditioned dip of the head or wiggle of the hip. Operating in half-light on ultra-senses, above normal, to avoid high kerbs, low, unseen fences, no sprawling on the ground or having one of four bottles knocked out of my hand. Kicking dead leaves that waft into and out of the air, the giddy crackle and crunch as your feet joyously wade through, the following day they are wet and dangerous as ice. The van, a mixture of low, back-of-the-throat, sickly throb of diesel and the sour reek of days-old milk spilled or dropped. Sometimes low mist would hang, the smelly dirt clogging nostrils, lungs never quite filling. 'Appen, in the mist, rain or snow, the milk-float was like a trawler at sea, to be battled back to. Spiders' webs constant in certain places, but ultimately unpredictable, spluttering the molecular from your mouth, hand out front scything through silk, trying to avoid the pointless task of picking the strands of the web from your face, something I never got used to. So, where anything corridored the hand spasmed out front, perpendicular to the face; now I know where Bowie got the inspiration for the front cover of *Heroes*, he'd walked through too many spiders' webs. Spiders were obviously a bit of a theme with him, an influence on his first 'hit' album, and half the name of a much later and probably crap tour.

Communications from customers were varied, revealing, usually written, tubed and popped into the top of an empty bottle. Rambling, semi-apologetic changes of orders, next to concise, economical alterations. Angry notes about milk left three inches too far to the right, just far enough to bathe in the morning sun, or long, 'official', bank manager letters from people with too much time, broken up into paragraphs and sub-sections, **Chapter 1. 'The Need For The Milk To Arrive Before 6.30 am.'** Notes left in ripped and halved envelopes, cheques in coin bags, small change and bank notes in formal envelopes marked 'Mr Wood', all these things, mixed and matched, in any combination. The battle with the birds constant in some customers' minds. Little cups and specially designed caps, the lids from detergents or fabric conditioners, small lengths of wood or Perspex left to cover the milk – don't forget or the note will be scathing. They may even slide out of their door, 'Excuse me love, don't forget to cover the milk, you can take these two from yesterday if you don't mind.' Silver lids speckled by the ratta-tat-tatting of a tiny beak, or shredded by something larger.

Semi-skimmed milk was exotic in the 1970s. We carried them all, all manner of milk with different-coloured lids. Silver, red, gold, speckled-yellow and speckled-green, holly and berries for Christmas. Full-fat was where it was at. Silver lid was proper milk, none of your girly and slightly weird semi-skimmed, we sold some semi but full-fat was king in the 1970s.

Carving my initials on the silver lids of bottles to say 'Hi' to a friend.

On the milk-round, some people, you see every morning, 'Good morning love. It's lovely today, isn't it?' Often faint envy in their eyes, they made me aware of the golden time of life I was passing through. I couldn't say whether they were envious of youth, possibilities, lack of stress, the fitness and activity, or the perceived freedom, but they were like package-tour holidaymakers, being shunted on to a bus as they watch the backpackers pass by.

Houses with no people living in them, just disappearing milk. Some people, mysterious shadows, slipped past the invisible boy with milk, gone as you turned. Followed by a friendly face, a familiar, a mother with an urge to mother, 'You should be more wrapped up in this weather.'

'No, I get too hot.'

The milkman tried to avoid every morning the bellowing of a big voice, 'Woodward, here. WOODWARD.' That wasn't even the milkman's name, he wasn't even a customer, I never worked out who or what he was, but every time the milkman was clocked he skulked over, like a school kid to the headmaster's office, to receive his bollocking.

Sometimes you round a corner and it's just not right, something unseen stalking, just behind or where you are heading. Something you struggle to understand or define suddenly fills your head and surrounds you, it falls from nowhere, not quite physical. Semi-used senses pick it out, questioning logic, a presence, an atmosphere, benign. As quickly as it drops, it evaporates, it has been moved through, all that remains is the pronounced senses, the beads of non-movement sweat and fast blood.

It may seem obvious but there really is something elemental about the weather that in these days, for many, of popping from door to car, car to door, door to car, we may miss. Often bus stops have shelters and even radiators need love. The milk-round reinforced elemental nature, there was nowhere to hide, you can't fight the 'is' of weather, it *is* cold, it *is* wet. All you have contra, paradoxically, is the acceptance of the 'is'. The weather wins when your head disrespects it, when you lower your head, hunch your shoulders, tighten your body. Sometimes the wind or rain is so aggressive that it simply wins, you have no choice, it is elementally unpleasant. The milk-round taught me that when you give yourself to the weather, 90% of the time it is a glorious union. Accept that it is how it is, open up to it and enjoy it or at least deal with it. Sometimes things just are, you can spend a lot of energy fighting or wishing they weren't but they simply are.

I have never felt more alive, more fully part of the universe, more attuned with microbes than when the weather beat my semi-naked body. So wet that the sweat from your body steams at minus ten, cloaking it in a seemingly chaotic coat of mist that rushes with or against the wind at speed, disappearing as it leaves your body, laying a faint trail of vapour and salt. I'd arrive at a place every morning where I could run boundlessly, constant breath, no fatigue, I could run forever, no maintenance, I was air. It was the heat generated through constant, burning movement that allowed this elemental partnership, this breaking down and merging of forces. I could lift and jump from the back plate of a moving van and my feet would automatically hit the ground at ten, 15 miles an hour, the micro-delayed jolt of the weight of the milk would ground and move with me. Pushing the wind back in the direction it howled from, a wall of energy you move through, pinning your skin to bone, drawing muscles to the fore. You are hard, you are powerful, forceful, exhilarating, exhilarated and elemental. You are wind, rain, heat and carbon, just that. Whooshing through gaps in space, gushing through the gullies, evaporating the wet overcoat of the world, burning distance and motoring from point to point. It is your body that is battering the driving snow, not the driving snow that is battering your body.

Out in the real world, where extreme exercise was not wrapped around me as a protective cloak, the weather sometimes reminded me that it was an unstoppable force – elemental nature could kill. During my youth it was much colder than it is now, cold days today were a refreshing spring morning in the '70s. As a by-product of my milk-round attitude, I often left the house in winter with absolutely no thought of the weather. I'd simply pull on whatever coat or jacket and leave, or just leave. My main concern being rain, this may have led to occasional, slight discomfort but it wasn't usually an issue. During my early to mid-teens I used to travel to quite a few away games to see Leeds United. I set off to see Leeds play Oxford in the League or Milk or Coca-Cola or Simon's Spam Cup with no thought of anything but football. Going to the coach I became aware that it was a bit chilly but the walking kept me warm – three-and-a-half hours later I was cold through my bones and out the back, had it been snowing I would have climbed inside a snowman for the heat.

It was minus 10, -10, don't say it never gets that cold, that was the temperature. So I grabbed my thick coat, over my three woolly jumpers, with my begloved fingers, and snuggled up against the bite. In the real world, being a slightly effeminate but hardened milkman, I stood in thin boots that weren't fully attached to their soles, wet, thin socks, a shiny, thin polyester coat, designed more for the look than any coat-like features. A thin, tank-top-shaped, pink-and-grey, cotton-shirt-type thing, that only just covered my belly if I didn't move, wondering how you know that you are about to die of hypothermia. I mean really thinking, 'At what point do I alert a steward that he needs to contact my mother to make the funeral arrangements?' Leeds lost 3-0.

Another time coming out of Gipton onto Easterly Road, it was cold but I was about to get a bus. I didn't require the luxury of the thin tank-top as, being a milkman, I didn't feel the girly evening cold, it is never colder than just before sunrise. The bus never came and I had never experienced heat. I later found out, sitting in a little old lady's house that I met for the first time when I knocked on her door saying, 'Please no more cold, let me in. I'll marry you and bear you children', that the buses had stopped running due to adverse weather conditions, bloody bodybuilders. After these two times I realised that the weather could kill young, hard milkmen. What annoys me is that one came before the other and I didn't adapt, I can be a bit simple like that, me. Primates in jungles or on mountainsides learn and adapt, not me.

Blue, red, green, white, black gates, slatted gates, horizontal, vertical and diagonal, solid gates. Gates bolted, on a catch, hook, hinged or sprung, gates that could be jumped, gates that became jumpable as I grew, and gates that demanded opening, opened and closed, over years, fifty to a hundred thousand times, gateless gardens. Large gardens, small gardens, front and side gardens, back gardens, no gardens; gardens that were micro-manicured and gardens that were thoroughly independent. Rows of gardens that could be sneaked through, spaces squeezed through, hedges straddled, barriers limboed, fences hurdled or stepped over, drainpipes swung, pole-vaulted.

Sweat on my topless torso, melting hail or snow that encircled my every step and encased my legs to the knee, breath constant and solid out front. Everywhere virgin snow, trodden, slid and scattered. The warmth of the sun peeping over roof-tops, static cars and horizons, tanning my body before breakfast, before the first communal shit of the day. It was spooky how many people crapped at the same time. Synchronised shitting. I'd know to the minute how early, how late we were, no need for clocks, always fifteen minutes either way. Maybe one of the boys was late, a delay at the dairy, maybe a lot of eggs that day to be doctored with feathers in the box to persuade the punters that they were farmyard fresh – they were in fact farmyard fresh with or without the feathers. Were the punters reassured into feeling wholesome and healthy by the downy presence of hen? We may be made late by volumes of notes and changed orders, maybe the milkman had spent longer at his 'morning stop', that over time moved houses and times. At first his stops were a mystery, we'd move like light for the hours of the round but at some point stop and listen to the radio for ten to twenty minutes for what seemed like no reason at all. I soon discovered the reason for the stops.

The existence of a wife, young children and home had a profound influence on my pre-pubescent mind. To my young senses, battered by Catholicism, it seemed all wrong, a fundamental betrayal of everything, no nuances, it just shouldn't happen. As I grew I gradually saw a pattern of men, fathers of friends and acquaintances, who had an affair or a series of affairs. It didn't just seem bad but very sad, pathetic. I bumped into a neighbour in a strange setting – he winked and said, 'You haven't seen me.' There was no honour, no respect, they weren't just being unfaithful to their wives but to their children and, to an extent, to their extended family and friends. I saw a number of distraught families at first-hand, it was pitiful and cruel. In my young, judgemental, black-and-white head I would never do it. Why did they do it? Over time I heard stories of people marrying young, having no knowledge of others, no comparisons, no experience. I slowly decided that, given the chances, I would experience the sexual world to the full, new women would become normal, I would be unfaithful to all who tried to stop me, until I committed. I would not have an affair, I would exorcise the 'other', the 'not you' before I came to a serious relationship and bred. Obviously some men were simply monogamous, no matter what their sexual experience. Fabulous, I could rut with abandon and claim moral justification. An excuse not to be passed by.

The whistling and shouting at women in the street, ogling half-dressed women in the paper to a fanfare of blunt, monosyllabic words, ratta-tat-tatting aggression, not seen elsewhere in any of our conversations, stripped the women of any sexuality, any attraction. I would later see the women in the street unnoticed by others and get an erection like a block of flats, but as soon as 'Look at the tits/arse on that' hit the air, any mystery, wonder or lust disappeared like a Man U fan waking in The Squinting Cat pub, Leeds......quickly. In my forming consciousness women did start to take on an air of being a tad seedy, base, unattractive, bit smelly, white and bulky. Pre-puberty, the selections made by editors, milkman and older boys, for a short while, set a high, be it completely socially dictated, standard. 'Normal' women were passed over for a pre-defined 'exceptional'.

As my sexuality ripened in the groin a gradual but definite switch occurred, genetically programmed, unstoppable, like a rhino in a corridor. 'Real' women became fascinating, where as the 'false', presented as perfect, became standard, over-groomed and dull. There was something so pre-packaged that they appeared like Smash or Pot Noodles. All E numbers and gloop; after two mouthfuls you just knew there'd be a nasty taste and texture across the roof of your mouth, like sucking a perfume bottle or licking a lipstick, and an unsatisfying absence in your stomach. (Can I just say here that I think Pot Noodles are grossly misunderstood and underrated - respect to The Pot.) Here cometh the second fact I know. **The 2nd Fact What I Know: '70s TV Dinners were absolutely and unquestionably shite.**

There she is again, it's 'disappearing behind a door' girl, slotting a key into a door, opening it and disappearing, as she does. Well, well.

Back to my developing, early perception of women, real women, ordinary, average, normal and all other terms of equilibrium that women would punch you on the nose for if associated with directly. These women seemed appetising, solid, wholesome, you could imagine the full feeling, the warm and contented belly. They were mysterious, magical and fascinating, they drew you in closer and closer until you could sense the naked skin, warm and soft. You just wanted to dive in, mouth and body open.

Every morning on my milk-round I'd hear, 'Look at the tits on that!' I'd just look at the picture or woman and shrug. I never got tits – by the time I'd been sexually active for a couple of months, I'd worked it out, legs, thighs, the gateway to genetic conquest, primeval urge. Tits, breast-feeding and socially constructed male obsession. Men wholeheartedly promise me that they love tits, I don't believe them, or I believe that they believe it but years of indoctrination have led them there, like a Pavlovian dog; whereas legs, thighs, butt, draw a wild-dog response to spread genes.

The only thing tits may do is signpost health, but logic dismisses this – my 'A' cup byrd (she won't marry me until I get a personality and a penis extension) breast-fed our son for 18 months. Tits, 'Eh, what?', but legs, the length, the curve, turned me on like *The New Avengers*, alone, in a darkened room. I think deep down they always did, legs in socks, tights or stockings seemed to have an added layer of mystery and intrigue, picked out and accentuated lines and dynamics that reduced my breathing to short gasps. In my early pubescent mind medium to dark tights danced and excited, moving up them with eyes or mind focussed the blood exquisitely and filled my head with a beautiful absence, so full of all that existed of any interest in my world, women's legs.

When I finally came to touch them, it was more exciting than I'd imagined, small head-explosions gradually gaining in intensity. Even now, all people of the world, men, women, gay and straight must agree that there is a nice feeling to an attired leg; tights/stockings over legs feel smooth and nice, a wonderful texture under your touch that is not replicated anywhere, it simply generates electricity. I sometimes tire of my beloved David and listen to '60s New Orleans funk or classical guitarists doing Greek film music but the touch of an attired female leg is a constant and eternal obsession, on my death bed my final words will be, 'Thighs in my face....please.'

15
(What? No chapter 14?)

Remarkable though it is, I was no top totty aged nine/ten/eleven. I was aware that other boys were popular with girls and harboured a half-acknowledged jealousy but it really didn't matter that much, I had my football, Airfix models and music. Fun wasn't female. I was seen as average, ordinary and everything we all hate to be – there were a couple of special friends, one that encouraged me to put my hands down her knickers and one that I played marbles with, but girls largely left me alone.

1976 was a good year for a sun tan, in preparation for losing your virginity, and I had the best tan in Britain. Outside school it wasn't necessary to wear a top, so for hours on end of an evening I didn't, and I'd have two to three hours in the sun most mornings, on the milk-round.

I'm sorry but the 13-year-old was stunning, live with it. Bestowed with a multitude of genetic gifts, too many to list here, the mixture of my parental genes created a thing of rare and extreme beauty. Just with me, not my siblings – they were dogs to the last. Pick the nicest features of each of my brothers and sister, combine them and you'd still be left with a rat-faced buffoon as compared to my genetic cocktail; measured to perfection, just the right temperature producing a flawless sensation.

One of these genetic wonders, which has passed through me and down the line, was perfect teenage eyebrows.

As I came through my teenage years it was clear that a lack of height diminished my irresistible sex appeal – it's hard to be a universally fancied adult at five-foot-two. Had I gone into acting I would have needed to carry around a box of fruit. The teenager was magnificent. Toned, tanned and usually topless, short, spiky, blondish hair darkening my tan. I didn't know that my totty rating was rising, but it was being pointed out by girls my age, who'd developed a weird look in their eyes, a look that was a bit scary and less neutral.

Now maybe you shouldn't read this. It's so outlandish that you really won't be able to stomach it, you'll regurgitate it like a cat eating grass. Gut convulsing, trying to wretch the words out of the pit, but again it's true, so I'll say it. I could talk, God could I talk, and I did, about anything, N-E-thing. You may find it highly implausible but I could babble for England, babble after having listened. Listened to what the other person said and respond in an interesting manner, at length, and with sense and perspective. Let the other person speak and comment on their comment. Hard to believe but I enjoyed it, talking, still do.

What was it that drew the girls in? Why me? It started before I came out, but intensified with coming out. It was possible that as I was tapping at the side of my cocoon women could sense it, sense the elements of Michael that I was, divining-rod in hand, trying to locate, to mine. There was so much at play. The world of Leeds, Yorkshire, England; the girls of Leeds, Yorkshire, England, were in a completely unique position and frame of mind. A small window in history that I just happened to coincide with.

I mentioned earlier that 'disappearing behind a door' girl hadn't just come out as Barbarella, in Leeds, Yorkshire, England, with the sexy space-age costumes and a vague, sexual curiosity mixed with a passive acceptance. What if she had, or some other female had? I promise you that no matter what they looked like – as long as it was not extremely unattractive to the average boy – they would have been fighting off male attention with an alligator and bullwhip. Picture a teenage girl in Leeds, Yorkshire, England '77/'78 coming out as Barbarella, boys would be falling at her feet begging, 'Please, let me come on your spaceship.' She would be number-one male fantasy, bar none.

To some extent, this is what I did by coming out as a Bowie fan in Leeds, Yorkshire, England 1977/78. I nailed, without the aid of a hammer, the female fantasy of a majority of girls of a certain age group. This elegant piece of joinery was not intentional but thoroughly unconsidered and it intensified the strange look in the female eye. I was already, by the time of my 'coming out', being led astray by many girls – with my change they became merciless. There was no need for me to chase girls or even show that much interest – they wanted me. Like the new copy of *Smash Hits*, they had to have me. By pure chance or the compulsion of 'coming out' I captured what every female within three years of my age wanted.

Who were the male sex symbols? Where was the glamour? Girls between 13 and 15 had come to their sexuality amongst images and memories of Marc Bolan, Bowie, Brian Ferry, Jimmy Hendrix, maybe Phil Lynnott. They were all 'exotic', unordinary, not average, not like the boy bands today. The girls could no longer admit to Donny Osmond, David Cassidy or The Bay City Rollers and retain even one iota of peer respect. These, largely pre-puberty icons, were 'clean'. Bowie, Hendrix, Bolan, Ferry, Lynnott were not the kinda fellas who wanted to hold your hand. The girls of East Leeds, Yorkshire, England needed 'the exotic' and by pure chance, some strange warp of fate, I gave it to them and with little competition.

The memory of feeling average stayed with me throughout my slagging times, so even as the tenth girl that week was removing my underwear, I half-expected them to laugh and walk out shouting, 'I'm not shagging you, you're plain.' They never did.

I was a naïve, young man being taken advantage of by too many young women – they only seemed to be thinking about one thing. It was hard. I tried to talk to them and they'd feign interest, while all the time trying to manoeuvre the conversation around to more suggestive topics. They didn't want to know what was important to me, what I thought, what I felt, my passions.

'Football is boring' or 'I don't like Leonard Cohen.'

Few words, just plenty of eye contact, hair-flicking, lip-licking and manipulation, fleeting, playful touches. So resolute. Doggedly tracking and hunting me down, not to plumb the depths of my soul but to superficially explore my outer shell. Ignoring the pearl to eat the flesh.

I know you don't believe it but what can I do? Rewrite history? I have the sword of truth in my hand and it really doesn't matter what you or even I think. I could pretend that girls weren't queuing up at my bedroom door, bottle of wine in one hand and The Pill or Durex in their back pocket, but that would be a lie, they were. I had to beware girls bearing wine and no bulge in their back pocket.

Attentive, but only as a means to an end. Often too focused to allow even a bit of flirting. No interest in the real me, just the gorgeous exterior. There was no real respect for or interest in my personality – I wanted to scream, 'I am a person; inside what you want is a real person, a being, a consciousness. A boy with feelings and emotions, not just an object to be used.' But I shagged them instead.

It was never enough to just see me, to spend time with me in company. Constantly trying to isolate me, planning a way out of the social group, waiting for me to go to the toilet so that they could follow. Feeding me a non-stop supply of wine and trying to break through my defences. It was hard and it was relentless, they used and abused me. They were savage and focused, pushing past other people as if they weren't there to get to me. They were fast and furious in their pursuit, while I was a little slow at running.

I was as slow as a rocket, while they were as fast as lead balloons. I was a yellow, plastic rocket being carried by a little boy to the park.

On the way he drops it over a barrier onto a building-site where it gets encased in concrete and lain as the foundations to a house, soon to be occupied by a young couple named Maria and James who breed six years later. They were lead balloons being carried on the bullet train by a scientist, specialising in dermatology. He is taking them to a colleague so that the level of lead can be tested and they can judge whether that is the likely cause of a little girl called Jessica's skin problems.

The lengths to which the girls would go to get me onto a bed was chilling, they were out of control. What shocked me was that older girls hunted me down and seduced me, cruelly taking advantage of my young innocence. They were breaking the law. Mid to late-teen females just wouldn't be seen dead with a boy a couple of years younger, that was a teenage law, punishable by complete social ridicule and banishment to the dark corners of the public spaces. Yet these older girls would happily take me out in public and wear me like a new pair of trendy shoes. As I became more blasé (about the age of 14) in one-off sexual encounters, older girls would be using all their advanced feminine wiles to coax me into taking their phone number. Once you're in this place of not caring, not trying, not planning, it's a self-perpetuating, ego-boosting situation. If a girl had absolutely no interest or urge to see me again, due to some strange, mental frailty or awful lack of taste, it went unnoticed as I wouldn't ask for a phone number or another liaison anyway.

This nonchalance was expected, part of the unspoken arrangement. Only when the woman was planning more was it noticed and my status as top totty, a heaven-sent gift to the women of East Leeds, subconsciously underlined.

The fact that I didn't keep in touch with girls wasn't to do with them, it was down to the reality of the situation. I may bump into them again and that would be fine, if they seduced me, they seduced me, if they didn't, they didn't. Life was relatively spontaneous and arrangements were to be avoided, I wouldn't keep them.

I owned my life, everything was mine. I was young, funny and vital, opinionated and witty, cock-sure and positive, destined for rock 'n' roll stardom, and I spurned more attractive females than Bjorn Borg (not that Bjorn is female, I mean more females than him). Honest to God, I swear on your life, David Cassidy called me one day, in tears, 'Mick, my record sales are plummeting, the female stalkers are disappearing and I hear that they are all outside your house. Will you stop hogging the women? Please give me back my girls. '

'David, get a grip. Technically, when you do it, it's paedophilia.'

How funny, I am lying on straw. It is hard to pull away from the numbness that draws my concentration to my groin alive and dancing. How does she know this place? Did she play here as a kid? I look down at her face but can mainly see the top of her head, close my eyes and rest my head on the shiver. I look down again and see her face, she looks uncertain and uncomfortable, like she feels compelled. I take a few seconds out to concentrate on my tingle, to enjoy it for a moment, and then pull her head up – she looks confused, has she got it wrong? I kiss her with an intensity that is designed to purvey appreciation. I pull away slightly, she nervously scans my eyes and is reassured. Rolling her over onto the hay, she is so long and lithe, I stroke between her legs, legs that, were we standing, would reach my belly. Legs the result of years of good breeding. She pulls herself up slightly, eyes open, and moves her lips to mine.

Can she trust me?

She is taunted every morning for a passing resemblance to a soap star. A soap star she would not choose, a soap star to which, for me, she has added an element of sex appeal. The boys taunt her because they cannot have her. She is thoroughly sexy although she clearly does not know it.

'Shall I use a johnny?'

She kisses me more.

'Yes. Is that OK?'

'Course it is.'

Her leg is up at an angle, foot resting on the ground. I move my hand up the length of it, as we kiss, my other fingers lost in her hair, cupping the curve of her skull. I'd guess through the nervous tension that she is a virgin. The nervous tension adds to the moment and intensifies my calm. We kiss softly as I move my fingers around her valley, around her hill. Lightly stretching and bringing moisture up from the well, I tickle gently with two fingers. Kissing around her neck, the breath is deepening, body starting to fade into the brain, where the sensors map and pick out every physical sensation. Pulling me onto her, we kiss and break slightly so that I can roll on the Durex.

She grips my arm tightly as I move inside her, not to the base, a short, predictive gasp. Slowly probing, more circular and horizontal than penetrative. She raises her legs and draws me further in, a slight loosening across her body, moving her hands to the back of my neck and pulling me closer, deep, flickering, oxytocin eyes. Building intensity feeding the tension in her body, she is fighting the low groan, like the early onset of childbirth. Distracting, strong hands moving across her skin. Nowhere near orgasm, I will not witness that moment, she will not go there, that is someone else's honour, as it should be.

Lying in each other's arms, slow caresses, I usually avoid this level of intimacy but it is all that is appropriate for her and I like the girl. This is her childhood haunt, not mine – her time.

It wasn't easy for me. Sometimes I felt like screaming, 'Please no more sex, I'm only human. How can you expect my penis to be constantly erect? There are only so many pretty, young, fresh-faced girls that I can deflower.' The pressure was awful, while I wanted to lie back and read my new copy of *The Beano*, girls were demanding that I remove their underwear, no concern for the exploits of The Bash Street Kids.

Sometimes I'd sit back and ponder the girls tempting me away from the path of righteousness and monogamy, forcing me to deceive my one, true love or steady girlfriend. The callousness of these girls was staggering, how could they do it to her? They tempted me into extreme sin, nailed me to the cross of lust and procreation. We had no choice, I was so damn fine. Like Jesus in the desert, they could battle the constant temptation, the overbearing ache to get into my pants, but alas, like me, they were only human. One look, one glib one-liner, one meaningful stare into the distance and they were helpless, led astray by my vibrant splendour. The choice was not theirs, they were female and they saw me, easy. In line with Eve they were weak, led me to sin and made me betray my love, my faith, for forty seconds, and forty seconds I'd resist. But still, through my majestic agony, I managed to absolve them, 'Forgive them Father for they know not what they do.'

I can feel the tarmac hard on my head, beneath my coat. It is spread out to avoid car-park burn; we had not made it to the full shadow. She cannot be comfortable, she only has the thin coat and fishnets to protect her knees, I look up to check, she could rise up off her knees and squat but most of her weight is falling through her flowing hips and pelvis. She is not in the mood for conversation. Orange is fast winking behind her head as it obscures and reveals the light, tight-curled, auburn hair dancing in shadow and glow. It falls forward over my face and flicks back up into the air as her face is bathed in moonlight, eyes closed in prayer to the sky, bottom lip held tight between teeth.

She is pushing off my chest as I hold her pelvis in a vice, one hand on the base of her back while the second palm is hard against her bone. She bucks at speed pushing hard against my hands, trying to throw the imaginary rider, or break the stubborn horse. She slides further back in the sticky saddle, leaning back, using my top as reigns.

I stroke her hard, she is muscular and solid, no waste. No straight lines, just perfect curves, arms, shoulders, thighs, buttocks, waist, hair. Her skin glistens in the half-light, smooth and almost lucent, blood flowing fast, muscles igniting.

When I was mid sex period, a lad a few years older, who was also known as a bit of a lad for the lasses, got annoyed. He heard a friend, who had lived with me since he was about 14, taunting me about my sex life. The guy started saying, 'He can't have been with that many. Bet I've been with more.'

These sorts of conversations always made me cringe and I NEVER commented on ANY of it, I may have smirked, slightly embarrassed, but I would never get involved. I would never even confirm whether or not I had actually had sex with any but my steady girlfriends. These two, semi-joking but with serious undertones, sparred over it for a while. Until my friend said, 'Go on then, how many have you shagged?'

'No, how many has he?'

'He says he doesn't know. Lying shit will never say.'

'Roughly.'

'He doesn't know, or the wanker's not saying. How many have you, roughly?'

'I know exactly.'

The guy, who by the way was a good lad, he smiled constantly and was quite a wag, gave a number. My friend raised his eyebrows, blew out air, while winching his chin back into his neck.

'I'd say about two months' worth.'

'No way.'

'Yeh seriously, easy, two months an' he'll shag that many.'

With self-image, there are times when it catches you by surprise, where the back-slapping, no matter how you try to fight or disguise it, gives you a small buzz, but it's inevitable that your brain kicks in.

My friend was exaggerating, as one does in that situation. While they were talking, I'd done a little calculation, using equations and estimates, recent averages and shit. Not that many, not in two months. Realistically, it was almost certainly more like two-and-a-half to three months. I don't know what happened, girls didn't seem that interested in me until I was about twelve, and then from about 13 they just kept offering to remove their underwear – constantly, for a seven-year period, I swam in women. I have no idea of an amount of different women that I actually poked. Sorry, I couldn't resist that bit of Man Fucks Woman: Subject Verb Object. It is not an achievement, productive, creative or a source of pride. There is no boast, there is just how it was and it confuses me, in my head I've always brushed it off. I could only estimate, and I couldn't estimate with any certainty, to a closeness of 500, the actual figure.

I'd never talk to anyone about it and never think about it, so in some ways there was no need to deal with it, get it into perspective, to justify it to myself or anyone else. I just ran around, like one of those monkeys who spend all day shagging any member of their troop apart from their mother. It could have been, on a subconscious level, me feeling that I should have sex, that was my role, I had to live up to a reputation, social duty, gender stereotype. Or it could have been that I simply liked shagging. For various reasons I would avoid sexual contact with some girls, didn't trust them or thought they'd get needy, perhaps they were politically motivated, maybe they'd read too many *Jackie* photo love stories and stank of that fucked-up view of gender roles.

Shackled still by my gender straight-jacket, this promiscuity frowned upon and ridiculed. If it was a woman writing, stating a vast number of men over a seven-year period, at least she could celebrate it with, 'It's my body and I chose to do as I liked with it.' I sense no concern for me or the possibility of emotional scarring, long-term consequences. If a woman shagged thousands of men while she was between the age of 13 and 21, would a large proportion of the men be seen as being abusive, taking advantage of a woman with low self-worth and esteem? Men are not, generally that attractive, or should I say that men and women are fundamentally different, the wiring is different. I believe that men's fundamental, primal, hard-wired, urge is to spread genes like a gardener with a hose-pipe. This genetic weakness is what the girls located and cruelly exploited, I gave up the battle, I was helpless in the face of the onslaughts. Men can fight it, we can train it out of ourselves but that is what it is, it is fighting nature and few would hold out against a constant stream of young women in safe scenarios. We may get to a place were the urges are well and truly under control but they are alive and well, just captive in an intellectual and habitual box, consequence being the real gaoler.

Do most women select, choose genes that they think will give good offspring? Obviously women often have sex just for recreation, not to breed, but how much of the basic, primal wiring still leads to men that would give their children some kind of competitive edge? I think that many more men are fundamentally led by penis than women by fadge. Women often 'go off' attractive men that have no sense of humour, no conversation or banter, are a bit stupid, vain, insensitive. Whereas most men would still chase or shag what they see as an attractive female and hardly notice those traits, they don't care, they simply want to shag. I'm sorry but we are different.

This gender-wiring, this urge to spread seed, may have protected my self-esteem, convinced me what I was doing was alright, natural. Also, there was a social climate of 'boys will be boys'.

'Mick, what y'doing in here?' Smiling, this girl is always smiling, she's my smiling friend, my laughing, talking friend.

'They're queuing out of the door in the Gents and it's disgusting in there by this time.'

'You are naughty.' She is moving towards me, still smiling.

'What? I'm always in here.'

'Yes, I know, you are naughty.'

She is up to me, face cupped in her hands, tongue forcefully into my mouth. Her hand is behind my neck while the other is straight down my pants. Still kissing me, she has moved her hand from behind my head and is moving her knickers to one side, drawing her body closer and easing herself onto me. My hands are up her long, black skirt, one pulling her gently down at the hip, the other easing her knickers further across and out of the way. She is taller than me; I am leaning back against the wall as she flings and grinds her hips, one hand pulling at my buttocks, still smiling, her stocking-tops flashing against her thighs with each backwards motion.

'Jesus you two, you could at least use the cubicle.'

'Anita, you are such a stiff. Leave them alone.'

We stop, laugh into each other's eyes, and fall into a cubicle. She pushes me back onto the toilet, hitches up her skirt and pulls her knickers to one side as she climbs on top. It is hard for me to move as she rocks forwards and backwards with increasing speed, her arms bear-hugging my head close to her chest, her breath quickening. She leans back, grasps my knees behind her and drives from the hip with more speed, small forceful thrusts, she is gone. Short, breathy pants, building in intensity. The downward pressure and fast rocking action on the toilet seat is slightly uncomfortable, allowing me to fully appreciate the pure animal that is riding me. Sexy as a thread of magic mushrooms on a cool September morning. She shudders to a sudden stop instantly flicking out erratic spasms from the hip, I rise and grind. Pulling in breath, she is gently rolling her butt, smiling.

'Haven't you come yet?'

I say nothing but mirror her rolling butt, breaking up the rhythm, and throw in a slightly thrusting motion, she smiles, I smile.

'Let me up.'

She gently pulls herself up and moves over, I slide behind her and hitch up her skirt. She has one hand on the wall and the second on the cubicle, forming a crucifix. She raises her foot onto the bowl and I slide in below, with slow circular stabs, just moving in, just moving out, breaking the cycle with sudden speed and penetration, then easing back. My hands slightly pulling at hips, stroking the inverted V inside the top of her thighs. She starts to push down and wiggle in time. I pull harder at her hips as she twists slightly, moving her hand from the cubicle wall onto the wall behind the toilet, taking leverage and force from the confined space of the 45-degree angle of walls. Her hips are locked tight and pushing against me as we move at speed, fast moans, my hand grabbing at her hip while the other strokes her clit, fingers tingling with the rapid, moist friction.

She is still smiling, stood with her trendy mates. As usual, we have both pulled.

'Who's that?'

'Who?'

'That girl, there, with the bleached blonde hair.'

'Just a mate.'

'What did she say?'

'Don't know, she's a long way away. Just, like, "see y'later" or "goodnight".'

'She looks like she's always smiling.'

'I know. She always is, she laughs and smiles *all* the time.'

I did all sorts of things but sex was one of my basics in life, probably my dominant drive. After a few years it became the norm and sometimes a bit dull, but I was a 13- to 21-year-old male for God's sake, and my body and soul appreciated this newly explored sensual fun fair. Breath, food and drink, consumption and disposal, sleep, never enough, all arranged around sex. We are dominated by the body, by biology, and I wasn't fighting it. Of all these 'basics' I think I correctly selected the one to do to excess. I didn't eat, drink or sleep too much, I didn't breathe too much, just the right amount for the action being carried out.

Sucking in the sharp, dry, angular air of a crisp winter's morning or drinking in the soft, moist, rounded air of a humid summer's day. The air was particularly dry in '76 and hot enough to explode tennis balls. Feasting on Bachelor's Savoury Rice with brown sauce and two eggs on top; deep fried and battered prawns. Swilling tomato juice around my mouth or, later, tickling my taste-buds with a pint of Tetley's. Sleep was to be snatched at any opportunity and indulged in. These were some of my sensory delights, these and slowly moving up a woman's thigh.

16

In retrospect, my early schooling seemed to revolve around one central principle, the school motto, 'Let us fuck up young people's view of their sexuality,' worn on blazers in the form of the school badge. It was in Latin so no one understood it, but the clear statement of aims was there in one little phrase: 'Junoros perspecta o rutta il distortes.' They obsessed about repressing sexuality and making sure the children were taken to at least one funeral a week. There were medieval threats to ensure decent behaviour, which was tempting, but the pervasive sadness that hung in the church dictated that we just sang and didn't mess about.

The junior school was run and dominated by manic nuns, locking 'naughty' children in cupboards and if the cupboards were occupied you went in the chest on the floor.

'Touching yourself is a sin.'

'Beware the curse of self-abuse, it is the disease of the devil.'

Why they were speaking to young children in such a way is a mystery. It was always there, they didn't seem to start the indoctrination just before the onset of puberty, no, get 'em young.

'If you have impure thoughts you must ignore them as they are the shameful work of the devil.' This is a weird thing to say, I'd say disturbed, but to say them to seven- and eight-year-old kids is proper poorly. It was a constant undercurrent; sexuality is the dirty, shameful domain of the sinner. As soon as I had any understanding of sexuality I knew it to be the glorious gift of God, although my relationship with God was under negotiation.

The nuns were hypocritical and dishonest in many ways; they lived in luxury in the big house at the top of the hill while telling us that we should give as much money as we could to poor black babies in Africa. You never saw them driving a car less than two years old and this was in the '70s when new cars were like dog-tusks.

Around the age of eight, I forgot my PE kit. I loved PE, it was great. I never forgot my PE kit. The headmistress and scariest of all the nuns, Sister Dolores – that's not Sister Dolores 'protector of the meek and mild' of Lille, but Psycho Sister Dolores of Leeds, 'torturer of the smelly and downtrodden' – anyway, The Mad One decided that all children forgetting their kit that week would do maths. All kids except members of the netball team, the champions, pride of the school netball team, they could watch PE and perhaps join in without their kit. Now, being a good Catholic child and having been taught the worth of justice, sacrifice and the path of righteousness, I raised my hand. It was ignored. It remained in the air. It was ignored. It remained in the air.

'Excuse me Sister Delores, why are the netball team allowed to watch—'

'Be quiet McCann.'

'But sister, it hardly seems fair that—'

Shouting nun say, 'SHUT UP, don't you DARE question me.'

'But sister, they have forgotten their kit just as we have.'

By this time she was right on top of me, probably four-foot-eleven and fat but to an eight-year-old she was a Rottweiler. She swung and took in as much force as she could, gathered a lifetime of frustration into one, fat hand and slapped me across the face with all her might. I winced, it hurt, made my eyes water.

'I like PE; I wouldn't forget my kit on purpose.'

'BE QUIET.'

'It's not good.' I would not back down to an oppressor.

The secularist in me thinks she must have had a seriously fucked-up childhood. The Catholic in me thinks that if I saw the 95-year-old nun now I'd kick her fucking face in.

I returned home after school.

'What has happened to your face, have you been fighting?'

My face was puffed up and bruised.

My dad taught in a rough Catholic comprehensive school. I didn't know at the time but, even though he never got promoted in his life, his teaching methods were seen as revolutionary. A couple of teachers, years later, told me that when they were at a Catholic teacher-training college in Leeds my dad's methods were often discussed as the way forward in rough schools. Which was ridiculous because no one could have made the kids quake like my dad did, and no one could make them laugh like he did. I later played his school at rugby league and expected a battering; they looked hard as nails, but they all told me how they loved my dad. They didn't use those words but the sentiment was clear. By the way, I took a battering but played really well, had to, couldn't let my dad down.

So when he got home, he asked me what had happened to my face, I told him. He went to school to speak to Sister Delores. The following day the crime against humanity was compounded. She came sidling up to me,

'Michael, you have told your parents that I slapped you. I did no such thing.'

She also tried to get me to feel guilty for 'telling tales'.

'They asked how I got the bruise.'

'Where did I slap you? Was it your right side or your left side?'

She spent the next five minutes trying to confuse me with some spurious defence of her being right- or left-handed and trying to get me to say the wrong side of my face; she failed, I may have been eight but I was not stupid. My, how injustice lingers, and I've suffered very little.

My dad only went to school twice to chastise teachers. The second was at senior school, I was probably 14/15. My grammar school had merged with the secondary modern next door to form Cardinal Heenan High School. Obviously coming from a grammar school we were all a set of snobby, swotty softies, whereas in reality it was probably a 60/40 mix of working-class and middle-class, just like them. There was a series of fights between boys from the schools which I tried to ignore. Lads from our school also had away games where they travelled to other schools to fight; my only question was, 'Why?'

Coming around a corner at the back of the school straight into a gang of 20/30 lads from St John Bosco's. I was with a mate from their school, he kept walking, didn't blame him. They walked straight at me, I didn't change direction, why should I? They'd changed track. Right into the middle of them, I knew I'd take any one of them on their own, 'cepting p'raps two, but I'd give it a go with either of them. One was just supposed to be quite hard, their 'leader', but the other I knew by reputation and really didn't like what I'd heard. He'd been expelled from St Kevin's, quite an achievement, for fighting. St Kevin's was on my side of Leeds, in Whinmoor, and I knew quite a few chaps there.

'Mick watch him, he starts on anyone. He got expelled cos he wouldn't stop fighting with Mulligan, a real nutter, really hard. The fights were mad – they'd just keep going until one of them was unconscious. When one was, they'd jump on the other's head until someone pulled them off. If he hadn't got expelled one of them would have got killed.' This prognosis was repeated by kids in my year, who knew Mulligan. His psychosis was legendary in 15-year-old, male Seacroft, as was his family's in different age-groups.

Anyway moving through the centre of the gang, as was my right under English law, I heard, 'Ooh the fuck d'y think you are? Y'fucking puff. Ooh you looking at?'

112

I turned and there was a line of lads; although I had no idea who was speaking, I returned the traditional response practised for years by many full-blooded, proud Englishmen, even though I'd come from Irish/Welsh/English and no doubt Scottish/Lithuanian and African stock: 'Nobody. Don't hit me.'

I didn't really; I returned the traditional response practised for years by many full-blooded and proud Englishmen et al, 'You, y'cunt.'

There was no real space for any other response, it had to be basic and slightly uneducated, I felt like pointing out the chain of clichés and saying '"Fancy a fight?" works better for me', but resisted.

The wheel spun – please be red, please, please, please be red.

My old dad used to say, during Tarzan films or nature programmes, 'There's nothing more dangerous than a wounded animal.'

'What, not even a nuclear bomb?' I'd ask, amazed.

'Don't be daft, an animal is at its most dangerous if it's trapped or injured.'

What he was talking about was fear, fear is a drug that dulls the pain receptors, heightens the senses and concentrates the aggression.

'Well don't or I'll knock your fucking 'ead off.' Aw great, it's black, out of 20 to 30 kids, guess who stepped out? Go on, guess. Yes, that's right, it was one of the gobby little shites that I'd put to sleep with a solid right. *Get in.* Phew what a relief. Oops no, it was the lad with the reputation. My skin prickled, my arches flexed, my head zoomed to a stop at pure concentration. 'Fuck!'

He stepped up to me, eyes fixed and manic, his first punch skimmed my chin. That was his last punch. I was possessed by something primeval. Fear and ancient survival reflexes gushed through my body, he must not get through to the village. An absolute corker of a right that travelled from somewhere south of Brighton and gathered force on the journey bent him from the knees, a couple of out-of-sight blows later I saw the opportunity to ram a finger up each nostril and rip. Where did that come from? I was dancing around him in a frenzied trance and blacked out. I re-entered my body pulling his head back from a wall for the third time, his face pouring blood onto the ground shouting, 'I'm in a perfect position to be kicked. KICK ME.' I stepped back, leant forward onto to my left leg and looked up. I could see from the gang of faces that it would be one blow too much, so I patted him on the head and walked.

Later, that moment scared the shit out of me. I hadn't stopped out of humanity or pity, even though any threat had gone. Although he was still standing, which was disconcerting, he was not conscious. I had stopped because I saw the threat of a gang of 30 kids. My fear and survival instincts were screaming, 'This one you must kill!' and had I not been under threat I have no idea when I would have stopped.

Later that day I was summoned to the office of one of the teachers from St John Bosco's, I didn't know him, PE teacher who took the football team (our footie team got through to the English schoolboys final – they were good – got beaten at Elland Rd by some southern team). On the way I saw the lad with the reputation. He looked at me grinning through a purple, red and black face, topless, clutching his dripping, red shirt to his face. His pure, white torso striped and blotched with purple. 150 yards away he cackled, I swear that the haunting sound was not distant but right in my head.

'Come in.'

It was immediately apparent that the teacher was not interested in my version, just violence. He had not a professional but a wild look in his eyes. He couldn't wait to get through the preliminaries to the main event. I could not win this one. He would have battered me in a fight, no contest, too big, too powerful and too fit. I asked for a witness to be present, he snorted, 'Put out your hand.' He looked me in the eye as he swished and carved the air with a thick, bamboo stick, like Errol Flynn on speed. I looked him in the eye and raised my hand. A little jump and a skip and he whipped the stick down onto my hand; I maintained eye contact. Not a flinch crossed my face, not even a twitch. 'No way, you fucking bully.' The smart thing to do was to shout 'Ouw,' and blow my hand but this was not a contest of intellect.

His blood vessels expanded a hair's width more and he struck me again with increased velocity, holding eye contact. He couldn't hurt me; I was elsewhere, boring into his soul. He repeated it a couple more times until he was furious, he didn't understand that I had all day. It stung, but my hands were hardened by lifting hard, plastic, heavy milk-crates and, by this time, I had more chemicals running through my body than a smack-head in Afghanistan. He looked at me with murder in his eyes, not a bit cross, but real murder. He focused all his agility, muscular build and hatred into the end of the stick and like John McEnroe serving to win Wimbledon crashed it down onto my hand. The stick could not take it, it cracked, snapped and half of it whipped back into the air, while the sharp stump missed my hand by a millimetre.

He had lost it. He wanted to 'break' me. He knew nothing of my secret weapon – I had seen *Cool Hand Luke*. The film with the gorgeous man with the eyes. It is quite scary to see a man in power lose control. I wasn't scared, we had gone too far for that. I had society wrapped around me like a bullet-proof overcoat. Had I been in a South American prison, that man would have certainly started to remove finger-nails, proper pain and everything. I hate proper pain and would have sold out my family in about 1.6 (or maybe 1.7) seconds.

The following day I returned home and my mother was holding a letter, looking perturbed. 'What is this? Why didn't you say anything? "The most violent fight the school has ever seen." What is this? Was it really that bad? Are you alright?'

'Yeh, I'm fine. It was just a fight. A kid at school started on me.'

'He started it?'

'Oh yeh, he started it.'

'But it talks here about the police and being expelled. What happened?'

I described the happenings but left out some of the gory detail, she interjected with the occasional 'Ooh my giddy aunt', 'Hell's bells and Batley Buses' and 'Ooh love'.

She didn't like this, she was confused, she really didn't like this. For years she had told me to walk away, not get involved. How could this be? I was a good kid. But it was a dangerous world, maybe too dangerous for me to ever be let out again.

'Why can't he just spend the day crawling in the toy cupboard with his cat, like he used to?'

Next day, my dad told me not to get the bus home, he'd give me a lift. I waited in the corridor outside the office, I heard the antlers lock, the young stag against the Lord of the Glen. My dad came out with a 'jobsa a good'un' look and we went.

'If that lad starts again, you defend yourself.'

'I'll get expelled.'

'No you won't, if that lad starts again, you defend yourself.'

After morning assembly, the PE teacher came up and said, 'Touch him again and you will get expelled.'

'He started it.'

'Touch him again and you will get expelled.'

'I won't start anything.'

'I'm telling you, you will get expelled.'

'So what am I supposed to do if he starts again?'

'Walk away.'

'What?'

'Walk away.'

'Walk away? Is that what you would do, if someone came up and started punching you, sir?
'Yes. In this circumstance. This is his last chance; he's had a tough time of it.'
'I won't start anything.'
'You will get expelled.'
'I won't start anything.'
Something scared me in that fight and brought about a fundamental change. It wasn't violence or pain as such, more a killer that lurked in the dark corners of my being. I realised that I was capable of things of which I was ashamed. From that moment I considered myself a fully committed pacifist. Anyway I had two more fights with the lad but not with the pure violence of my soul, which was a hindrance. It simply meant that the fights were a bit messier, lasted longer. Every time I had the opportunity to inflict serious pain on him I resisted. I remember having him pinned to the ground and saying, 'Come on, this is pathetic and I don't want to knock you out again.' I realised quite quickly that he couldn't really hurt me, he didn't have the power and I could 'take a punch'. Obviously physics dictates that if someone hits you in a certain spot with a certain force they will knock you out but he didn't have the force. I could control the fights relatively easily but it would have been more sensible to just knock him out, to finish him. Had I just chinned him the first time, rather than absolutely battering him, I could have just chinned him on a weekly basis which was what he wanted. I was scared of that fury lurking in my gut, I was scared of death and he wasn't.
I came into this through the nuns and I have to say that I did meet one good nun, Sister Catherine, at senior school. She used to cover me if I legged off lessons and played guitar in her anteroom. She gave me a list of lessons she didn't want me to disappear from, but for the rest of them, including RE, if any suspicion arose, she'd just say, 'McCann? Oh, Michael, yes, he's helping me with a few things.' I could always say, 'I was helping Sister Catherine, ask her.'
Unfortunately she got killed in South America by putting herself in front of gun barrels aimed at women and children.
I loved Sister Catherine but Catholicism seemed totally unambiguous. Thou shalt not have impure thoughts. Thou shalt not touch yourself. Thou shalt not look at girls. Thou shalt not cover your body in Greek yoghurt and invite a goat to lick it off. Thou shalt not have any sexuality at all, just like the Blessed Virgin Mary. Jesus was conceived outside fun, love or sex, or so the story goes. They even

tried to enter sexuality within marriage, the missionary position being the only position without sin. Excuse me; do you really think that you are so important to God that he gives a fuck about the positioning of your copulation? Is God that trivial and anal? I think not. Obviously, being a teenager this sexuality bullying enraged my penis and attitude to sexuality, I was often asked:

'Mick, as you came, why did you shout, "This one's for you, Sister Delores"? Is it some weird fantasy? Do you want me to dress up as a nun?'

'CHRIST, NO!' Which in retrospect was probably a bad decision.

At the time, girls seemed comfortable with me. I was a confusing mixture of cute, fun, considerate, pretty, fluffy and dangerous, selfish, disinterested, dark, physical, detached from serious. My excitement for the here and now, the moment, this moment, a special, glorious moment, a splendid moment, this conversation, this life being celebratory, fun being a crucial universal element, somehow made young women want to take me.

I liked parties, partying, drinking and tripping, I liked loud music, laughing, talking and messing about. I liked fun, serious conversations, the universe. I liked sex. Awful though it is, sometimes I just couldn't be arsed. I'd go to a party and simply want sex first and socialising second. I'd walk into the house, straight upstairs and listen to girls bitching and fighting on the stairs or outside the door, to be the first one in. I couldn't even be arsed selecting. I'd probably get round most of these anyway. In general, I felt like I was trying to grasp a sacred opportunity, this was *my* time. Although often, a few mates, bottles of wine and I was happy, I also sometimes wanted to party arrogantly, like they did, in my imagination, at Temple Newsam.

I grew up in the shadow of Temple Newsam House, a stately home, birth place of Lord Darnley, second husband of Mary Queen of Scots and father of King James I. It was the backdrop of my youth. Opulent and grand, my mother used to walk us kids there, probably a three to four mile round trip, while I was still in a pushchair. Tempsey was a constant. A stuffy, old ghost during my young life, transformed into a historical pleasure palace as my hormones kicked in. I suddenly caught a whiff of the absolute decadence of the place. In my imagination the mushroom, opiate and alcohol fuelled happenings of centuries sparked visions of the wildest parties, a hedonism that my teenage brain could only stand and marvel at with an envious longing. I would try to recreate some of this self-centred abandon, a homage to

117

partying giants of the past. I was not from a rich family but I could play the dandy, you no longer needed money to play and party to the extreme. Coiffured dandies in fine silks, embroidered jackets, elaborate wigs and basic, deadly make-up with 'Joker' lipstick and beauty spots haunted my spirit. Women with huge hair, frilly undergarments surrounded by dress scaffolding, hiding a young child to tickle their clit. Attitudes concerning children may have shifted but not towards pleasure.

The reality of the times did not matter, only my vision. There must have been wild parties there, but if not, it was real in my head and no historian could change that, they would probably be wrong anyway. It stank of old money and freedom. A 'let them eat cake' freedom from social conscience and responsibilities, fuck the poor and rut local serving wenches with abandon.

Obviously I grew knowing that Temple Newsam House was haunted – which stately home wasn't? There was a blue lady, living in the house and grounds, who was sometimes grey. I decided it depended on her mood. There were all sorts of stories to be told of this woman's life and history but I didn't listen, it didn't seem relevant. That she was there in the present was relevant to me, not her past. Anyway if I saw her I'd have her knickers off in no time, she'd be helpless and ecstatic.

I felt a real empathy with the coiffured dandies of old. I didn't think I was, or wanted to be, a woman. I was a fully hetero boy in effeminate clothing, not dresses but something that felt unique. A new form of dress that simply didn't accept the boundaries, it obviously wasn't new or unique but it felt like it was. I sometimes worried that it may be slightly shallow, a fashion, a bit of a whim not the proper compulsion of transvestites or homosexuals. Yet I had been compelled, I couldn't have resisted stepping out of my door on that first evening with greasepaint, silver hair, a kimono and my mother's white fur coat. I was driven.

I made some stands, like going in for the Miss Cardinal Heenan High School competition 1978/9, in full drag. I came third and demanded a recount; I was clearly the most attractive creature there. Walking behind some of my mates, after the competition, 'Fuckin'ell, that Lady Stardust w'fit wan't shi? Who wa'she?'

'Dunno, but I'd shag her.'

'Ay lads, it w' me.'

'Fuck off, it wan't.'

'It wo, ask Joe, he saw me getting ready.'

'Fuckin'ell y'queer bastard.'

'Scuse me, it wan't me who wanted to shag a man in drag. Let's talk later, when no one's around, I'll dress up fo'y' and everything. Anyway, don't say that, some of my best friends are bastards.'

I hadn't just presented as a woman, but as a male fantasy of a woman, short tight skirt, fishnets etc. I cornered one of the judges later.

'Miss, that was such a stitch-up. I was much more attractive than'er who won.'

'What?'

'The competition, I should have won. Do you know how degrading it is to come third in a beauty competition?'

'Michael, what are you talking about? Were you in the competition?'

'Lady Stardust!! That w'me.'

She laughs, 'Ahh, I'm sorry, if I'd have known it was you, you'd have definitely got my vote. I thought she was a confused adult.'

'But third? I ask y'. I was gorgeous.'

'Well, you had me fooled; I thought it was someone from outside school.'

I was entering into a fine tradition that started with the first Neolithic Man to smear red across his face and strut through his cave. I'm sure that throughout history there has been cross-dressing or displaying. I felt a certain guilt for not having to struggle and fight like historical dandies, say, Oscar Wilde, Byron or Quentin Crisp. Surprisingly, I hadn't really suffered as a consequence, I should have had to fight, scratch and accept the loss of relevant people. I did lose friends but not on the scale that I should have and I had been rewarded by an infamy that drew too many girls and seemed to give me the respect of people whose respect counted to me.

I was more of a Beau Brummell, other than the syphilitic death, although I have no idea how I will die. I was due to die in my 21st year, due to drowning, I knew the exact date and by some scary coincidence was scuba-diving. I think the pre-warning stopped the panic as the aqualung seemed not to be providing enough oxygen.

In some ways I wanted to battle, to face up heroically to bigots and oppression. As I'd never been battered, I had a false mental image of my hardness, my indestructibility and my immortality, I was Jimmy:

Jimmy looks sweet cos he dresses like a queen
But he can kick like a mule, it's a real mean team

Maybe it was a simple difference in my age, or that my appearance/confidence was, in some strange way, threatening or reassuring to other males but I definitely had less fights after coming out.

Those lines from 'All The Young Dudes' remind me to point out that no song, that I'm aware of, gets into the teenage head like 'All The Young Dudes':

Billy rapped all night about his suicide,
How he'd kick it in the head when he was twenty-five,
Ooh that's speed jive,
Don't want to stay alive, when you're twenty-five

Wendy/Lucy's stealing clothes from Marks and Sparks/unlocked cars
Freddie's got spots from ripping up the stars from his face,
Funky little boat race,
The television man is crazy saying we're juvenile delinquent wrecks,
Man I need a TV when I've got T-Rex, I'm a dude dad,

All the Young Dudes
Carry the news…

Jimmy/Ritchie looks sweet cos/though he dresses like a queen
But he can kick like a mule, it's a real mean team
But we can love, Oh yeah, we can love
Now my brother's back at home with his Beatles and Stones,
But I never got it off on that revolution stuff, what a drag, too many snags
Well I drunk a lot of wine and I'm feeling fine
Gonna race some cat to bed,
Is that concrete all around or is it in my head?

Brother you guessed I'm a dude dad
All the Young Dudes
Carry the news…

The only realistic competitor in the teenage head-state stakes that I can think off is 'Here We Are Nowhere', by Stiff Little Fingers, but I haven't given it that much thought, and neither will I.

17

120

At the heart of the Arndale Centre was the Wimpy Bar, obviously an integral part of the architect's original plan, the heart, the beat. Perfect design, a crow's nest elevated and open, perfect positioning, perfect look-out tower. Situated upstairs, mezzanine, on the inside angle of the 'L' of the arcade. The corner table was the best, positioned as it was on the outside angle of the Wimpy Bar, allowing both catwalks to be surveyed, not right to the ends but most people walked through. The perfect hide from which to set my sights upon the plentiful game.

Long periods could be spent daydreaming and looking down on the shoppers, teenage girls shopping for something not ordinary, something exotic, just for them, something not anchored in 1970s Leeds, Yorkshire, England. A magical emporium of women looking for me.

Ra-ra skirts, pencil skirts, skirts that looked like Laura Ashley wallpaper with a length of lacy material across the middle. Three-tiered skirts with fake underskirt like the ruffled petticoats of the Temple Newsam serving wenches. Some pencil skirts, like school trousers, went shiny after too many washes and were often too tight. The girls were growing and still thought the skirt fitted just as it had on the day of purchase.

Olivia Newton John style, skin-tight, Lurex pants, brightly coloured, pastels, or black. Blouses and T-shirts, jumpers and buttoned coats, long socks over tights, woollen tights, ribbed tights, multi-coloured stripy tights. Tank-tops and flared denim jeans, Levis or Wrangler were the make to have.

Every male under the age of 25 owned a denim jacket. I'd owned one since the age of eight; I chopped the arms off and painted an absolutely stunning likeness of David on the back panel, in black and light blue.

For us kids of the 1970s there was a huge *Da Vinci Code* type mystery that straddled the decade.

'What was the relationship between Jesus and cheese-cloth?'

The paradox was alarming, there couldn't possibly have been one, but there was. In the '70s Jesus wore cheese-cloth, as did Bjorn Borg and probably the Holy Spirit.

This was ridiculous, had Jesus come again in the 1970s he would have certainly modelled himself on Ziggy Stardust, not a tennis player.

Here's a moment, not of 1970s Rock'n'Roll history, but of Rock'n'Roll history: 'Not only is this the last show of the tour, but it's the last show we'll ever do.'

'Oh my God, he's killed Ziggy off.' Hammersmith Odeon, London, England, 1973, the last time Ziggy would ever appear on stage. It is of course bollocks, a Rock'n'Roll myth. It was obvious where Ziggy had to play his last show. Leeds, Yorkshire, England that is where Ziggy died, at the Rollarena, 1973. Obviously David wouldn't have the heart to kill him off without first giving me the opportunity to see him. But do you remember? Age nine? I didn't know how to use a Yellow Pages, an A to Z and a compass? Thirty years later I still hate my mother and live beneath the park keeper's hut on the Temple Newsam estate?

Bowie didn't 'break up the band' for a while and *Pin-Ups* was a fitting farewell to 'The Spiders' – a classic, basic, old school, R'n'B covers album. On *Pin-Ups* that band are tight, the tightest pop/rock combo I've ever heard. Although he replaces the fine, original Spiders drummer, Woody Woodmansey, the album is Ainsley Dunbar's, there is nothing that excites and drives a band like a proper sweating drummer, right there, cock-on and knowing it. All bass players in rock/pop combos should force the drummer to study *Pin-Ups*.

Mick Ronson got *Slaughter On Tenth Avenue* a belting album, that Bowie produced and wrote some of.

God bless The Spiders' beautiful, Yorkshire soul.

As I've named *Pin-Ups,* as tightest ever rock/pop combo album, (this obviously pre-dates programming) I'll have a stab at tightest bands ever seen. There are two. The first is Wishbone Ash, tighter than a virgin's inner flaps. The second shocked the pants off me. I'd always had a mental block with three-piece bands, they never seemed to kick up quite as much of a rumble. I saw The Police pre Roxanne being a hit and they were really tight but for some reason, in my head, three-piece bands never cut it. Anyway The Police are not my second tightest band ever, this was a three-piece that sounded like a 24-piece band. They were scarily tight, so tight that they simply played, no thought, no sign of concentration, tighter than a foreskin that's been introduced to super-glue, I mean watertight. Nirvana, they were tight, really tight, and heavy like a proper punk band. That was a very exciting little giggle.

The one adjective to describe the non-street hair of the '70s was big, the second would be airy. Female hair, like waves going out to sea, went the wrong way. Farrah Fawcett Majors and Betty Spencer, wife of Frank, had a lot to answer for. Hair would flick this way then come back underneath, while getting bigger at a random point, little boys in canoes would set off at dawn and never be seen again. You knew that hours of patience and a structural engineer had been employed.

And in the male role model corner we had Kevin Keegan, Starsky and Huggy Bear, Leo Sayer, The Bee Gees, David Cassidy, Bjorn, David Essex.

The none street barber's motto was 'air in hair'.

Metal buttons and large pockets. The male shoe of the '70s was not the platform shoes, it was the Ox-blood Doc Marten. Platforms only covered a three to four year period in polite society, whereas Ox-blood Doc Martens straddled the decade. It was a good time to have shares in Doctor Martens. The main thing you needed to know about Docs is that they were a footwear disaster when used in conjunction with segs. I knew a lad who tried it, the air-way soles didn't react well to the sharp, multi-stabbing segs and flat docs are simply an uncomfortable shoe. I never had Ox-blood Doc Martens, I had black Major Domos, they were more substantial for the milk-round, better wearing, went higher up the leg and looked cooler.

Necklaces of shells, melon seeds or small, round brown and cream hoops.

Loons, flared hipsters, usually in purple, yellow, green or brown, made from a felty, crushed cotton type material were early '70s and completely gone by the mid to late '70s, as were the two coloured kites inserted in pants to create the flair. Oxford bags were in the residual by '76, as were trousers with buttons going up the waist band. The numbers of rows of button determining, for some, how cool the kegs were. I only ever went as far as two; I didn't fully embrace the button stacking. At junior school, as well as my platforms I had some brown and cream, crinkled, soft plastic wedges, they were exciting.

As I was saying, by '75/'76 these multi-button stacking pants, star jumpers and Oxford bags were in the residual unless of course Newcastle United were in town where apparently they were all the rage. What? It's true. It was the first moment that I became fully aware that I was fashion conscious, seeing hoards of giddy Geordies wearing the season before last's fashions. It wasn't boot-to-boot team shirts in them days, no, it was the era of multiple scarves. I've nothing against Newcastle fans, their passion is the same as mine, just a different colour shirt and a different city. If you see a Scunthorpe United or a Huddersfield Town fan, you know they are genuine fans, there is no question. They are obviously not glory hunters. There may also be some genuine Man United fans, who are born into following the team (but they are a rarity at Old Trafford), I'm always surprised to meet a Man U. fan who is actually from Manchester, but meet them I have. I like Man City fans, although some of my mates are scum so I'm not prejudiced or owt.

The Arndale Centre was my hinterland, I'd display across my territory, my mane of hair clearly recognised as that of the top predator by the whole pride. My land was not ruled by the laws of the Serengeti; there were no cubs or genes to defend. The primal genetic laws were in play but under the administration of the modern world. There were stronger males around but they lacked the experience and charisma to maintain such a large pride. Less beautiful males may just be friends but some clearly had an eye on befriending me to chip away at the edges of my land, loose females roaming around the perimeter. I was egalitarian with my pride, we could do whatever we liked, there was no arrangement, it may be years before I'd return to them, if I ever did. The fact of the matter was that I could look their way and they would come over to smell my furry balls. I had no real need to expand my territory as rogue females would constantly travel in to see me preen and strut, top of the pose chain.

Often I'd go 'casual', make-up slightly touched up from the night before, clothes loose and rough, although always very eye-catching for late '70s Crossgates, Leeds, Yorkshire, England. Sometimes I'd put on a display, perfect hair and make-up, carefully chosen garb and *slightly* affected manner. Alone, with a mate or small group we'd always flit between people while there. At least as important as the pursuit of the females was the pursuit of a laugh. Messing about and chit-chatting with friends, serious discussions and playful banter.

Although I was not aware of it I had become a male bird of paradise. Strutting through my lek, polishing the shop fronts with my ego to make sure the reflections were true: 'Yes, I truly am gorgeous.'

Flicking back my ruff into a black backdrop whilst flashing large, electric-blue eyes concealed within my feathers. Head bobbing and flitting from side to side then held in sudden stillness when the perfect angle coincided with the decisive display. Popping throaty yet guttural calls into the air and flashing brilliant, electric colours around the margins of my display ground.

As with all animals, successful displays led to mating.

A constant stream of girls passed by or hung around, checking my span. Cocky girls, shy girls. Forward girls and girls who sucked you in with small, incessant glances. Girls who exuded confidence while others stapled their gaze to their shoes. Overblown gestures and laughter just louder than it should be or hiding behind arms like a toddler on a leg. Typically, they had spent time preparing to come to the shopping centre, not usually as much as me, but enough to signal intent.

Small groups or large gaggles of kids, someone always knew someone,

'Do you know who j'm'call it? Hangs around with what's her face?'

Moving through the Arndale looking particularly good, dragging girls along the ground as they gripped my ankles, there's a small gathering of kids, I move closer. It's her, it's 'disappearing behind a door' girl with someone I know, someone I've been half hanging around with, someone I can't walk past and ignore. *'Get in'*.

'Mick, how y'doing?'

'Fine thanks Liz, you?

'Yeh good.' She turns to 'slotting a key in a lock' girl and says quite openly,

'Watch him. He's a bad 'un. Mick don't even speak to her, she's a nice girl.'

'Aren't you all? A'right, I'm Mick.'

'I know.' She looks away half interested. She's good, very good, I'm almost convinced but she can't fight Mother Nature long-term, none of us can. I mentally thanked Liz, I couldn't have got a higher recommendation had I bribed the Queen. 'He's a bad'un.' The girl was female, surely she knew that that was a crucial element in my babe-magnet sexual aura, I was a bad 'un, what else did a young girl want? They'd read *Jackie*. They wanted a bad 'un to turn into a good 'un. What did I want? I wanted to get into the knickers of 'disappearing behind a door' girl.

In general, with girls, I appeared detached, not needy, I didn't care. There is nothing that frightens women more than a man wearing his penis on his sleeve. Being lustful, these are probably the most honest of men, but women don't appreciate the honesty. They like games, never mind what they say, they do. Are 'games' interaction? Are games flirting? Sparring? Foreplay? Obviously we are talking percentages and generalities, there are NO universal, emotional gender traits. Well actually there is one: if a woman doesn't know a man, and sniffs general, desperate, sexual drooling, no matter how attractive he is, he won't get laid.

I was discreet, no doubt this was a plus. In '70s Britain, girls would be quickly and easily labelled 'a slag', a term I never accepted. Kids can be cruel and should any details of sexual encounters spill, they can be a powerful weapon to use, exaggerate, twist and batter. In a strange way for the girls, it may have been quite emancipating. Mick was safe to shag, there would be no strings, no one would find out, unless *they* decided to tell someone.

If there was one thing that I learnt about women from all this, one defining female trait, it was that they spoke to each other more than men and in more detail. I slowly realised that they certainly spoke amongst themselves, often asking me about certain girls I was supposed to have been with. I'd say nothing and the girl would say, 'They've told me all about it.' Sometimes there was a slight twinge of betrayal but, due to gender positioning at the time, I knew it wasn't usually done with any malice. I was male and in that social climate had a very different reputation to lose, I would not be negatively judged for sleeping around. If the girl didn't want to have sex, it was fine, no pressure, most times they'd change their minds anyway, I don't remember openly persuading any women to have sex with me, other than at the flirting stage. It wasn't like I was being considerate or sensitive, I'd often just move on to a different quarry. If it didn't feel right to a girl that was because it wasn't right, I discovered that their radar for the right or wrong time was much more finely tuned than mine.

Anyway, as I knew 'disappearing behind a door' girl lived halfway up my hill, by some strange coincidence we left the centre at the same time. I caught her up and befriended her, in the socially agreed sense of the word. Over the next few weeks it became normal for me to disappear behind the door of 'slotting a key in a lock' girl. There was a cool back room, with a powerful music system, good lighting and an understanding mother. This along with my bedroom became *the* place to hang out. My bedroom was out of bounds to my parents and not simply a place where I was taken advantage of. I'd often return home to mates, sitting in my room, listening to music and hanging out, people often let themselves in.

There were a few lads who seemed to stop visiting 'slotting a key in a door' girl when I started. I was a bit disappointed, I wanted to get to know them simply because they were black and I didn't know any black people. I wanted to hear what they were into, chit-chat and share the record player with them. Fitting the race stereotype, Glenroy was, apparently, a seriously good 'disco' dancer. Anyway the few times I saw them, they would be leaving. I was friendly and chatty but Glenroy seemed a bit nervous and flushed. Perhaps he was a complete homophobe and wanted to smash my gayboy face in – he wasn't, just a bit shy until he got to know people.

Nig-nog, wog, sambo, nigger, Paki, coon, black bastard. These terms were everyday, normal, often said with scarcely an eyebrow raised, rarely questioned by people afraid of the unfamiliar, the unknown. Folk often thought you were a bit weird if you did question them. Rednecks are not good with change or development. In the '70s, I never questioned the phrase 'going to the Chinky' and still can't decide if it's racist.

Racism was great, there was a simple right and wrong, no grey area just the smug feeling of knowing, for sure, that you were right. Also the levels were predefined, you couldn't have a slight leaning towards being a bit racist, a smidgen anti-racist, it was all or nothing. You had to decide which side you were on and I was firmly, completely through to my bones anti-Nazi. I'd grown up arguing with my dad about it, he slowly changed, but from a very young age I bickered with him about his phraseology, as no doubt my older siblings did. I could never work out if he was genuine or just trying to wind me up, get me debating.

I didn't really do anything other than question at any opportunity, buy and wear the badges and drop coins into buckets. I didn't know anyone who I thought of as black, not one person, but I knew plenty of people who supported the NF. I could see that, to them, it somehow felt like the obvious, uncomplicated thing to do. For teenage, working-class white males in white areas there seemed to be some subtle, unseen pressure, almost a social compulsion, pushing them towards the easy and obvious distrust, dislike or hatred of the unknown, the different, the other.

Winning arguments with racist friends was easy. I'd argue, tease, taunt, threaten, offer out and ultimately stop hanging around with them. I tried it with a stranger at a funfair in Crossgates, I was fairly sure that he could batter me but I didn't know it.

'That swastika T-Shirt's just fashion in't it?'

'What do you mean?'

You know, like Punk and The Pistols and that?'

'What if it isn't?'

'Then I'd argue with you about it.'

'That's one argument you'd lose.'

127

It had struck me while talking to him that there was absolutely no question about whether he could chin me, he stank of an ability to chin Mick McCann, very easily and very seriously.

'Well no I wun't, you might batter me but I wouldn't lose the argument. Anyway mate, sorry to bother y'.' I backed away almost bowing, thinking, why do you do it? Think before you confront people. You take it for granted that you can chin people, why? You can't, you can chin some people, if they're not that hard, and if they're that hard you'll get battered.

'Mick,'

'What?'

'Mick,'

'What?'

'I din't know you knew Mini Pedro.'

'I don't, I know *of* him but I don't know him.'

'So what were you talking to him about?'

'Who?'

'Mini Pedro, what were you talking to him about?'

'Is that Mini Pedro?'

'Yeh.'

'Ooh lord!' I gulp like a cartoon character, tied to track, facing a train.

'What?'

'Oh, nowt.'

'So what were you talking to him about?'

'I wasn't, nothing, politics and that.'

'Politics?'

'Yeh politics…that's all.'

Every subsequent time that I met Mini Pedro he came across as a lovely, gentle man – he was so hard, or so self-assured, that he didn't need to growl.

There was a punk/reggae crossover and some punks moved over to dub and reggae, no doubt influenced by listening to John Peel and the reggae bands that played with Punk bands. Croby, and a few punky mates like him started going to 'blues', it was one of the few ways that they could delve deeper into the music they loved. The first few times they'd have to sit in a dark corner and try to become part of the wallpaper as the dub tried to bounce them into the centre of the room. I got invited to blues clubs a few times but I was no good at sitting in corners, my whole reason for going out was to giddily move around and babble with people. It was not in my nature to try to blend into the background.

One time a party ended abruptly with the return of parents, pity, it had been a promising party. I came out a bit after the other kids after thanking the parents, manners cost nowt. They weren't pissed off about the party, the house wasn't wrecked or anything, just, in their heads, it was time for it to end.

As I came out onto the Ring Road some of the lads were doing monkey noises and shouting, 'Fuck off home, y'niggers.'

A quick rabbit punch to the side of a head, one knuckle extended so it jabbed.

'Ott.'

'Shut the fuck up, y'stupid twat.'

There were six or seven black lads over the other side of the road. They were about our age, maybe a year older, standing and staring at a gang of 25 to 30 fascists taunting them.

Without thinking: 'Stay here and shut up.'

I walked over to them. They stared at me furiously, fuming, a tad vexed.

'A'right? Listen I'm really sorry lads.'

They just stared at me.

'They're just pissed and some of them are a bit backward.'

They just stared at me, although I sensed that they were reassured by the fact that I was right up to them and my 'mates' were 40 yards away.

'I don't have to take that.'

'I know you don't. I'm really sorry. It's not all of them, some of them are just ignorant tossers.'

'Yeh but we don't have to take that, off anyone.'

'No I know you don't, I'm really sorry, it shouldn't have happened.'

I think they were a bit confused by a short transvestite emerging from a bunch of, what appeared to be, fascists. They almost wanted to laugh.

'I appreciate that you're sorry, fair enuf, but you weren't shouting were you?'

'Listen, if there's one more word out of them, I'll personally drop whoever it is, then and there, for you to see.'

A lad who has kept quiet looks confused. 'You will?'

'Yes.'

'Are you sure? You can drop any of them?'

'Probably, but I'll give it a go with any of them.'

'Well if that's the case maybe we should fight.'

His mates laugh, I laugh.

'Fair point.'

'Nah, sorry, it's good that you've apologised.'

'Well remember my face, I know we all look the same, but try. If it kicks off I'm on your side.'

They carry on laughing. I was the only male within a half mile radius who was wearing full slap and tight shiny clothes, not easy to miss.

'Listen I still don't think we should have to take that.'

'I know, it's not right, but give us a break. Look, if it starts, three or four of them will run, there'll be a few who won't get involved in this kind of malarky. Most of the rest will fight because it's a fight, not cos you're black. But I don't fancy our chances. '

'Not with you on our side, but if you keep out of it we'll be safe.'

'I'll remind you a that when I'm saving y'butt.'

We laughed and they agreed to watch us walk away.

'Disappearing behind a door' girl, became a mate and occasionally tempted me away from the school bus stop to her house for hours on end of mad, passionate Monopoly playing, listening to music and drinking coffee with abandon. Her powers of persuasion were remarkable, I'd beg her to let me go to school, but she'd give me a look and say, 'Looks like rain.' We'd be off faster than lightning from a storm cloud. We were occasional lovers but constant mates, give or take little times of typical teenage-drama-based communication.

I discovered that while she was a very presentable middle-class girl, responsible, intelligent and funny, she was also the kind of girl who got kicked out of Brownies. She was a good girl who started a fire in the Brownie hut. It wasn't just this that condemned her; there was also the persistent misdemeanour of hiding the mushroom that Brown Owl used as her seat of power and constantly calling her Brown Cow.

I joined the Cubs probably around the same age, eight or nine. My friend was in the Cubs and they were going for a trip on a boat across the Humber, how exciting was that?

'Mum can I join the Cubs?'

'The Cubs? Why?'

'They've got a trip to Hull.'

'Hull?'

'Yeh, on a boat down the Humber.'

'Well I don't see why not. Is that the only reason you want to join?'

'Yeh.'

'OK.'

My mum couldn't see, she had cataracts, talking books, a magnifier that turned single letters into houses, a white stick that folded up and everything. When crossing a road she'd wave her stick in the air, count to three and walk. Today, within a morning, she'd be splattered across the cattle grill of some 4x4 that lived on a council estate. In the '70s it worked, mostly.

On the day of the trip, at Crossgates station, mum was panicking. She was unable to see where I had sat, waving randomly at the train, at all places on the train, no idea where I was. I was banging frantically on the window shouting, 'I'm here. Mum I'm here. It doesn't matter that you can't see me, I know you're waving. HERE. MUM. MUM I'M HERE'.

She couldn't hear me, she couldn't see me, didn't know if she had waved at me and looked liked she was trying to mask distress. I wanted to help her. I wanted to get off, put my arms around her and tell her that it was alright, I could see her waving but the train was leaving the station. She stopped waving just as my carriage was pulling by her. The high window was slightly ajar.

'BYE MUM, SEE YOU TONIGHT.'

Words pummelled out of existence by the low growl of the train, she looked helpless, tears rolled down my face like a tragic wartime kid, train juddering away to the countryside or gas chambers.

I could never have imagined that someone would have been so excited to see a bee, but as the post-operative bandages came off, she was staring out into the garden, at home.

'Look, look a bee, look, it's beautiful, the bee, there, look. I haven't seen a bee for twenty-five years. Look at the flowers, the colours, they are stunning. God Michael, come here, let me see you.'

She cups my face in her hands one long tear starts inside her eye and stretches to the end of her chin.

'No, your looks haven't improved, definitely not' is what she should have said but she said nothing, just gazed into my soul, irradiating my chest.

'Disappearing behind a lock' girl was a good girl with a lot of personal freedom. She came and went as she pleased, smoked in the house and had been smoking in front of her mother since the age of 14. She cooked a mean stir fry which to me seemed ever so cosmopolitan.

We discussed things, she could keep up and contribute and everything. More importantly, she felt comfortable doing so. I'd met shed-loads of girls in our age group who'd built a persona around being more stupid than they actually were. A honed dim-wit gaze, while pretending that they didn't understand things that they quite clearly did. Don't ask me. In the immortal words of Toyah, it's a mystery, a mystery but true. I'd often punch them square on the nose and say, 'Wake up, I know you're not that dumb.' Their reaction was always predictable, anything to avoid an intelligent conversation, down to the toilet to get tissue to mop up the blood, avoidance, avoidance, avoidance. Maybe I was a bit daft and they didn't want to waste time on inane conversation but rather sit quietly and think about particle physics or the influence of Munch on Gothenburg town centre. They weren't thinking that, for some reason they were just pretending to be less articulate and intelligent then they actually were. Don't ask me, I'm not that interested.

Anyhow, 'slotting a key into a lock' girl, she did have opinions and would express them and challenge mine. There was a rumour and I must stress that it was only a rumour, although I knew the truth of it, a confidence I kept. The rumour was that she even read books. It was true, she bought me a couple. I was Dean Moriarty or Holden Caulfield for weeks.

When I was 'in character' she often knew who I was. There were certain characters that I enjoyed so much that I'd allow them to possess me for short periods. It was nice being someone else for a while. My absolute, absolute, complete favourite was the king from *The King and I*, I can't think why.

'Sit, sit, sit. I wish to make a royal decree. All girls, women, ladies, etcetera, etcetera, etcetera, must show an interest in football at least three times a day, whether I am present or not.'

I really liked Peter Ustinov as well but couldn't do him.

She made interesting connections and asides, coming at things from angles and going off on tangents. Coherent chains of linked thought stretching back over an hour and moving forward to intriguing rests or conclusions. Unpredictable and fresh.

I'd make obscure jokes and she'd get them, and answer with a further layer of obscurity. She sometimes even saw them coming and set me up – that's a gift. We agreed on most things musical, although I later really struggled with *Gentlemen Take Polaroids*. If we didn't agree we'd give the other's music a chance, she sometimes even allowed me to play Wishbone Ash, now that's friendship.

I'll tell you who she was, she was a best friend, no choice or judgement, that is what she was, what she was born for. We forged a bond, discussed all the pressing issues of the day, the big philosophical debates, agreeing on most of the important, crucial things in life, like tongues are weird. Tongues are simply weird. Stick it out and leave it out and it gets really cold on the outside and tingles while the inside still feels warm, tell me that isn't weird. The length and volume of a tongue, the smooth underbelly, the coarser belly, the colour and texture. Tell me, do we have a fact what we know? That tongues are simply weird?

I'd just like to clarify something, similar to the 'Soul Mate Convention', you don't have to have one best friend. Although I did, and a best mate, obviously the best mate was male. In the '70s you couldn't call a bloke a best friend, he was a best mate and Dosher was one of mine. (Details of my mateship with Dosh can be found in the story of my musical life, none of which is contained here – that would be way untidy.)

Frequently sitting till late chatting and playing, music always on, sometimes until the dawn. Often as the sun was coming up I'd reluctantly return home to get changed for my milk-round and go straight out delivering milk. Going for walks to Temple Newsam at midnight, alone, with friends, spotting Little Owls, drinking wine from a cold bottle, chatting, laughing and flirting. Sometimes I'd take my twelve-string, sometimes not. 'The last one into the lake is a girl.' My mate Andy flies down the hill, never once checking to see if anyone else was running, mindst you, he was very pissed, stupid get. He'll stop before he gets there, SPLASH. Oops.

'Andy, what y'doing? It's fucking March, y'tit, it's cold.'

'I know but once y'said it, I couldn't resist, the lake looked so nice. I'm cold.'

'All y'clothes are soaked. Didn't y'think of taking y'coat off?'

'No, listen I'm really cold.'

'Yeh, that's because you've just jumped in a freezing lake, it's two in the morning, middle of March. Jumping in lakes is probably not a priority.'

'Eh? It was your idea. Honestly I'm cold, I'll just have a little sit down.'

'He's really pissed as well, which isn't good. We need to keep him moving and get him home'

'Andy, come on, wake up. Andy, come on we're off.'

'In a minute, I'm just having a little nap.'

Shaking like an Elvis fan on speed and teeth chattering like a pneumatic drill, we were starting to get really worried for him; I almost gave him my coat. Anyway the funeral was lovely.

There were often spontaneous art installations in the area, Fox's Wood adorned with fifteen disabled cars, we counted them. God knows how they got there but they were beautifully arranged, the wood bejewelled with light-blue sunlight bouncing off windscreens.

One of our number decided to rearrange diversion signs. He altered them in such a way to send traffic round and round in circles, so that he could sit and watch the confusion of the drivers. He was also intrigued to see how many times they would pass before deciding to ignore the signs.

Sometimes when the mother was away we'd play Choo-Choo Trains, six in a bed, sandwiched, front to back, making train noises and messing about in an innocent fun kind of way. One time one of the girls started to get frisky with me. I said stop, moved to another carriage on the train. She followed, trying to plunge her hands down my pants, I said no and moved again, again she followed. In the end she was chasing me around the bed giggling. If I stopped she went straight for my groin while trying to pull me close, I'd carry on pushing her away and saying no but she wasn't accepting it. In the end I ran and locked myself in the bathroom, which I didn't want to do because, until she started, I'd been having a laugh.

After a few minutes I slowly opened the door, she was still waiting and tried to barge the door open, I closed it. This repeated a couple of times with the space between the openings lengthening. In the end I waited about twenty minutes – she was very drunk and I thought she may have got distracted or crashed. I edged out, it was quiet until she jumped out with a blanket wrapped around her and dropped it to the ground, coming towards me stark, bollock naked. I returned to the bathroom very perturbed, it had been quite amusing for a short while but now it was harassment.

An hour later I sneaked out, everyone was asleep in the same room. The girl hassling me obviously didn't mind shagging me in the same bed as everyone else. I went to a different room just in case she woke in the night and saw me, by the morning she'd be sober and less bold.

I'd said no at least 40 times, I ran away, locked myself in the bathroom, I did not give my consent – and awoke with her on top of me, being ridden past the point of no return.

Here's a question, is an erection consent?

Just because the penis is mechanical does that remove choice?

Here's another question. Can a woman rape a man? Yes? No? With the use of a gun or a knife to the throat? Via blackmail? Under no circumstances? I don't think these questions should trouble the world, they are not that important but I thought I'd ask them anyway.

My slapper years probably only lasted around seven years. This was a burning-hot period for sexual freedom generally, schoolgirls had access to The Pill and it was pre-AIDS. I struggle to think of any period of time in history where there can have been more sexual freedom than late '60s to early '80s, probably a ten to 15 year period. I think that the '60s did the spadework without really, across society, feeling the consequences and that AIDS brought the period to a sudden and definite end.

Sandwiched in the middle of this unique period of sexual proliferation were my slagging years. Years in which I had a lot of controlled, disposable time that, outside the aristocracy, royalty and artists, I can't imagine anyone else having, at any other place or time on earth. Prior to the Industrial Revolution no males, outside capital cities, would have had access to the quantity of females that I had. This freedom, time and constant availability of women/girls leads me to think that, for that period of time, I was historically a top-five tart. Also, Gainsborough or Casanova weren't living at home with their mum and dad while they were faffing.

Even with my free time there were people that I couldn't fit in, that I would have, had the day had more hours, it was often a number of different women/girls a day. Sometimes, as one went out the front door, another came in the back.

I think that a strange combination of things led me to be probably one of the most promiscuous ordinary men/boys of all time. I realise that's quite a big statement and why make it? I say it in all seriousness and believing it to be true, Mi'Lud. For this statement to be true I would need to remove men with clearly defined power imbalances over women. I think there may have been men in positions of power who got close and maybe some who were more so. The people I slept with, to the best of my knowledge, always did it from a position of equality, of choice, I was not a dealer or a pimp, I did not move to Thailand, and I had no hold over them. I was not a director or a theatrical agent, they would get nothing from me but a few laughs and sex, maybe good, maybe bad.

Shit, bollocks, we've hardly even started. Ah well, I can't stop it now. No point crying over spilt milk. The hard brick scrapes my elbow, the orgasm sudden, brief and unsatisfying. I would apologise but she is too pissed off. There is something very sexy about the situation, the casualness, her butt and the way her skirt backdrops her hips, thighs and stockings, something very sexy about her disdain. We could go again, very soon and for a long time, if she'd chill the fuck out, but she scowls, tuts and pushes me away. Suddenly I can smell piss on the wall and feel the crunch of broken glass beneath my feet.

We're speaking less than when we decided to come outside, which is quite an achievement. I was going to speak to her but she is sulking like a sister. In my head I make the excuse that she seemed pissed off when the initial agreement was made. This was what she wanted. Remarkable. I'm a proper bloke, with a proper bloke's denial.
'Premature ejaculation, it was all her fault.'

I laugh out loud, which pleases her not. She looks at me with a tight face, turns and walks away with a downward pressure in her feet. I want to shout 'I was laughing at myself, not you'. But we only know each other well enough to shag, not converse. I hold my head low and feel like shit not through guilt, but selfish paranoia lest she tells tales. Something else hits me slow and definite.

'Oh my God, have I developed premature ejaculation? Is that it? Will it always be this crap?'

I have something to prove to myself. The next woman that night thinks I don't fancy her as I take so long to come. She quite liked it for the first hour but by now she is bored and sore and I have replaced my premature ejaculation phobia with a 'I'm never going to come again' phobia. I'm not having one of my better nights.

Now and then I was left with a gnawing, empty feeling, hard to define. When I was a child I sometimes had a through-the-bones lack, something chemically essential being missing, a craving in my head – I later decided that it was milk. My instinct, no more than that, was that when I had this strange, psychological, empty feeling there was an absence of some element in milk, or something associated with it, perhaps breastfeeding. It's a very young memory and always night-time, a fundamental sadness that I couldn't explain. I can imagine it being similar to a sad version of pregnant craving, although women can usually pin down what it is they crave. My mother, when pregnant with me, craved tar. She walked until she found new tarmac being laid and hovered around the periphery of the workmen drinking in the fumes.

Occasionally, after a one night stand, or a one hour faff, something akin to this childhood emptiness would be all-pervasive, filling my gut with a disrespect for both of us. A purely animal act, much less than that, a realisation that you didn't even like each other, not a bit. Yes it felt seedy, but more, it was like someone had hacked off a huge chunk of my soul, my body crawled, *the* bad trip in a thousand, a dehumanised shell. Often there was nowhere to escape – if you couldn't leave, you just had to tough it out, avoid conversation and pray for sleep. If it were my place, you'd will them to say, 'I'm off now.'

I'm afraid to say that this emptiness wasn't usual, it was occasional; slagging around was, most often, fun. I usually messed with people that I liked, I'd be drawn by something beyond the skin. It may be that away from the slagging I'd ask myself questions but the opportunity would arise and I'd accept like a thief with a wrap of brown. The strange thing I learnt about the 'one night stand' was that it rarely, maybe even never, came close to someone I felt for.

The 'bad trip' seemed to arise if the person had a preponderance of that element of absence in me, and we just kept missing in conversation, craving milk. It will have ebbed and flowed, had it been a different time or day we may have got on spiffingly. Conversely, it often felt like it was something in the other person, separate from me, despite me, that allowed it to be a positive experience. Where we were, how it would be, was almost completely dependent on the girl.

Sometimes you would stroke their hair and they'd be on the verge of exploding, but that was their spirit, not my touch. I could make it bad, on occasions did, but couldn't guarantee to make it good. Try to make it pleasurable but 'appen her head said no and no matter what I did there may be no discernible change in pulse rate. I could coax, relax, and try to distract by showing them my collection of Esso 1970 World Cup coins with pictures of the England squad on, which obviously helped it along. But women are not mechanical in the same way as men, the clitoris was handy, but sometimes it was defended like a one-goal lead – 'this game will not be entertaining'. They got turned on with their own unique, personal switch and sexual preferences, likes and dislikes were often, confusingly for a simple lad, different, even opposite. Bloody women. It was not a choice the girl made, they wanted fun, I could sometimes sense internal battles, frustrations and resignations, guilt, nerves, fear, uncertainty, regrets.

When I first became aware of the fight of the female head-sex, I took it personally, it was me, I was crap, which I probably was, am, but it wasn't about me. At last I'd found something in life that wasn't about me, it took me years to accept it. You could slow it down or break it up, and return to it, which may help; create atmosphere, reassure, have a laugh, make it obvious that it really wasn't that important, which, to me, it wasn't. Now and then you could see the head-battle being won, relaxation and tension gush through the body, or you could inject fourteen pounds of heroin through the eyeballs and they'd still have a tense and controlling head.

People say 'all men are the same' which is clearly a ridiculous nonsense of a statement; you can't make such a sweeping generalisation about a whole gender. Boy George and Vinnie Jones are the same? I think not, Boy George could handle himself. Here's a fact – all women are different. In fact I do believe I have stumbled across **The 106th Fact What I Know: All Women Are Different**.

Don't even think about thinking 'No they're not' because they really are.

What about self-respect? Because of my socialisation, I don't think it did any lasting damage to my view of women, self-respect or head. Sometimes it just felt a bit seedy, not right. Sometimes, with a stranger, there would certainly be a feeling of, Why am I doing this? It is all right to go home on your own.

In the time of my coming out, David, like my obsession and coming out, seemed to be coming from a place that was his own, Bowie was right out of time, elsewhere, slightly dislocated, other, apart from. Unless you saw it from that place, it is hard to fully explain, so here, if you can be arsed, is a little exercise that we can all do together. Place 'Sound and Vision' on your turntable (a revolving plate on which you place big, plastic CDs called records, that play both sides of the disc – i.e., you have to turn them over halfway through – and are usually by the same artist all the way through. Also, you must not spread jam on records, damn it, you're not even supposed to touch either face of them, just the thin edge) and listen. Now, consider that this was recorded the year following 'Bohemian Rhapsody', there doesn't appear to be just over a year between the songs, more ten to thirty years. 'Bo. Rhap.' is a rock operetta. What is 'Sound and Vision'?

Consider the form not the content. Opposed to the grandiose nature and structure of 'Bo. Rhap.' is the understated and newly structured, to *popular* music, 'Sound and Vision'. There is no emotion; it is very clean, no dirt, no smudge. Remaster it and I'm sure that it will sound, at least, contemporary today, almost thirty years after it was recorded. It may even sound quite fresh next to all the dirgey guitar bands around at the moment. This contemporary feel is what may mask the fact that, almost thirty years ago, it didn't sound even slightly of it's time. It is timeless.

This whole thing relates to my obsession with Mr David Bowie and as he hides away, I feel him slipping away into history, he's becoming a bit of a footnote, compared to Elton John for example. Elton John is half a songwriter and, although I don't like admitting it, I really like some of his early stuff, but he is not a lyricist. Elton is Mr Establishment, whereas, when David was asked if he minded the fact that all his contemporaries were being honoured with knighthood and the like while he was being overlooked, said, 'I wouldn't know what to do with it. It's of no use to me; it's not my kind of thing.' Elton hardly led popular music by the nose for ten years. As a single, 'Sound and Vision' completely changed the musical landscape. The only question is where was black music at? I'm not qualified to say.

The songs are so far apart that they couldn't possibly be contemporary. Perhaps that's what makes 'Bohemian Rhapsody' such a good song – as well as being unique, it *is* 1975, and 'Sound and Vision' is *not* 1976/77. Everyone loves 'Bo. Rhap.', and rightly so, public surveys place it as the most popular single ever made and who am I to argue with Mr Joe. Mr Joe is wrong, obviously, I can't claim to have vast experience of singles released prior to the '70s, but I bet I know most of the highly rated ones. Anyway, the top five singles released in the '70s were, in no particular order:

1) Emma (Hot Chocolate)
2) Life On Mars (Mr David Bowie)
3) Red Light Spells Danger (Billy Ocean)
4) All The Young Dudes (Mott The Hoople)
5) Anarchy In The UK (The Pistols).

Obviously, if I collated a top five singles of the '70s tomorrow, the songs would change, other than 2 and 3, 'No. 1 Song in Heaven' (Sparks) would replace 'Emma', 'Alternative Ulster' (S.L.F.) would replace 'Anarchy', 'Another Girl Another Planet' (The Only Ones) would replace 'All The Young Dudes' and so on. Also, I didn't listen to enough black music to be able to comment with any authority, but 'Boogie Wonderland' would be in one of my top fives, as would 'Superstition'. Ooh and don't forget 'Bohemian Rhapsody', that's got to be in a top five singles of the '70s. I love 'Bo. Rhap.' but don't tell me that Mr Freddie Mercury (God rest his beautiful soul) didn't have 'Life On Mars' in mind when writing the first passage of 'Bo. Rhap.'. Like some of us other mere mortals, he held Mr David Bowie in awe. Some would place 'Imagine' at the top but it just hasn't got the emotional intensity of 'Life On Mars'. Mindst you, perhaps the understatedness, along with its sentiment, is what makes 'Imagine' such a popular song. It's not about the greatest song of all time or people like Cole Porter, Jacques Brel would enter the fray and what would the average Poll Voter know of these? We are all commenting and voting from a position of ignorance.

Excuse me dear reader, as I go off to have an internal debate, back in a minute.

'How the fuck do you know what Freddie was thinking when he wrote the first passage of "Bo. Rhap."?'

'It's a gut feeling.'

'A gut feeling?'

'Yes, I feel it in my gut.'

'You can't include that on a gut feeling, the intros are not even similar.'

'Similar mood, similar feel.'

141

'Yeh similar to "My Way" and a thousand songs written before then. You've put it in cos it's tidy, because you can, because it's controversial.'

'I'd say thought-provoking.'

'Yes, thought-provoking, it makes me think you're an opinionated twat.'

'Freddie looked up to David.'

'You mean respected – he wasn't like you, dribbling at the mouth every time a new album comes out.'

'He might have been.'

'He wan't.'

'How do you know?'

'I just do.'

'How?'

'Mick, what about all the care you've taken with the rest of the book, all the research about the tiniest, unimportant things, all the interviews carried out to check the minutiae. You're just trying to big up David without "due process".'

'No, I'm not.'

'You're worrying me.'

'What?'

'This obsession is taking over.'

'*What?*'

'It's interfering with your life.'

'Don't be ridiculous, *interfering with my life.*'

'Mick you've written a book about it f'fuck's sake.'

'No I haven't.'

'Yes you have, you're not in control. Have you thought about attending Bowieholics Anonymous?'

'There's no such thing.'

'If I get the number and arrange it, will you go?'

'There's no such thing.'

'Will you go?'

'I'm not talking to you, you're mental.'

The only songs that could compete with 'Life On Mars' for the best ballad of the last 35 years are 'Loving You' by Minnie Ripperton, perhaps 'Angels' by Robbie Williams, at a push 'When I Need You', Leo Sayer. Although I personally, for obsessional reasons, prefer 'Life On Mars', I have to include 'Angels' really. I would put 'Life On Mars' as top five of all time.

Auxiliary possible top ballads: 'Wishing on a Star', 'Me and Mrs. Jones', 'All Is Fair In Love', 'Above The Clouds'.

Bowie reckons that he wrote 'Life On Mars' as his version of 'My Way'. He wrote the first English version of the French song that became 'My Way' but it was rejected by Sinatra or his people or maiden aunt or someone, Paul Anka wrote some new lyrics. So David wrote 'Life On Mars' in anger – that'll learn 'em. 'Life On Mars' is a slightly obscure song in 2006, not the national treasure that it should be, like say 'Bo. Rhap.' Ask a cross section of one hundred 25-years-olds to sing 'Life On Mars', I think you'll be looking at less than a 10% hit rate, sad really. Especially as I think the hit rate for 'Radio Ga-Ga' would be around 63.85%. I rest my case Mi'Lud. Middle of the road, commercial radio stations, Virgin, Real Radio etc. don't seem to know that Bowie has a sparkling back catalogue. You're not likely to hear 'Life On Mars', 'Sound and Vision' or 'Young Americans', more 'Lets Dance', 'Starman' or 'Rebel Rebel' over and over again. I know, I have been subjected to days on end of 'commercial radio'.

Low, the album that contained 'Sound and Vision' – what a brave and noble move. David was relatively skint, through being really crap at business, a liking of powder and extravagance, not in a Michael Jackson, buying objects, kind of way but in a musical spend kind of way. He'd managed finally to really break America, with his *Young Americans/Station to Station*, soul stuff. Picture the scene of him walking into the American office of his record company, their biggest-selling artist, a wiry, off-his-trough, self-obsessed, white Englishman, playing soul music and getting away with it, the first white artist to go on *Soul Train*, American TV's biggest black-music programme.

'So David, lets hear it,' the record executive awaits the audio dollars of white soul music to rustle through his head.

'Yeh, here. You're going to love it.'

Weird ambient music fills the room, the track ends.

'What the fuck was that? Where's your stuff? Not the stuff you recorded from the elevator on the way up, David you've been in the studio, right? What have you recorded?'

'That was it.'

'When are you putting the vocal on?'

'There are no vocals.'

143

'Excuse me?'

'Yeh, there are no vocals on that track. Side two has no vocals at all – well there's one bit of, like, sort of chanting, sort of monk stuff.'

'Are you fucking kidding? You can't have an album with no vocals.'

'There are vocals on most of side one.'

'OK, OK play me some. Play me at least a single, that we can maybe record an album around.'

'A single?'

'Yes, a single.'

'Well I can't see singles. What do you mean? I have just recorded an album.'

'Yeh, yeh, play me a single.'

David puts on 'Sound & Vision'.

'That is not a single.'

'Well I said I can't call singles. What do you want?'

'The Plastic Soul stuff, that's what you do. That last thing. Do you realise that there was no main vocal line for a minute and a half? The song was less than three minutes long and for the first half of the song there was no real vocal line. David, how are they going to play that on the radio? You've got to grab them in the first ten, twenty seconds. David, pop songs need a verse, a chorus, middle eight, they always have, that is what pop music is, verses, choruses. The Beatles, Elvis, or say Marvin Gaye, everyone, all pop music has a verse and a chorus. Where are they?

'That's got hooks.'

'David give me your soul music, not this weird, cold, mechanical, arty bullshit. Give me songs with verses and choruses, save that other shit for your bedroom. Who's going to buy that? No one.'

'I'm quite happy with it, I think it—'

'David, let's forget this, we'll write it off, I'll give you some more money, go and save your career. Your fans want your soul, you know? "Young Americans", "Golden Years", "Fame", they love it, you're huge, don't throw it all away.'

'No, you've got your album, listen to it, it'll grow on you.'

'David, you're not listening. We sell music, that's what a record company does. That is not music to sell, it is not pop music. We'll delay the release, go back to the studio.'

'No you've got your album, listen to it and give me a call.'

'David I can tell you now that that shit is not going out on this label, it's commercial suicide, so you think about what you want, come to your senses and give me a call.'

20

Being fundamental Christians, many of the neighbours did not approve of the developments at the house with the door to be disappeared behind. There was constant surveillance – one woman, rather rudely, stared right into our room from her stair landing. As she had little excitement in her life, she was a seemingly constant fixture trying to hide her presence. I'd wave whether I could see her or not, if she wasn't there it didn't matter if I waved, did it? There were constant complaints and calls to the police but we never had the music *that* loud. The mother used to go away digging most school holidays, and I'm sure that sometimes the music was quite loud, but they were large, stone-built Victorian semis with at least one hallway, a closed door and thick wall for sound-proofing. My neighbours had to put up with my band rehearsing in our cellar. That will have been loud. The neighbours wouldn't have commented had it been adults, they would have hardly noticed it. Some adults from the surrounding houses were friendly and would chit-chat. You got the impression that these had lived more of a life and thoroughly approved of young people having fun and didn't mind saying so as the oppressive neighbours took around their petition.

As the house of 'slotting a key into a lock' girl was often under the administration of teenagers she had a pretty much open door policy. It was like a full-time party that rose and fell in intensity, the calmest it would get was the morning after but through the day new people with new energy would arrive. If it was snowing there were bound to be snowball fights and there were regular water fights that spilled out from the house and onto the street to protect the house. We didn't understand what the neighbours were complaining about – we never charged them for washing their cars. For some reason people often hung out on the garden wall without coming into the house. There's obviously the eternal, acceptable adult prejudice that more than three teenagers in a group is always a threat, they are always 'up to no good' and should be oppressed. We had youth clubs. I'd hate to be a teenager in the 21st century – your age alone seems to be a sign of guilt.

Not all teenagers are bad, and pensioners can be talented flirts.

''Scuse me, can I help you with those?'

'No, you're alright lass, I'm just having a little rest.'

'Yeh, well when you've finished resting I'll carry those, I'm on mi' way up the hill anyway.'

'Eeh, I can manage a couple of shopping bags I'm not planning on tidying mi' grave yet.'

'I know that, you're a fine looking young woman, I'm after a date.'

'Eeh y'cheeky young beggar, my courting days are long gone.'

'Aye but you've still got the twinkle.'

'Ooh, stop it y'daft aipeth. I'm sorry I thought you were a girl earlier, my eyes are not what they used to be.'

'You're alright, I get it all the time, the lipstick confuses people.'

'And you've got such a pretty face.'

'Well, thank you.'

'I suppose I should I say handsome.'

'No, pretty's fine.'

'Come on then if you're carrying mi'bag, I can't stop here chattering all day. Eeh lad, you do look handsome with y'make-up.'

'That's what all the girlies say.'

'Eeh love, I bet the'do. I bet the'melt with that cheeky little smile. My granddaughter sometimes comes to visit me, she's about your age.'

'Yeh, well you don't want to introduce us, I'm a bad 'un.'

'You seem like a lovely young man to me.'

'These things can be deceiving.'

'Well she's big enough to look after herself.'

'Mmm?'

There were often new people who visited the house of the girl with no name and they sometimes, usually through nerves, created a bit of a strange atmosphere. The standard dress code for most of the males visiting in the late '70s was drainpipe jeans, blue or black, with turn-ups, Doc Marten boots and a black biker jacket. Underneath was usually a mohair jumper or a T-shirt with a band on it, very lazy. On the way home, these new people visiting were usually stopped and questioned by the police who watched the house for a couple of years. At this time glue sniffing was legal, as were freshly picked mushrooms and they could hardly kick down the door of a private house cos a few teenagers might be drinking; anyway that would blow their cover. I didn't really get into glue sniffing, it seemed too dangerous. I tried a bit of Zoff, a trade name for a plaster remover but didn't take it up as a pastime.

Whilst out picking mushrooms I noticed that my nicest boots had been very badly damaged by the constant September damp, the continuous bending and standing motion, and the cross country miles of walking. I wrote a little gem of verse in my mind, analogous of teenage excuses, failure to accept responsibility for our actions and ultimately, my explanation for spending more time tripping than doing school work. Shakespeare, Wordsworth, Coleridge, any of them would have been ecstatic to have had a moment of such genius, sadly they never did.

Ode to a Boot.
The boots that I have ruined are few and far between,
It is not to me they owe their ruin,
More the places they have been.

Yes, thank you. Kiss mi'neck, that's good. No really, thank you. I know, the depth, the layers, it's staggering. If I could just say a few words. I'd like to thank my parents, friends who have supported me through the years of struggle. There's a whole team of people, who work away in the background unseen, without whom none of this magnum opus, this work of unrivalled brilliance, would have been possible. This poetic gift is not really to do with me, it is heaven sent. I would ultimately like to thank God for giving me such unprecedented talent. Jesus, thank you for my radiant gift. And perhaps one day, God permitting, I may write a teenage ode to the washing machine that makes everything pink.

As I said earlier I was the best with make-up on earth, no contest except for the short-sighted girl. I got an awful shock, years later, in the early eighties, when 'slotting the key into a lock' girl came home with the first Culture Club single, 'White Boy'. Seeing the cover made my stomach churn. Looking back was a guy who was better with make-up than me, I had to hand over my title, no discussion, I was no longer the champ. I consoled myself with the fact that he probably had the aid of a make-up artist, although in reality he probably didn't. It wasn't like the later Duran Duran make-up (excluding keyboard player) done for the cameras. This boy obviously lived the lifestyle and, like me, had done for some time, he was authentic. He'd been brung up right. It wasn't just the make-up, he had a thoroughly coherent look that worked. I was jealous as shit. I, by this time, had moved away from different spikes, long held together with hairspray (only a certain brand in a pink can would hold it), short and shaggy, different angles etc. I had started messing with very long hair, sometimes spiked, with ponytails in different combinations, side, top, around the back.

147

I had taken it for granted that I would be successful in music and, at the expense of all other options, had dedicated my life to making that a reality. This felt like it should have been me, I'd missed the boat. It was a hideous moment but also a kick up the arse. I'd been quite lazy in promoting my music; I arrogantly thought it was some kind of destiny. Although, for a split second, I hated Culture Club through to my bones, the single was alright. They were certainly going to be successful, no doubt at all and no way could I vault them, I wasn't even in the stadium.

Boy George brings more doubts into my head, specifically about my later assertion that the mid to late '70s 'New Romantics' were an outside London movement and, likely, northern. He most probably went back as far as me and probably further, you could tell by looking at him that he was no Johnny Come Lately. I'm sure Boy George is a bit older than me and his image is so clearly rooted and real. He must have 'come out' somewhere; I 'came out' in Leeds, Yorkshire, England, where did he come out? And was there an infrastructure for him to come out into? Bowie/Roxy clubs in London 1977? I don't know, I'll research it and get back to you.

(I'm back. I borrowed a couple of autobiographical books by Boy George and could not find any reference to Bowie/Roxy type clubs, '77/'78/'79, in London. If they had been there I'm sure he would have mentioned them. He and his extravagant friends used to skirt punky places and he only makes reference to Bowie/Roxy/Electro/Non-Punk type places like The Adelphi, Precinct and Primos from the early eighties. I did not read the books cover to cover so I may have missed something but I had a good scan and used the references in the back.)

What I can say for sure is that Bowie used 'New Romantics' in the video for 'Ashes to Ashes' – mid 1980 – and that these people were seen as 'new', congregating at Blitz.

What about Sheffield? Cabaret Voltaire, The Human League, Vice Versa/ABC, Artery, The Extras and more all came out of Sheffield. There must have been a 'coming out' scene in Sheffield, Bowie/Roxy clubs. I don't know this scene, but there appears to have been a club called The Limit Club, where these people congregated. Sheffield has answered one of the main questions about these scenes being part of a youth culture – cultural production. In '77/'78/'79 there did not appear to be people from Leeds producing the style of music suited to Bowie/Roxy clubs, synths and studio time/production values seemed too expensive and prohibitive; somehow bands from Sheffield seemed to solve this. Perhaps Sheffield City Council was supportive of bands. This difference between the two cities seems strange as in the late '70s Leeds and Sheffield were very similar places. There probably were bands in Leeds doing electronic music, just not with the same success; I may have also been too young and arrogant to pay any attention to them.

Was the Leeds scene much more image based, much more clothes and make-up based, while in Sheffield production of artefacts was central? It's probably too tidy to point at the historical background of the two cities, with service and tailoring in Leeds and the more solid, industrial, useful object production of Sheffield, so I'll ignore that.

I should add at this point that I have a vague memory of Bowie/Roxy nights in York and Bradford that people from Leeds would travel to, I never did, too busy partying to make arrangements. So are we looking at a Yorkshire scene? The Yorkshire Dandies? Was there a Lancashire scene?

It will have been harder, more dangerous, to come out in Sheffield than Leeds, in the mid to late '70s. I've always imagined Sheffield to have a higher concentration of the elements of 'hardness' than Leeds. Essentially the same, just more profuse. I am certain that a Leeds accent in Sheffield is a sign of homosexuality. Although my older mate, a 1970s Leeds United football hooligan and football thief swears blind that in about 1976/77 Leeds fans 'took the Sheffield end at Bramall Lane.'

Cabaret Voltaire were a band that I always knew I should listen to, always wanted to, but never did – I was a teenager and it would have required effort. I don't know what they were like, what they looked or sounded like, when and where they were coming from, they were certainly around in the mid to late '70s and hailed from Sheffield. Still, I'm sure they were 'out there' and will have been Bowie influenced. Obviously it is possible that they were not influenced by David, but his influence on that era is so huge that it is almost inconceivable that a band that were a bit 'left-field', were not influenced by him to some extent.

His influence straddled the '70s, it touched all youth culture. I would argue that he is still the most influential artist of the last three and a half decades, on everything, any medium, any cultural expression. Obviously this is just my opinion, but who else is there to touch him? Come on, put up or shut up. Look at Madonna's shifting image and musical output, do you think that she noticed David surviving popular music's vagaries with sudden changes in musical form and image? I have no idea if she used to listen to David but obviously, she did. Here's one silly, obscure example. I think that the influence of Prince is way undervalued, especially on 'black music'. Now don't even think about arguing that Prince isn't influenced by David, he simply is. I would like to point out here that Prince is one of the few artists that I consider to be in David's constellation. I could understand Prince becoming an obsession, though not for me, I came to him when I was too old. Obsessive behaviour has deep roots.

Sadly, by the late '70s you were completely defined by your look, that is who you were. Punk had always been very elitist and Johnny Come Latelies made it even more the case, probably the nerves of being exposed as an 'X-clothes'/off-the-peg punk or not authentic, old school punk. Newish dandies made out that they had being wearing make-up for years, they hadn't. To most kids, if someone was 'stiff' they were unknowable or at least a dark secret. There was a pressure to 'belong'.

'Disappearing behind a door' girl didn't really take part in any of the youth culture dress codes or fashions, neither the big-haired, TV, magazine influenced 'glamour' girls or the 'alternative' punk, Bowiesque looks. She was more understated, classier, '30s or '50s short jackets that came from flea markets. She sometimes got looked down on or hassled by 'punky' girls. This was ironic as she'd been into the music longer, knew it better and had a love of the music rather than a passing interest to allow a shallow pose. The number of times that we would be the only people dancing to tracks that, weeks later, filled the dance floor, or an album track or a single earlier than the 'hit'.

She really didn't give a shit who saw her dancing to what, if she liked the track she danced, if she didn't she didn't. There was an incident in the early eighties that summed up the bitchy head state of the kids of East Leeds and 'slotting a key in a lock' girl's ability to rise above it. The Staging Post, Whinmoor, Soft Cell were hot, tracks had the dance floor heaving. The pianist from Marc and the Mambas was DJing there and Marc Almond had come to visit his friend. People were pointing and raising their hands to their mouths:

'Who does he think he is? He's so full of himself.'

He was in fact having a quiet drink with no strutting at all. The DJ played a Soft Cell track that, week in, week out, filled the floor. That night the tumble weed blew. 'Disappearing behind a door' girl grabbed my arm.

'Come on, dance with me, this is appalling.'

I didn't normally dance to Soft Cell but agreed and we enjoyed the freedom of the dance floor, putting on a performance for the sad fucks. We may have been scabs but we were happy, contented scabs.

The other thing that 'disappearing behind a door' girl had, late '70s, was a house that was visited by many interesting and fancied males, which confused much of her female peer group who thought of themselves as being more glamorous or more worthy. She faced many envious looks and bitchy comments as she also had the prize visitor for the whole of East Leeds – me.

I once heard the girl with no name getting goaded by vindictive girls with Farrah Fawcett Majors hair.

'Mick would never go out with you, you're not pretty enough for him, he'd never have you as his girlfriend.'

The sad thing was that these girls were right. Not for the reason they thought. It was weird how some people couldn't see her beauty, especially girls with too much air in their hair. Hers was short-cropped almost shaved at the sides, with longer, flicky, spiky bits at the front, not at all Dallas glamour. No, I wouldn't ask her out because I had too much respect to place her in that unenviable position. Anyway I made a mental note; never shag either of those air-hair-girls or anyone else who hinted at the same opinion.

New friends, girls who had ignored her for years, suddenly walking with her and linking arms.

It wasn't just semi-strangers that 'disappearing behind the door' girl had to watch out for. People who should have been most protective of her seemed to try to nail her. One joyously telling a room full of people how some older boys tried to rape her when she was seven:

'Ooh it was so funny.'

'The door' girl got upset at having such a traumatic experience blurted out for the entertainment of new friends and was taunted with, 'What's wrong with you? Y'pathetic cow.'

People who were close were jealous of her slim, yet curvaceous figure, making constant reference to and fun of her smaller breasts, 'her two fried eggs'. I couldn't really see who she could trust. 'Friends' running around the house after having found her diary, shouting out and laughing at her innermost thoughts and feelings. Teenagers can be cruel. The lad who'd instigated it felt suitably repentant afterwards and wished he could make amends but it was too late.

I would not share with anyone else any secret or confidence that she had shared with me. I would try not to gain personal information that

151

she didn't offer me, if anyone tried to tell me a secret I'd walk away with my fingers in my ears:

'I don't want to know.'

I would not take part in the 'playful' bullying and cruelty. And I would not bullshit her. I would be a true friend, a rock, for no other reason than I cared. Also she might shag me more.

There was certainly a sexual tension between me and 'slotting the key into a lock' girl or 'disappearing behind the door' girl as she's more commonly known. One day her older sister told me that 'door' girl needed to lose her virginity, tonight was the night and I was the person to do it. I wasn't told this with a quiet word in my ear but in front of a group of people. Anyway she knows all about it and is 'up for it'.

'What time's the appointment?' I asked.

Later, me and 'disappearing behind the door' girl found ourselves alone, lying on a bed – my memory is that she was naked but hers is not. She looked sexy as a Bowie album still in it's cellophane, a snapshot that stayed with me, but was stiff with tension, as was I, but not with tension. It was unspoken but obvious why we were there. I really wanted to shag with her, but we talked the night away, had a little cuddle and saved the deflowering for another time, when perhaps we may play a role in the decision. We made the decision very quickly.

Her relationship to me was unique, compared to all the other females, even steady girlfriends. They came into the situation as girlfriends – this arrangement was different, we sometimes had sex but she was first and foremost a friend. A friend who gave me a horn like a bull elephant. I could have fucked with her for weeks with nothing but toilet breaks and a radio to check the Leeds scores. We had sex when she made it obvious that she wanted to, although she didn't realise that this was the deal.

This passivity heightened my sexual anticipation, we could be alone with her looking as alluring as a new Bowie album still wrapped in cellophane and I wouldn't know whether she was going to take me. I could flirt and hint, but the coffee cup may still be clutched close to the breast, the ultimate contraceptive. The fourth cig lit in an hour barbing the approach, I don't think she was aware of these barriers and was hoping I'd make a move. I would not, not until she made it plain that she wanted that.

She believed that I showed more interest in her when she had new boyfriends, although I thought that she just gained more cocky confidence and flirted harder. Although she could have been right, maybe I'd flirt harder, maybe I needed some kind of reassurance that she still fancied me. In my head, nothing changed when she got a new boyfriend, it was her who dictated the sexual contact, not me. I could not and did not comment on her love life. I would occasionally say, 'I don't like him.' Or 'I don't trust him.' But usually she chose nice lads, though obviously not good enough for her.

The two of us were trapped, happy but trapped. If our relationship became in any way more formal I'd lie and cheat, she knew it, I knew it. I could have pretended to become the bad 'un turned good, but never wanted to lie to her. As the situation stood I could be honest, supportive, almost honourable. If she was upset, needed to talk, I could have Kate Bush in her Babooshka costume on my bed but I'd leave her to go for a walk with the girl with no name. After family she was the most important female in my life.

This tenderness was repressed and a few spiteful people persuaded her that she wasn't 'good enough' and that I was using her. I'd regularly point out, indirectly, that these people were Iagoing her (as in Iago/Othello), that the situation dictated our friendship. Words of love or affection were never spoken between us, it was better that way, although sometimes a look or a touch carried much more information than words. Also I needed to mature, to discover and find myself by shagging boat-loads of byrds.

We knew we had a special bond. We were doomed, just like a classic first love, which for her, it was. This wasn't the '50s where you married your childhood sweetheart; we had ambitions, things to do, places to be in five years' time. We both knew that we wouldn't even consider a long-term, marriage-type relationship until, at the earliest, our mid-twenties. We may live with people, have relationships that may develop into a life-long partnership, but in the here and now our lives did not include real commitment.

21

Concerning my shameless shagging and betrayal of steady girlfriends there was no perspective, there was certainly a denial, or at the very least an avoidance. It had to be secret to protect my steady girlfriends whom I'd always try to warn that I was completely untrustworthy, an extremely accomplished liar and cheat but somehow they didn't seem to believe me, or didn't want to.

'Stand still, don't move.'

Two large Dobermanns were snarling and threatening, sucking in the fear of my steady girlfriend and channelling it into raw, predatory, pre-kill, aggression.

'Don't scream.'

Her whole body spasmed as I moved between her and the dogs, top of the food chain. I held eye contact with the dogs and growled deep and low. I later discovered that they should have attacked me for this threat, but they never did. I had a deep fear of dogs after being bitten by an Alsatian, as a five-year-old, while defending my cat's food, but her hysteria brought out the male defender of the cave in me and fear was banished. I slowly ushered her back to the safety of the behind-the-closed-garden-gate space, she was shaking like a child on a go-cart. Safe behind the gate I goaded the dogs.

'Come on then, put your teeth where your bark is, you slavering, over-legged, scavengers. You're all bark and no bite, you arse-licking, deformed wolf. Shuurd-up before I come out there and remove your canines with my teeth.....GRRRR.'

They barked back insanely.

We went inside, she wanted to go to my bedroom and have sex.

'No, come on. You'll be late.'

This dance with the Dobermanns was a twice-monthly performance for 18 months. Each show original, the dogs jumping over the gate or bounding through open gate, with my partner in slightly different parts of the lane. Sometimes she'd scurry past the gate unnoticed, but most often, if they were out, the dogs would pick up the perfumed air of fear. Like a gladiator confronting the lions, fear never stopped her from leaving the safety of the garden. The expression 'being thrown to the lions' might explain their situation, bravery explained hers. If she was late, the back-door dog route would be taken, full of nervous glances and quick movement but faced nonetheless. I'd watch from the kitchen window ready to run out in my undies and slay the dragons. I'd sometimes walk her to the bottom of the hill, stepping backwards and shielding her from drooling, snapping dogs. After she'd gone, I'd return back up the hill, they'd growl slightly, flat ears, and lollop back to their garden with an occasional half-hearted yelp at me and a 'well we made you look good' side glance.

During the time of the dancing Dobermans I awoke with a burning sensation stretched across my back, tensed my body and cursed. I was going round to some friends' flat and wanted to get to the bookie's in time to meet one of them, scrambling out of bed I pulled on some clothes and went. Usually went to bed in make-up and had great skin, what a fucker. I was in time to place my bets and we returned to the flat he shared with his girlfriend who was also one of my best mates.

'Jesus my back's smarting.'

'What have you done to it?'

'I don't know, it feels like I slept on a bed of nails.'

'Let's have a look... Fuckin'ell, have you fought Zorro and his three amigos? Come here, look.'

I looked in the mirror and there indeed were carved the initials of at least four people. But unlike generations of children before me, I knew the name of Zorro, she was called Alison. What the fuck! She hadn't seemed that into it. From the back I looked like I'd been prepared for crucifixion, flogged to within an inch of my life. As soon as I saw it, rather than being a bit uncomfortable, it stung so much that it brought tears to my eyes. Ain't the mind weird?

'What have you been doing? Oh, wait a minute, you dirty little shit, what have you been up to?'

'It can't have been last night.'

'What – didn't you pull?'

'Yeh but look at it, I'd have felt that.'

Laughing. 'You're a dirty little shit, you're gonna get what you deserve, you've brought this on yourself.'

'No, John, I've been scarred by lust, she dragged her long claws down my back, like the Romans marking the doors of those –'

'You're a cunt.'

'Lust is a cruel mistress, she is untrustworthy and clever. She seeks out your weaknesses, tempts and cajoles, offers you everything until you find you have nothing....'

'Bollocks.'

'.....but her. Stripped of honour, she has prepared you for her next enticement, luring you in to suck out your worth.'

'Shud up.'

'Lust consumes you until she is all you are. Addicted to the buzz, the warmth of her thighs, her hair across her face...'

'Mick it's your choice.'

'Yeh but –'

'You choose.'

'I have no choice, she dances before me and I am entranced by her swaying curves, I can smell her delight.'

'Fuck off. It's all excuses.'

'Yeh I know, I'm a twat.'

'Why do you do it?'

'Ask a mountaineer.'

'What?'

'It's there.'

'Shud up, why do you do it?'

'Lady lust sidles up, forbidden fruit in hand...'

'Don't start all that bollocks again. Why do you do it?'

'A'RIGHT, I like shagging.'

'What – like Karen doesn't shag you, all the time?'

'Yeh but she's not always there.'

John shakes his head, 'You're a twat. I like Karen, she doesn't deserve it.'

'I warned her.'

'Oh, fair enough, that makes it alright then, you had a brief conversation, 18 months ago, telling her that you were a bit of a bugger. She deserves everything she gets then. You're a twat.'

'I'm not well, John, I've got a hormone imbalance, I need to see a doctor.'

'Oh, classic. "Doctor, I can't stop shagging different women" "OK, Michael, how old are you?" "Seventeen." "And the problem is?" "I can't stop shagging different women." "You're seventeen and like sex, how unusual. That is a concern, let me rush to my medical textbooks and see if I can find this obscure syndrome. No, nothing here. Give me a minute, I'll phone my colleague, he specialises in time wasting twats."'

'It's genetic.'

'You're a twat.'

'I know, it's great. Anyway, what am I going to do about my back?'

'You're fucked, she can't miss that, it's really bad. I know.'

John returns with a dripping shirt and drapes it across my back.

'That'll take some of the soreness out, but you'll still have the marks – they'll be there for weeks.'

There is one crucial factor in all this I should mention, no matter how I try to dress it up, I loved sex, the warm feel of skin, the hand moving slowly but definitely up the skirt, the tingling in my groin. You know the kid in the sweet shop? I owned the factory. I had to filter them somehow, it got to the point that unless they brought wine, they didn't get in. There is a buzz that comes with 'the new', the first months of a relationship are supposed to be the most sexually active, not that I had many relationships that lasted that long. I usually had a 'long-term' girlfriend, so avoided the 'other' from getting anywhere near serious. They all had their sex appeal and I'd often go for the less traditionally 'attractive' because they were usually more fun, had more about them. Obviously, there were T.A. women that were intelligent, witty, interesting and fun to be around but my experience was that there were many more where their perception of their tidy looks made them socially lazy, quiet and dull.

After a while I definitely selected more on 'laugh' than 'attractiveness', this helped to stop it from being awkward and seedy but more fun, we could talk – perhaps I was deep down lonely, insecure. The irony is that at the moment of my coming out it was socially dangerous, I could have been left friendless, absolutely isolated and I simply didn't care, yet I was very needy. I liked to be liked, craved approval in a Hitler/Nuremberg kinda way. I'd hand out badges to my friends with a photo of me on with the inscription underneath, 'Mick's cool, I like him very, very much and, if you ask me, I'll happily tell you all his good points, but it may take a number of days'. The man in the badge shop tried to get me to edit the text but, as you have no doubt discovered, shortening text to concise statements is not my strong point. However, we did manage to cut it down to, 'Mick's cool, I like him very much and, if you ask me, I'll happily tell you all his good points, but it may take a number of days'.

'Well, Michael, it looks like you're in for it now.'

My friend and John's girlfriend, grinning with approval.

'Let's have a look. Jesus, that's bad. Errrrr, is it sore?'

'It wasn't but it's getting sorer by the minute. Can I get rid of it or cover it or something?'

'No way, you are fucked, you're busted, she can't miss it. That's bad, that could get infected, you could lose your back with that.'

'What can I do?'

'Pray, or accept that your balls may get nailed to a gatepost. Don't worry, it won't hurt that much and it will solve the problem.'

'Jesus it's dry, pass it to me and I'll wet it again.'

We spent the next few hours replacing dryish shirts with wet, I was thinking of hiring my back to the launderette. John was right, Karen didn't deserve it, she was a little gem. For one so young she was confident, independent, funny, full of life and sexy. Although she was a scaredy-cat, she had balls, she'd taken up a part-time job at The Squinting Cat Pub, Leeds. That took balls. She was a nice girl from a nice family who lived in a nice area but a friend of the family was trying to gentrify The Squinting Cat Pub, Leeds! Gentrify The Squinting Cat Pub, Leeds – you've got more chance of getting Elvis to crack a nut between his knees; I'd like to point out that, as he's dead, that is highly unlikely. What they meant by gentrify, was getting the clientele to fight in the car park rather than behind the bar, getting them to shag in the car park rather than behind the bar. 'Anyone caught with a shotgun could get barred.' 'Stab your friend and we may call the police.' Black on white bolted to the door. This excessive, totalitarian regime led to 'The Revolt of '79' where like-minded, working-class people banded together in unity to fight this middle-class oppression. It was their life, their community, their rights, and no mealy-mouthed, authoritarian rulers would stop Doreen from singing, 'I Will Survive' at the top of her voice while hitching down her tights and knickers and crapping on the pool table.

'WE WILL FIGHT FOR THE RIGHT TO GET PISSED AND CRAP ON POOL TABLES WHEREVER WE FIND THEM, IT IS OUR BIRTHRIGHT.' The politicos were in raptures, chanting and clapping as Doreen proclaimed her freedom all over the green baize.

Karen was with the dictator as the fascist moved in, 'Please don't shit on my pool table.'

'Aye, fuck off, it's only a bit o' fun.'

'Aye, if she wants t'shit ont pool table, she c'n shit ont pool table.'

'No...'

'Get behind the bar where you belong.'

The pub erupted into riot, Karen had already run for the door to the upstairs, with 'Phone the police' ringing in her ears from the bobbing landlord, selfish and oppressive to the end as he dodged bottles, glasses and chairs. The only phone was by the bar next to the stairs.

'Touch that phone and you're dead' came from all angles.

'Pick up that phone and you'll get acid in your face.'

Would you make the call? She made the call. The police arrived, and arrived, and more, until they stopped getting battered and stopped getting their cars set alight. Still, today, the National Union Of Pool Table Shitters fight for justice and their annual general meeting has lectures such as 'The Importance of a Flat Table', 'Knowing Your Angle of Delivery', 'Getting the Turd In The Pocket', and 'In Off The Brown'. But apparently their one-day workshops are more helpful. The freedom fighters somehow worked out where Karen worked through the day, and she spent the next few weeks receiving death threats, she was genuinely scared. As the French proved, line up with the oppressors and you get what you deserve.

Anyway, the day of the Zorro and Co., wet/dry/wet/dry shirt fiasco, we were meeting up in The Station pub, which was unusual. I'd spent the day with John and Jo and we were waiting for my girlfriend Karen. The main topic of conversation being actions, consequences and now, after a lifetime of shitting on perfectly nice steady girlfriends, how much they were going to enjoy seeing, or hearing second hand, just how I got it. After years of bullshitting away evidence such as female underwear and jewellery in my bed, at last there was no escape, the only question was how bad would it be? The consensus being that it wouldn't be enough and that perhaps they should arrange a medieval torture chamber. The other concern around the table was how it would affect Karen and just how guilty they could make me feel.

She arrived, my heart beat a little faster, I was flapping like a midge, colour seeped into my cheeks, again masked by make-up. This was weird, I could usually control these obvious clues. Build-up and guilt had me flustered. I'd always tried to semi-protect my girlfriends by ensuring that as few people as possible knew as little as possible. Worse than my actions of the early morning was this situation. She didn't know what the other three people at the table knew, which was more her business than anyone else on earth.

She sat, removed her gloves and coat, smiling. 'Hi.'
'Hi.'
'Hi.'
'Hi.'
'How you doing?'
'Yeh I'm fine, you?'
'Yeh, I'm OK.'
'Anyone want anything from the bar?'
'Yeh, I'll have a Tetley's, ta.'
'Are you sure you're alright.'
'Yeh fine. Y'know those bloody dogs?'
'Yeh, I hate them.'
'Whose dogs are they?'

159

'Don't know. They live on our street.'
'Two big Dobermans, they're horrible.'
'They got me tonight.'
'What?'
'Well no, they didn't get me.'
'What happened?'
'They just caught me by surprise. Came right up behind me and started barking.'
'Yeh?'
'Yeh, they came from nowhere.'
'I hate those dogs, could we poison them?'
'You can go in their garden, I'm not.'
The thought of entering the garden flicked open in Karen's mind and slammed shut with a shudder, 'So what happened?'
'Well, y'know I usually stay dead calm.'
'Yeh. They should keep them properly controlled.'
'I know, they're horrible.'
'Sorry, so what happened?'
'Oh nothing really, they just freaked me, I wasn't expecting it. I was daydreaming.'
'That's the worst one, when you're not ready for them.'
'I know, I crapped mi'self. It just made me go BRRRR and I ran.'
'Didn't they bite you?'
'Well that was it, once I'd started running I knew I couldn't turn on them.'
'How big are they.'
'They're full-size, big, nasty Dobermans, aren't they? Two of them.'
'Yeh, they're big and really vicious. They drool while they're barking. I hate them.'
'So what do you normally do Mick?'
'I just stare them out, and they lose interest.'
'Aye Mick you shouldn't make eye contact. Ar Lucy would go for you. Aye, something else, now they've seen you run, you want to be really careful next time.'
'Anyway, what did you do?'
'Well I got a good start but they were gaining, and I couldn't stop and try to stare them out, they'd have ripped me to pieces.'
'Shit.'
'A'know.'
'Go on, what happened?'
'Y'know the gate at the bottom of the hill?'

'Which one?'
'The one right at the bottom of the hill, facing you as you go down.'
'No.'
'Little gate, about so high.'
'Oh yeh, the really overgrown one?'
'Yeh, no one uses it. Well I just hurdled that, one jump, I was like Dick Emery.'
'He wasn't called Dick Emery.'
'Well y'know who I mean. What was he called? The hurdler, won a medal in the Olympics.'
'I don't fucking know.'
'Anyway I flew over it.'
'Didn't the dogs follow?'
'No they just stood there barking, so I went round the other gate and escaped.'
'Are you alright?'
'Yeh it just shook me up a bit.'
'It does. You look a bit shaky. I hate those dogs.'
'Yeh, I think I caught my back on the way through the hedge. It's really overgrown.'
'I know, I've seen it.'
'I twisted on the way through, to protect my face.'
'Is it sore?'
'Yeh, it stings.'
'Let's have a look.'
'Naa, I'll show you later. It's nothing, there won't be any marks or anything.'
'Anyone want anything from the bar?'
Karen went to the bar.
'Shit you're having a bad day Mick, that woman last night and then the dogs, I'd go and see the owners.'
'Jo-ohn.'
'What? You should. You've got to control your dogs.'
'Jo-ohn, a' you stupid?'
'What? Why? I keep our Lucy well under control.'
'There was no incident with the dogs.'
'What?'
'It's a line, an excuse, an explanation for the marks on my back.'
'Ohhhhhh. You bastard. You are a complete twat. I'm off to help Karen with the drinks.'

161

'GET IN!' I was the man. No one ever had the gift that I had, to bullshit and lie to someone I cared deeply for. I sighed long. The relief was more for her feelings than the perfectly executed crime. I was also very happy that John, with full knowledge of the facts, went for the dog story. It showed that I had a gift for deceit and that Karen wasn't necessarily stupid. I blew air out, deep, long and hard. I hated the idea of people dragging around my secrets with them. It was wrong in so many ways.

'If you get away with this, I've a good mind to tell her myself.'

'Let her without a greenhouse throw the first stone.'

'What do you mean?'

'You know what I mean.'

'No I don't.'

'I think you do.'

'I've done nothing, I've been completely faithful to John.'

'Hmm, people without sin shouldn't live in glass houses.'

'Shut up, I've got nothing on my conscience.'

'That's what you say.'

'What do you mean, that's what I say? I haven't done anything.'

'Everyone's done something.'

'I haven't done anything.'

'Is that why you're so mad with me?'

'What?'

'Because you haven't done anything and I do things all the time.'

'No. Don't try to get out of it, I've done nothing.'

'Prove it.'

'What?'

'Prove it.'

'How can I prove it? You know very well that I haven't been unfaithful.'

'Prove it.'

'How can I prove it?'

'Well if you've got an element of doubt, you won't get away with it.'

'Get away with what? I haven't done anything.'

'That's what you say. Ssshh. They're coming back, let's just call it our little secret.'

'There is no secret.'

'What are you two talking about? What secret?'

'Oh nothing. I was just winding Jo up.'

'What's the secret?'

'Karen, there is no secret, I was just winding Jo up.'

162

'You better tell me.'
'There's nothing to tell, I was just winding Jo up.'
'Mmm, something's not right here.'
Part of the payback for these kinds of situations was an acute feeling of extreme guilt but this emotion was easily repressed. I sometimes got a bit of a twinge when I saw exes with new boyfriends but it was only fleeting. I had a strong suspicion that one of my steadies was messing me around but annoyance was as much at play as jealousy and I had to let it go – who was I to comment?

And although she goes grazing a minute away
He tracks her all night and he tracks her all day,
Full blind to her presence, except to compare
His injury here with her punishment there.

Now the clasp of this union who fastened it tight?
Who snapped it asunder the very next night?
Some say the rider, some say the mare,
Or that loves like the smoke, beyond all repair.

Nothing compared to when 'disappearing behind a letter-box' girl first had sex with another man, it killed me, I was as jealous as a punk outside a glue factory. It hurt. I had not prepared myself for it, it was completely unexpected although was obviously going to happen. She denied it to everyone but me. I wanted to scream, 'How could you do this to me?' but knew it to be indefensible jealousy, all-consuming but totally inappropriate and repressed into a speechless, damp-eyed shrug. She'd had a party that I didn't think I'd been invited to: had she planned it? Did she enjoy it? More than with me? Does she love him? Want to marry him and have children? Do you hate me? Do you still want me? Are you still my friend? Can I still see you? The questions were endless and silently grasped within a body in pain. The sad thing was that I knew it had to happen but avoided it until it punched me on the nose.

She had had to watch a series of 'girlfriends', one-night stands, week long liaisons. Almost every female was a possible shag and she could not protest, she could throw looks of disdain but little else. She owed me nothing, the relationship did not have any spoken or unspoken contract. As she was somewhere between a girlfriend, a best buddy and an occasional sexual partner there was no precedent. My relationship with her was unique. I had not kept a distance, protected myself, and I had a depth of feeling for her that felt like the real version of 'first love'. I was helpless, could exercise no control or influence other than masking the hurt.

22

It is difficult to explain what a dangerous thing my coming out was. When it was contained in youth, a kid obviously too young for grown men to beat, it was probably safer. There were certainly males, usually a couple of years older, who wanted to beat me to shit because I may be seeing someone they wanted to, or someone they fancied was dedicated to me or I just pissed them off. These slightly older lads, from around my home, didn't worry me in the slightest, because if it came down to it, they would underestimate me.

They would see a little, effeminate lad and as they had no background knowledge of me, would expect me to cower under the first punch, not expect a furious counter-attack. They would not recognise that I was very fast and agile, that they would be lucky to land a punch, that I had a fair amount of muscle, strength and good timing, leading to an effective punch. I was as fit as you could possibly be, they would have to knock me out because I would not tire, they would tire quickly, fighting is physically demanding on the heart. Also, if it came to close quarters and they were giving me pain, I would bite, scratch, stick fingers in eyes, rip at nostrils, grab at testicles – anything went for me, this was not rules by Lord Queensbury.

I would beat them to shit or that is what I told myself and that belief allowed me to face down any such situations. I had nothing to lose, I was a little, young, gay boy with no reputation in their peer group. I had a 'best avoid him' reputation at school as I'd finished a few fights without being hit once and by inflicting fairly serious damage on my, at times, fancied opponents. Harder lads would look the other way or just laugh at any cheek or challenge I threw in their direction, two reasons: 1. It was a no-win situation. 2. I think they liked me.

When I was 13, this was not the case with the cock of the school, whom I'd punched by accident. But punch him I had and in full view of the school. I'd seen him fight; he was vicious, made a pit-bull terrier look like Mahatma Gandhi. He was after me, I ran, too fast for him, flew through the chemistry lab window, he had to follow, got pulled by a teacher, could this get any worse? I was a renegade for an afternoon, couldn't go to lessons as there would be someone waiting for me at the end. By pure chance I got cornered by one of his side-kicks, who I chinned, not badly, that would have simply intensified my punishment. I could not run forever and didn't like running, I'd been panicked into it. The only 'honourable' thing to do was to find him and accept a beating. I had never experienced a beating before and the thought was scary, not the pain but the lack of control, should I fight back or just take it? I would get battered either way, best just take it; he's less likely to lose it and hospitalise me.

There were two sentries on the toilet door, they were obviously surprised to see me. Before they could grab me and pretend that they'd caught me, I said, 'Is Grant around? I hear he wants to see me.'

Not a word, they just pushed the toilet door open.

'You two been watching too many Clint Eastwood films.'

'Shut up y'little wanker before I knock y'fucking lights out.'

'Y'think? Y'want t'find out?' I turned on him, he could have knocked m'lights out but I was safe from him, I had the power, I was the property of Grant Webber and immune from any separate violence across the school.

'Look what we've found.'

'Y'dint find me, I came to speak to Grant.'

He moved his eyeballs in the direction of the door like Al Capone, or more a prison Daddy, and the room cleared.

He moved into my space and looked down at me, this was all wrong, my instincts were going mental, pulling my brain cells at the root, for one of this size I needed distance and space, I had neither. For the first time in my life I was wide open to a battering, no escape. He was a man and I was a child.

'Yeh.'

'You wanted to see me?'

'Y'fucking right I wanted t'see y'. What w'y'thinking?'

'I wasn't, it w'an accident. D'y think I'd have punched y' on purpose? Someone shouted charge, and I was the only twat that did and then I was right in the middle of y', looking at a battering, so I just started kicking and punching to get out.'

'So y'sorry?'

'Fuck, yeh, it wer'an accident.'

'It's a good job you came to me. Can you act?'

'What?'

'Can y'act? Cos if I hear even a whisper that you might have got away with it, you are dead. Do you understand?'

'I think so.'

'Y'better 'ad.'

'Yeh I do.'

'Ay, it wera good punch for a dwarf, that.'

'Nah, just lucky.'

He punched the paper towel dispenser – it crumpled with a metallic crack – kicked a couple of doors. I squealed and grunted a couple of times, whispered, 'Ta f'that,' and quickly left the toilet clutching the side of my face, sniffing, wondering if the punch on the towel dispenser would have actually removed my head.

But to these older lads from East Leeds, who didn't know me, I was a little gay boy and should I so much as get a punch in, their reputation would disappear faster than a lit fag in a headmaster's office. In my eyes they had to see no fear and a certainty that I would fight, this shocked them, suddenly this bullying situation was a danger to their standing, their position. They wanted to chin me but when they saw me turn, it was better to laugh and walk, with me gently goading them as they walked. I usually saw a big, slightly flabby, nowhere near fighting shape bully that had no experience of violence in their eyes, violence that I was only too happy to introduce them to.

Sometimes I could see, almost immediately, that I had little chance of winning a fight but I was a master at looking like it was a bit of a joke, showing no nerves while playfully pointing at the age and size difference without making direct reference to it. In dodgy situations it was always important to concede defeat, early. One, it took away any chance of 'achievement' from them. Two, you may get very lucky and they completely underestimate you, so you get a chance to punch or kick a couple of times and move away quickly saying, 'I don't want to fight, I know you'll chin me, you know you'll chin me, what's the point?' with the space and opportunity to run. The shin, not the bollocks, was my preferred place to kick, take a full-on kick to the shin and you can't move with pain, so then I could either finish it or get out of it. One very, very dangerous situation I remember saying something like, 'Yeh, you might be able to beat shit out of me, look at y', y' cave man, but you'll never, ever beat me at arm wrestling, come on, y' big lump o' shit, I'll arm-wrestle y'. Come on, you scared? If it's a draw, I win, cos you'll never beat me at arm wrestling. Come on.'

It was a bit of a risky ploy but he was going to chin me anyway, his mates laughed, he laughed. It was playful, it was fun and how could he not arm-wrestle me? When someone is being so cocky and cheeky you can't ignore it. He arm-wrestled me. I moved my hand immediately to the almost lost position, no resistance, he looked at me as if to say 'What were you talking about, you little shit?' and smiled. I smiled.

'Don't forget, I get the draw. Draw and I win. Come on finish it.'

I locked my wrist and while he applied immense pressure, I just looked at him showing no strain and smiled. 'Come on, all the way down.'

I don't know if everyone can do it, but when my arm is parallel with a surface I can bring my wrist up to about 40 degrees and lock it – to win at arm wrestling you have to put the hand to the surface – although I'm sure this would be illegal in a tournament.

He was twisting and pushing and straining but although I was feeling huge force pushing my wrist down and had to concentrate and strain to keep it up, part of the routine was to talk, showing no effect. I babbled at him, in what seemed complete comfort. I had to be careful not go too far, keep him happy and his mates laughing.

'D'y give in yet?' I'd wait for the lull in his pushing and pretend to counter-attack, to bring my hand up, 'Right here we go, I'm sick of messing about.' I knew there was no chance of me raising my hand but it was funny to try and also placed a little seed of doubt in his mind. Just as I was struggling to hold it, he gave in.

'Yes! I beat your mate at arm wrestling.'

'No you didn't.'

'Yeh, it's a draw, I get the draw, he gave in, not me.' By this time I was one of them, a mate, they were more likely to breed with a statue of the Duke of Wellington than beat me. If anything, they became guardian angels.

Leeds is slam-bang in the centre of Britain, put a pin in a map in the absolute centre of Britain and you've just stuck a pin in my head. It is hard to believe now as Leeds is a rich, trendy city but, in the '70s, Leeds was a bleak, poor, grim and gritty, northern industrial city, covered with a thick layer of grime. The slush splashing out from the wheels of vehicles was always a dirty grey-brown colour. It was a mucky, polluted city. We were too hard to have asthma in the 1970s but had we not been, every second child would have suffered from it.

If you are male, visit Leeds and a bus driver or taxi driver says, 'Yes love.'

Don't worry they are not questioning your sexuality or masculinity. Some men in Leeds, Yorkshire, England call everyone 'love'. Hairy-arsed solicitors or builders call 50-year-old, 18-stone men, 'love'. If taking a fare off Mike Tyson, they'd say, 'Yes, love.' This is something that I love about Leeds. Women first hearing it may think they are being patronised, they're not.

'Yes, Mr Lector? The Corn Exchange? That'll be 75p please, Hannibal.'

'Thanks, love.'

In my head the main threat was 40-year-old blokes. I had no idea how to handle them and felt sure that if I came to their attention in the wrong situation I was in for a beating. Contact with this group increased as I started to venture into town, also being a bit older I thought of myself as of chinnable age. The areas of Leeds I had to pass through to get to The Adelphi for the Bowie/Roxy night made the wild west look like a Women's Institute coffee morning at the village hall. The whole journey from my home through East Leeds was used by the SAS to teach survival techniques. Going from the market area of Leeds to The Adelphi was rough and probably the last place on God's earth you would wish to pass through in make-up and very effeminate clothes. It was a freak-unfriendly area, the locals organised freak-beating nights.

Chinnable age was a strange concept. Coming out of the FA Cup semi-final at Hillsborough '76, I was alone – on the way to the ground the milkman had got off the coach to piss up an alley and the coach drove on. It was a strange experience being alone at a football match, age twelve; it was standing and not knowing the ground, I was really struggling to see. The best place was no man's land right next to the police line by the Manchester fans and, although the view was perfect, a constant barrage of missiles, usually policemen's helmets, was flying over my head from one set of fans to the other. On the way out I was being constantly goaded by Man. U. fans and spent the whole walk to the coach saying 'Fuck off' to anyone who even looked at me. I had a white Leeds scarf around my neck, a blue one on one wrist and a yellow one on the other. Crucially, having just turned twelve, I was not of chinnable age. Halfway to the coach after being surrounded by Man. U. fans all the way, I saw three familiar faces. Three lads from the fifth form at school were standing on a wall. Without thinking I nodded, 'A'right'. I was completely unaware that they, apparently, were of chinnable age, they therefore spent the next hour being chased through the streets of Sheffield, desperation driving them through people's front rooms to escape a beating. They were ever so pleased to see me the following Monday.

'What w'y' thinking? You stupid little get.'

Strangely, although they were slightly miffed, my kudos rose. I'd had the bottle to walk through the Man U. fans with my scarves on, telling everyone who goaded me to fuck off. What the lads had missed was that I was not quite of chinnable age.

The point being 15/16 is, to some people, 'of chinnable age'. Travelling to town, tripping, in full make-up and unusual clothes through Halton Moor, skirting Gipton, past the Shaftesbury, through Cross Green and the market area of Leeds in 1978/9, and quite clearly being of chinnable age, was an extreme sport and gave me the instincts of a meerkat. Watching for the hard people of the hard places.

Charles Dickens once, apparently, described Leeds as 'the beastliest place', which I'm sure was right and up to the late '70s it had retained this Dickensian quality. He did not say dirtiest or ugliest but beastliest, an interesting choice of word, a perfect choice because there was a beast that lurked in the dark recesses of the city's soul. A snarling, snapping ogre stalking the dark, cobbled ginnels, ugly and drooling at the mouth, you could smell it coming and hear the lack of breath. Fortunately it was lumbering and dim-witted, so it never caught me but I often tasted its rancid, alcohol-soaked, aggression rank at my shoulder. Sometimes you really wanted to turn and bite its head off, rip it out at the poxy neck and dance on its blood-drenched skull but it was safer to walk. You never quite knew how many arms the monster had and you could get ensnared as it gained in strength.

This beastliness was everywhere, in us all, but it was the ascendancy of the beast, the concentration of it, that was to be battled. Even in the safe places we introduced elements of the beast that we'd picked up through a lifetime of association. That is one of the main reasons we were how we were, the battle with the beast, the concentrated harshness that had rubbed onto us from our surroundings, we were trying to scrub off. Wash out the testosterone, the hard, the intolerant. Remove the muck from under our fingernails and distance ourselves from the grit and the dirt of the people and the place.

There is no doubt that Leeds was dirty. Its murky sootiness was particularly blackened when it was raining; that seemed to be its natural state. The greyness in the atmosphere was the perfect backdrop and the perfect trait to frame and cloak the overlying dirt. This dirt seemed to have been internalised by some of the inhabitants, the years of grime seeping up through skin – underneath they may have been good people but harsh years mutated through generations to leave them bedraggled and growling.

Maybe it was my 16-year-old head but the Leeds city night life seemed to be dominated by people who should have been at home looking after their kids. There were few places for the bright young things or even the dull young things that the majority should have been at home looking after. To a youthful mind, looking for the beautiful, pubs across the city snarled through missing teeth, spit and sawdust layering the beer-soaked wooden floors. Sometimes I felt like a lamb skipping through a pack of wolves. I knew I wasn't helpless; my mind was quicker than the combined wit of the pack. I was faster, fitter and smarter but they had the added bulk, the years of experience and the safety of the howling hordes.

Most people seemed to go to town to drink, there were American, Chinese and Italian type eateries but not on the scale that they are in any city centre today and they were in their infancy; the beer, the alcohol, the drinking was the thing.

I do not remember the wine, 'themed' or refurbished bars that litter the 21st century city centre although there were a handful of safe havens. These safe havens were usually dressed in sparkling Victorian brass, mirror and dark-wood retro but could not guarantee the safety of the freaks. Tucked away off the main thoroughfares, they may offer sanctuary if you hit lucky with your time of visit but why would you? To a kid looking for adventure they had little to offer; avoiding arrangements meant that I would be out on my own and head straight for my safe destination, where the music was from another world, a world of dreams and otherness. Even tracks from *Heroes,* with its dark, urban, Berlin undercurrent, never quite equalled the shear head-bowing grit and drudgery of mainstream, main-town Leeds; with its beasts held captive by chains of ignorance and bigotry but ready to bite the wings off any innocent, oblivious butterflies that may flutter by.

This is the south-eastern quarter of the city centre and the beastliness congregates here.

23
(Top of the No. 40 bus, going into 'town'.)

'Aright love, what y'doing out on y'r own?'

Bollocks, don't sit next to me. NO. Top of Halton Moor – 10 minutes? I can't handle these two, they're proper blokes.

'A bottle o' wine all to y'sen, an'this early, y'out for a good night then?'

Fuck, should I tell them now before they go too far? Or will they chin me anyway? Just look out of the window.

'Come for a drink wi' us, we'll look after y'. What's up, y'shy?'

Shit his mate has got to suss it, he's right in mi' face. Just look out of the window like a girly girl would.

'A say love, you're gorgeous. Come fo' a drink wi' us, we'll show y'some fun.'

Aah, he's put his hand on mi' knee. I've got to do something, I am going to get battered.

'Come on Jimmy, ar' stop.'

'Listen love, we're int Irish Centre till 'alf nine, if y'get bored.'

Shit, how did he not realise when I moved his hand? I saw my muscles through my coat, I've got rough hands. Thank God they got off.

'Ayup love, what y'doing out on your own?'

Noooo, not again, shit, he really is built like a brick shit'ouse. No don't sit there.

'Bottle o'wine, all t'y'self. You out to get pissed up then? Fallen out wi'y'boyfriend.'

'Eer John, what y'doing? It's a bloke.'

'Is it fuck. What you on about? Look at her, she's gorgeous.'

'A tell y', it's a fucking bloke, art'y? Y'r a bloke, art'y?'

There's no point in the 'pretend to be a shy, girlie girl' routine now. Why couldn't they have been my age, or twenty or even twenty-five? I could have just done the, 'Yeh, wot about it?' routine and accepted the violent invitation.

'A'y? Are you a bloke?'

I watch them very closely, fix my eyes on the hardest one. 'Yeh, I'm a lad.'

'Aaaaaah.'

They're laughing, thank God for that.

'It took me ages to put this on, mi'hair took an hour and a half and you're pissing y'sen at mi'.'

His face straightened. 'But you look like a cunt.'

'Tony leave him alone, he's only a kid.'

'I'm a kid in women's clothes. No, no, a cunt in women's clothes.' That's it, got them, they're laughing too much to knack me.

'I only do it to give people a laugh, it's better than Morecambe and Wise, int it?'

The harder one, still laughing, has disapproval in his eyes, he doesn't like the way this is going, he's confused but he knows he wants to punch me.

'So a' you a puff then?'

'I don't think so.'

'What do you mean, you don't think so? Are you a bender?'

Mick don't wind him up, you're going to get chinned. 'Yeh, I'm a bender.' Shit Mick, shut up.

'Y'r a puff?'

'I don't think so.'

'You've just said y'r a bender.'

'Tony he means he's a gender bender, y'tit.'

'A'you getting smart?'

'What and get mi' face kicked in? I'm not, no.'

'So are y' a puff?'

'No, I don't think so.'

'Do you fancy women?'

'I'm fifteen, I get a hard-on every time I see a woman. Ay, and the'love it.'

'Who do?'

'Girls.'

'Love what?'

'Me, dressing like this.'

'Fuck off. Women don't like blokes dressed up as women.'

'The' do, the' love it. I've got more girls after mi' than I know what to do wi'.'

'Fuck off. Blokes in make-up. Fuck off.'

'Ay, Tony a bet thi' do. A bet ee's got loads o' birds. Ay Tony, no the' dote, forget it.'

'What do y'mean the' dote? Y'just said ee'll have loads o' birds.'

(Laughing) 'Ay, but I know what you're like. I don't want you going home and putting on y'mam's dresses and make-up just to get shagged.'

'Ay, I will if a'get mi'leg over all the time.'

'So a'you one of them punk rockers then?'

'No, I'm into Bowie.'
'I used to like a bit o' Bowie. Look after y'sen.'

I first became aware of the Bowie/Roxy night at The Adelphi through my older brother Martin when I was too young to go, probably thirteen. As he also liked a bit of Bowie and Roxy Music, he promised to take me down when I got anywhere near old enough to get in, which he did. At first, although I fell immediately in love with the place, I just felt a bit apart from it. As I started going more regularly I eased into it.

(In The Adelphi - Bowie/Roxy Club - '78/'79)
Music: Bowie, Roxy Music, T-Rex, Eno, Talking Heads, Iggy Pop, Iggy and The Stooges, Wire, Japan, Kraftwerk, Joy Division, Cabaret Voltaire, Simple Minds, B52s, Bauhaus, Fad Gadget, Gina X, Devo, Sparks, Magazine, Donna Summer, The Human League, Red Noise, etc.

The room was glowing, alive with a vibrant celebration, I was surrounded by beautiful people, even the people who were not traditionally attractive, like I was, were stunning. There were a few Ziggyish types, all with their own angle, 'Thin White Duke' types, bleached, cropped or public-school style with immaculate white shirts, some frilly, some straight with ties. Various Bryan Ferry look-a-similars. Make-up was individual but usually perfectly applied, a couple of hours old edge giving it a street smudge. The women were mostly, kinda Roxy or workings of '30s/'40s glamour, some bleached modern with veils, fox-furs and pill box hats.
    The Victorian flock, deep-red wallpaper was breathing with a gentle, organic, eternal rhythm, I was pulling together a kind of dirty, red-brick, crystalline, industrial, plinky-plonky sound and look for the band, probably inspired by the Kraftwerk drifting and twisting through the room filling lungs with otherness. My hair was spiked, thick with hairspray, to about three inches, bleached with permanent flecks of red, blue, green, purple, I don't know how many colours, I just trusted Paula with my hair, just Paula, no one else. I'd had too many Hilda Ogden cuts to know that when you find a hairdresser who kicks, you be nice and if she wants to go off on one, you talk through and adjust where necessary, but basically you go with her wherever she's going. She went to a beautiful place with my hair. I was wearing

black, Lurex, skin-tight pants and a gold-lamé, short box-jacket, with belt, that stopped around the crotch. I'd bought them from Miss Selfridges the previous week. I'd had the usual stares, giggles, people nudging each other. I explained to the shop assistant that I needed the right size, so the lack of male changing rooms wanted sorting as she had a male customer needing to try on clothes. It was a good job as well, the first pair she gave me were baggy and I needed Olivia Newton John tight with a little added tightness.

On vodka and orange, hallucinogens and a bottle of wine, I'd retired to the quieter, tabled area, near the bar to take a breath from half an hour's dancing. The room was lovely, warm, smiley; an inclusive, friendly sexy, not a cool, cold, distant sexy. I was battling my bladder's urge for the loo as I didn't want to leave, in case it changed back into a room full of human beings. I was also aware, after dancing for the first time in my new skin, that I wanted the tackle of Errol Flynn, not that of a juvenile chipmunk, but the women didn't seem to mind. Maybe my perfectly pert bum and pretty face was being read as enough conciliation for my lack of front-pant bulge.

A friend across the room was sweating, tapping two fingers on his lips; I threw a fag across the room like a dart, he caught it, don't you just love it when the world is perfect? I moved towards the stairs, my bladder had won the argument. Opening the door into another world, shiny brass, big mirrors, laughter, old men crowding together and tapping arms to make a point. I loved the lack of edge down here, no one pointed, no one sniggered, people just treated you like a friend. The search for alcohol upstairs would often spill into the better-staffed, downstairs bar. The young lad behind the bar nodded as he leant back on the pump.

'Eeh Mick lad, you're looking good tonight, a right Bobby Dazzler.'

An old lady with her hubby shouted out from the snug, I smiled and looked coy, she laughed. I'd chatted to her and her husband a couple of times but didn't know their names, I'd pop in and say hello on the way back up. The corridor narrowed and I pushed open the toilet door, noisily doing the female part from 'Rock Lobster' where she does the funny animal noises.

The noise subsided to a mumble. The room was cold and harsh. Six or seven skinheads turned and stared. The NF met every Friday downstairs at The Adelphi but they'd usually moved on by 7.30. There was a low, guttural growl. Should I get straight out of there? No, I really needed a piss. Please, cubicle, be free. No, there was a booted, crew-cut, large, Caucasian male pissing half on the floor, half on the seat of the toilet, I thought of giving him some hitting-the-water tips but decided against it. I had a quick look in the mirror and removed the eye-liner smudge, to try to disguise the fact that I was going for the cubicle. My mind instinctively located the two that I couldn't handle and the rest of the toilet faded away in a gentle wave of psilocybin.

The urinal was a large horseshoe with a distinct lack of any form of partitioning. There was a space by one of the two and I moved towards it, slowly. His boots looked blood red; they weren't. Although he was well-groomed and clean he stank of testosterone, fitness, fast hands and a hard head. His braces strained on the muscle between his shoulders and thick neck. On the top of his arm the British Bulldog was growling in my face, low and menacing. I wanted to tell him to control his dog, but thought better of it and it continued to growl. I'd been scared of dogs since an Alsatian bit me aged five or six. One of the periphery mumbled "King puff'. I looked over at him, I'd take him in about thirty seconds given the chance. The beast to my left glanced sideways, looked down and then stared straight at the side of my head. My face flushed, my make-up covered it.

Shit, I'm supposed to be pissing – I had my todger out but there was no fluid. Urinals generally work from left to right, and I was slap-bang in the middle, anyone downstream can tell by added volume if you're contributing to the flow. Let me tell you a closely guarded male secret, I can't claim it's universal, because it's not but it's certainly a percentage thing, if you get a no-piss panic in an open urinal it can traumatise you for life. Probably similar to premature ejaculation or impotence, once it's in your head, it's difficult to dislodge. Even now I look for cubicles, I will use urinals but my preferred space is a cubicle, it smells of home.

I was standing in the middle of a room, as far away from the exit as I could possibly get, full of very unfriendly men, who coveted my blood, with my tackle out for no discernible reason, tripping.

Please, fluid, water, someone turn a tap on, I squeezed my head and a spurt came out, then stopped. My brain said, 'Piss, pull up fly, leave room quickly.' My body said, 'Fuck off, danger, trauma, prepare for violence, put genitalia away and guard it.' I was trying to watch the room through the back of my head, scouring my primal, peripheral vision for the scat of an antelope or the shadow of a cat, listening for movement, trying to sense that increase in electricity just before a punch is thrown. My breathing stopped, my body buzzing and honed, I was there, I may be about to get battered but on the way out I will inflict pain. A door swung and I heard a couple leave. Good sign. The pure essence of threat, to my right, pulled up his fly, said the name of a pub and moved towards the door. He will have glanced at the mirror as he passed. He will have wanted a proper look, but you don't preen in public when you're a top skinhead. The door swung and I gushed, body tingling, stars flickering in my head, relief working it's way through my arms to my fingertips.

'Ayup Mick.' Yes, a friendly voice.

'Na'then Shaun, how y'doing?'

Five minutes later, 'Fuckin'ell Mick, that's a big piss!'

'No you don't understand, this is a symbolic piss. A heroic piss. This piss was avoided for too long due to beauty and warm vibes, scared and traumatised by the growling of hell hounds. This is a glorious piss, a monumental piss, a piss in the name of liberty, self expression and freedom.'

'Fuck off, you're full of shit, you've just got the bladder of a gorilla. I'm off back up, y'coming?'

'No, Shaun, wait. Let me tell you about my piss.'

'Shud up y'mad get, your piss is like y'fucking yabbering, never ending. Y'coming?'

'Yeh hold on, I'll just finish mi'piss.'

I said earlier or maybe later that something was kinda, but it wasn't, I don't think, so perhaps I should ignore it or not mention it again until I've thought about it a bit more, because it could be, almost, y'know? Having said that, I'm not so sure that it isn't less obvious than that, possibly. Not a good idea, I think you'll agree.

I get a bit pissed-off with documentaries about 'New Romantics': the youth culture that was given this tag of a soft, southern, safe, middle-class movement and suddenly changed pop music in late 1981/2 with Duran Duran and Spandau Ballet. It's roots were in a northern (to my knowledge), working-class movement that was around at least four or five years earlier and was a lot darker.

If I'm honest, my response was and is an emotional reaction to help me to cling on to some small sense of the eternal, distinct, ballsy, and – real or imaginary – golden period in time and life that had just ended. To me, what the documentaries log is the death of a youth culture. With Duran Duran and Spandau Ballet came the enslaving and slow execution of my youth. My cocky childhood certainty and outlook, my gritty, 'underground' cultural experience was being packaged and offered to the world as a pink, fluffy bundle of irrelevance whose only role seemed to be to generate money. Just as, by 1978, early punks will have been looking around at the new punks on the street and mourning the death of something that they couldn't quite express or justify. Our world had changed, we were no longer the same, the teenager in me lay slaughtered before me, coughing up blood and dribbling into the gutter. No one wants to witness the murder of their adolescence, the slow and deliberate removal of their colourful wings. Duran Duran, Spandau Ballet, Depeche Mode et al. caught my butterfly in their net and fed it to their parrot, *bastards*. It hurt – I almost became an adult.

Someone had read our diary and spread our secrets to all who would listen.

What was it that I had lost? Was it being part of something exclusive? Special? A sense of belonging? Maybe a feeling of owning or part-owning something that's been stolen? Had I lost it, my inner child, my certainty? Someone introduced the notion of grey into my head and, once there, it filled the space of childlike simplicity, of black and white, there was no longer truth, knowledge, just uncertainty and a questioning of all things, especially self. Say hello to the cynic, the loss of wonder, the death of the explorer. I mourn because overnight I went from being one of the coolest, most beautiful, flamboyant teenagers in Leeds to being ordinary.

Was it even a distinct youth culture that I experienced and mourned? That's how it felt to me and that's all that matters to me. I want it to have been a youth movement, so it was. What is a youth culture? How many youths does a youth culture need? Can its product simply be clothes, accessories, make-up and an ability to party hard? Is this too superficial and transitory? Or, like the Sheffield scene, does it need artefacts?

So, why don't the documentary makers research it? They get paid good money, probably Oxbridge educated, but they can't do a bit of simple research. If there were a documentary saying that the blues was born in 1952 in Cleckheaton, there would be uproar. But no, this movement, kinda my movement, gets a quick 'Bowie was a bit of an influence, but the beginning was '81/2 with Duran Duran and Spandau Ballet's first singles.'

The same as Elvis birthing Rock 'n' Roll, it's bollocks. The real artists, the real imaginations get ripped off and ignored by the media. They tag on The Human League's 'Don't You Want Me Baby' but don't appear to know that Phil Oakey's appearance changed very little from the late '70s when they were producing electro-pop in Sheffield. Songs like 'Being Boiled' and 'Empire State Human' ('78) were heralded by Mr David Bowie as the future of pop music, which, years later, they proved to be. Soft Cell (based in Leeds) had their first hit in 1981 and it wasn't their first single. Their first album *Non-Stop Erotic Cabaret*, was a dirty, seedy album, predominantly about shagging around and life in the 'Leeds scene'. Cabaret Voltaire's 'just do it' attitude being popularised by Punk. Am I being naïve? Or is *all* culture part of an evolution?

The early New Romantics, although they wouldn't have called themselves that, were in the north (and maybe other provinces) in the late '70s. A fusion of Bowie/Roxy clubs and gay clubs playing high-energy disco at clubs like Primo's brought a sophistication to the proceedings. I'd love to know if it was happening elsewhere, maybe Glasgow, Manchester, Liverpool, Appletreewick, Birmingham or Newcastle. It won't have been happening in London, as London is the centre of the universe and the shit, lazy, media researchers would have seen it.

The Adelphi and The Precinct had something of the street, and a number of punters who looked like Bowie, Brian Ferry, Marilyn Monroe, Hepburn, Dietrich etc., some with incredible attention to detail. There were many who had developed their own look, and many in between. Primo's had nothing of the street, it was mature and sophisticated, way above the street, half of the music you did not know, very few knew it. It was imported high-energy disco that hung out and mingled beautifully with the Bowie/Roxy-club music. It's throbbing, celebratory rhythms and pulsing tempo just made you want to dance and drink and talk and laugh and generally mess about in a happy manner.

The place buzzed with an extravagant arrogance but not exclusive, everyone was in it together. Mixed in with the Bowie/Roxy crowd were some of the exquisite creatures from The New Penny, a 'gay' pub that sat opposite. You may not know certain people but you could get to know them if you wanted, talking to strangers was the norm.

Everyone was special, not in a posy way but because they'd taken time to prepare not just for that evening but also over a period of years. Having had the courage to try things that might not work in a big way, in which they could look ridiculous, either ridiculous or spectacular. There were less people who looked like their favourite famous person. The essence was different. Different was where it was at, we did and would not huddle around brand names or the cosy biker-jacket type inclusions. People wore references to many periods of history, many places, sometimes a small signifier, sometimes the entire 'look'.

Here I was not *so* extraordinary, there were none more extraordinary but some were equally astonishing. I was young within the gathering.

The women appeared soft, feminine in traditional ways, little tomboyishness, but they were powerful and confident, older women. Glamorous and preened like edgy versions of the print models that I so disliked. It was often hard to tell if they were taking a little brother under a wing or had carnal intent and I had to leave it to them as if I made any kind of move and got it wrong I risked the friendship. I often had little understanding of what they did for work no matter how many times they told me, but mainly they seemed moneyed and professional.

The black walls meant that there were no boundaries, no perimeters, just swirling light surrounded by nothingness. The light, like man-made crystal, exact and sharp, constant deviation and movement, striping and slashing the revellers, slicing through the gathering. The light like the haze of forest light, picking out the dancing insects in the air, while smudging the colours into unique experience, filling the heart with a need to get the fuck down, grab the now and celebrate it with the full soul, the full being. Euphoria thy name is rhythm. Rhythm layered with surprise.

The music had a precision and production values that were impossible to find in the Punk/post-Punk, band-based music that I also listened to. It may have been the cost of studio time or highly paid producers but there was a sophistication in the mix that was rare. The sound system held the power to throb the bass through your bones; to differentiate, split, locate and balance the crystal-clear sounds, bringing new life to old songs that may sneak through onto the play list.

I know we like to classify and tidy things away into their neat little boxes but in doing so we lose perspective, nuance, and evolution. God vs Darwin, sudden spontaneous eruption of youth culture vs evolution of the collective brain.

Quiet Life, Japan, '79, the single of the same name, probably '78, sounded like Duran Duran and Spandau Ballet circa '82 but with a decent producer. They looked a damn sight better, make-up better applied, practised over years not put on for the first time that morning because they were going on *Top Of The Pops*. Tell me, Mr Crap BBC/ Channel 4/ ITV researcher, where does 'Quiet Life' fit into your history of popular music?

In my world Punk was a southern, middle-class, art-school, movement, involving a bunch of bored Bowie fans. I loved Punk, there was nothing wrong with those roots, they shook up the world, pure attitude in hard times.

There was a gap that Punk went a long way to filling, but it was a middle-class, southern movement, that's not bad, it just is, it may have been picked up by working-class, northern kids but they were not its roots. There appeared to be a bit of cross-over, Dave Vanian (lead singer of The Damned) would have fit in beautifully at The Adelphi or Precinct and some people with a Dandy leaning congregated around Punk venues. New Romantics, or the movement with no name, happened within touching distance of Punk and was a working-class, northern, hard happening where people from relatively bleak surroundings put a bit of glamour and Dandyism into their lives in a similar way to mods and skins in the '60s. Although I was hard, I am not claiming a hard, bleak, working-class upbringing. I have three older siblings who, like me, all think of themselves as, fundamentally, working class, but that's a complex one. On my father's side we came from immigrant Irish stock and my paternal grandmother was Welsh. My father could remember, as a child, pointing to a sign, as he and his father entered an establishment, that read 'No Blacks, No Irish, No Dogs' and being shushed by his father.

Why does this class thing matter? Working-class experience seems, somehow, more authentic, a certain kind of experience counts. A 1920s blues player from the aristocracy wouldn't quite work, would

181

it? Titles like 'I Say, The Servant Appears To Have Burnt The Toast Again'.

Ladies and gentlemen, pray silence for Lord and Lady Buckingham with their rendition of a self-penned little ditty, 'Dirty Britches Blues.'

I woke up this morning, Der-der-d-D
It's raining again, Der-der-d-D
Planned to go hunting Der-der-d-D
But there is mud on the lane Der-der-d-D
My man forgot Der-der-d-D
To take the crockery away Der-der-d-D
And when he'll return Der-der-d-D
It's hard to say Der-der-d-D

Yet how am I going to get out of bed without my man to help
I'm stuck in bed and below I can hear the hounds begin to yelp
And how am I going to keep my britches clean with mud on the lane
You can't understand my world, it is jolly well jam packed with pain

Don't you just hate Der-der-d-D
The dirty britches blues Der-der-d-D
Black, red or white Der-der-d-D
Can't decide which britches to use. Der-der-d-D

I have nothing against the aristocracy, but you wouldn't trust them with the blues, would you? A lot of, proper, American blues players settled in West Yorkshire, how bizarre is that?

Sorry I went off on one there, and I'd suggest, perhaps, that there was no need for you to come along. What was I banging on about? Class – that's what I was banging on about. In popular music, a working-class background seems more authentic. Did this authenticity come with the blues? You had to be pissed off to sing the blues, down at heel, so to speak, slightly broken. Maybe the past struggles involved in being working class, having a difficult life, inform the creative process and evoke empathy. Troubles, struggles and the harder/seedier side of life may be more interesting material and thus give the artist more credence, authenticity and drive. Why else would my beloved pretend to have more of a working-class background than he actually did? I don't personally believe that David Bowie was dragged up on the mean streets of South London.

Why does it matter? It's part of how we construct ourselves, the person we create for ourselves, we choose from the paradigm of stored character traits and build the syntagm 'me', a varying feast. We choose a persona to fit a situation, it might be a slight shift, but at extremes of situ it can be pronounced. Sometimes it can be a bit uncomfortable or awkward, if you slip into other 'mes' and it gets spotted. Often it can be very subtle, an aitch dropped or included here, a vowel rounded there, other times extreme, like a Castleford miner's wife trying to 'fit' at the Queen's garden party. It is not necessarily a bad thing. We may do it to try to put people at their ease, make them feel welcome, included, or we may be aberrant and challenge with abandon in an attempt to exclude ourselves without shouting, 'I am not like you and I don't want to be like you.'

Somehow being middle class seems a bit dull, safe, conformist, a bit boring. We don't celebrate the fact that perhaps they had/have a bit more freedom, strong work ethic, social conscience, are/were often politically active, wait for electrical goods to come down in price, are sometimes a bit kooky, and often don't really give much of a fuck what people think of them. Aspiration is what leads you to give a fuck, look up aspire in the dictionary, the entry is simple:

Aspire *vi* (with *to* or an infinitive) to give a fuck.

The working-class/middle-class thing, obviously, I'm generalising, but it seems to me that you can think and express without being dragged up on lard butties. My dad used to try to give me lard butties and he ate black pudding, raw.

A 1970s kids' joke around unpleasant animal products such as lard, dripping and black pudding:

'Does your mother keep dripping in the kitchen?'
'Yes, next to the sink.'
'Well you should put a bucket under her then.'

The New Romantics are seen as fluffy and shallow, and they were, because they were the Disney version of the real thing. I have no strong feelings about Duran Duran or Spandau Ballet, I loved 'Chant No. 1', but they were to the movement with no name what The Motors or The Rich Kids were to Punk, softened and commercially packaged. May I just say that I had no problem with The Motors or

The Rich Kids, lovely, edgy, pop and I had albums by both. The movement with no name did not have a manifesto, it did not have any representation, no leaders, and it was an 'organic' street movement. Even though it was starved of interest or acknowledgement, for at least four years, it lasted and grew. It was working-class and northern, so obviously it would be ignored.

Who defined what Punk was about? I love Punk, I loved Punk, I will always love Punk, but all that seems to be remembered is the spin and it *was* spin. Were The Pistols, to an extent, the BoyZone of their day? Malcolm McLaren claims that he manufactured them, they were a money-making scheme, a product, a business plan. They stood for and did some glorious things, happily Punk was and became more political, and the fact that it was largely a middle-class movement ensured that. Punk had power, representation, the media clamouring after interviews, blanket media coverage, manifestos, opportunity to express, and the world was mental, there was a lot to express.

The Dandies were very personal, very micro, about expression of self despite dangerous surroundings, questioning gender stereotypes and personal freedom out in the real world, in a real way, not in an academic ivory tower with dated '70s feminist theory. There is no doubt that they were hedonists and a bit wrapped up in themselves, how could they not be? The people I knew were astute and politically aware, had bollocks, often entrepreneurship, and a desire to change the world but not many were preachers. I was certainly more politically aware than any punk I knew, for sure, unquestionably, definitely. That could be **The 7th Fact What I Know**, but isn't. Who knows what the Dandies would have expressed, where their politics would have been, had they had access to the media to share ideas, debate, and expression in the way that Punk had?

I may be being, in some obscure way, a bit gayphobic or stereotyping but I am not aware of meeting any gay people who are a bit stupid, as in low IQ. There's a combined amount of bollocks, decisiveness and brain cells involved in coming out into the world, in isolation, and saying 'I'm gay, no discussion, it's genetics, I'm gay.' (I think this also applied to us 'coming out' during the late '70s.) This was concentrate in my youth, it didn't appear easy to be gay. It may be getting easier to come out now, but during my mid-teens at school I was approached by a few gay boys who took it for granted that I was gay and wanted to speak about how to be gay. Where to go and when, what were the places like? What should they wear and could I

184

introduce them to people? I sometimes escorted and introduced them to people or just gave them the info.

I always warned them about predatory males, I wasn't sure if this was real but one of my gay friends warned about men/older boys who would force fist-fuck with a vengeance, with graphic tales of ambulances collecting males suffering from prolapse, innards hanging out. It could have been a line. Apparently, you had to read the semaphore of the pocket handkerchief, the colour of hanky and choice of pocket informing you of the man's preferences – red and back left, or maybe right, was the scary one. A bit later in life I used to get stalked by what I believed to be people who, given the opportunity, would attempt rape.

I'm positive that the pocket semaphore was real at the time but, although I certainly got serially pursued, the violent, predatory, gay-men stuff was told to me by Bobby Bright Nose. He turned into Rudolph when he sniffed glue, his nose easily bright enough to guide a sleigh. He was a friend; mindst you this was a lad who stuck pins through my jacket pocket where I kept my Durex. He hated me or loved me, I was never sure which, but I took a lot of what he said with a pinch of salt.

There was certainly a link, a through-line from Glam to Romantics and it may be an age/perspective thing but was Glam Rock seen as being quite 'authentic' and Dandies seen as a bit fake? Why is that, is it what happened in between? Or was it simply the late representation of New Romantics as simply an image with no social background? If the movement was seen as a small, working-class, northern youth culture that ran pretty much concurrently with the popularisation of Punk (at the latest, '78) would it be remembered differently? From my positioning in this, and don't forget I was ten for some of '73 and most of '74, Glam Rock seemed a 'star' construction and experience, whereas, later, the Dandies came from the street.

A lot of the people I knew who were around in '78/9 in girly clothes were from gritty Leeds council estates, like Seacroft, Gipton, Whinmoor, Halton Moor. There were also people from other parts of Leeds that I didn't know that well but I'd guess, from the people, that they came from similar places. There was certainly a group of lads and lasses from Wortley/Armley. My mate Dale always thought I looked down on him because he used to be into *Saturday Night Fever* and wore the clothes and did the dancing. I didn't.

One day he came round to my house and said 'This Bowie thing, what's it all about then?' I played him lots of Bowie tracks and talked obsessively about it and he selected a couple of albums, *Young Americans* and *Aladdinsan*, to take away with him. A few days later he returned the albums, converted. What was it in Bowie that touched some people so deeply? Some people could say, 'Great album and I love *Low, Hunky Dory, Diamond Dogs*,' but then get on with their lives, no obsession – Dale wasn't one of these people. Within weeks he was looking more Bowieish and delving deeper, listening to bootlegs, rarities and B-sides. I didn't side-look Dale once, it seemed natural that with contact came obsession, I didn't see the relevance of him stepping out in a white suit and dance routines only weeks earlier, I liked him.

Fact 33 in life, the 33rd thing that simply is; **The 33rd Fact What I Know: Dale was very, very, very hard,** and then he learnt to fight. I don't think I realised at the time but he was really quite tough, not in the general street fighting kind of way but in the 'I have the physique of a light-middle weight and practise boxing and karate obsessively' kind of way. As a consequence of this leaning towards a purely violent outlook on the world, when months later he'd be walking through town covered in make-up, in a body stocking with a leg missing, woe betide any nutters who were unfortunate enough to stumble out of a pub as he was passing. He was their worst possible life experience. How could they not, seeing a complete freak walking through Leeds city centre, say, 'Fucking Puff.'? Years of interbreeding had led them to a dislike of any kind of 'other' and I mean **any**; gender, choice in clothes, race, height, profession, amount of time waited at a bus stop, side of hair parting.

In a way they were the victims in this scenario, ancient gladiators moving from the pub down the steps of certainty. If only they'd stayed at home that night, maybe started drinking ten minutes later or earlier, needed a piss, maybe not noticed Dale – but their genetically modified radar for 'the other' didn't give them a chance. They made no decision. Compulsion, they were drawn, no choice, uncontrollably, like my willy to my byrd's fadge, in.

Amongst a small group of my closest friends, these situations were legendary.

'Mick, 'onestly, there were three of them, proper blokes, looked mean as fuck, they were big and I thought "Please God no, we are going to get absolutely battered." And Dale turned on them, he turned and I thought, "Oh fuck, no Dale, you might be that hard but I'm not." Anyway Dale sez, "Keep walking and I'll catch you up." I sez, "I'm not leaving you to take three on, not on your own." "Keep walking and I'll catch you up," sez Dale. I sez, "I'm not going to walk away while you get battered." "Keep walking and I'll catch you up, trust me, I don't want to have to worry about you, walk, now." So I walked, and Mick, I swear, it was like *Enter The Fucking Dragon*. Blokes flying in the air or dropping from the knees, and they'd get up and they'd get knocked down and then another couple of blokes came out of the pub and tried to start and he knocked one clean out. Clean out with one punch, out. God, he was mean, a lovely bloke, never hassle anyone, he'd never start anything but he'd completely finish it, no mercy. I'd never normally leave a mate to fight four blokes but with Dale you just had to go ahead and get the beer in.'

I am only glorifying violence because in Leeds, Yorkshire, England ('78-present) violence could be a wondrous, life-affirming thing. A celebrating jig on the head of bigotry and ignorance. Did it achieve anything, anything tangible in the real world? Did it really change anything? Yes it did. It occasionally put pissed-up bullies in Accident and Emergency and made the freak beaters a tad nervous, which I'm all for. When mention of Dale and violence was made, there was an unspoken precursor, a screwing up of the eyes, a deep moan through pursed lips followed by 'Fuckin'ell ee' 'ard.' It was always 'Fuckin'ell ec's 'ard'. It was never 'He's hard', one adjective no adverbs, not necessary. 'Fuckin'ell ee's hard' was it, the thing, a pure essence, and not a description. There may be a tale or story to follow but 'Fuckin'ell ee's 'ard', with eyes, lips and moan was all that was needed, no levels of, no qualification, just statement of fact. Someone who quite fancied themselves might hear this and have comparison in their eyes, to which the tale teller would reply, 'No no, really, I mean fucking hard, don't even think it.' We are talking representing his country in the international heats of *Come Street Fighting* with Julian Clarey and Gloria Honeyford.

187

25

Sat on the bus going into town, mushrooms kicking in, wine, fruity, cheap, German and glorious, every drop savoured at the back of my throat. I was way too early, what had happened? Some weird time/space blip had warped through my dimension – either that or my make-up and hair had gone really well, first time. Whatever the cause, I was on the bus to town forty-five minutes early. No matter, I'll go straight to The Adelphi, it should be opening by the time I arrive.

Floating in mid-air past the rotting carcass of the dead dream that is Quarry Hill Flats. Hitler's nerve centre, the perfect place to exercise and impose the fascist control, grimmer than an NF rally, now stank of the battered 1945 Berlin. Hitler wasn't all bad, at least he recognised where the true capital of Britain was, sitting dead centre. Good lad.

I alighted the bus, my feet hardly touching the ground, taking my weight on the round, metal hand-rails, parallel-barring down the stairs, holding myself crucifixion-like on the bars by the door. I could do that, I was muscular, years of lifting full milk crates, sometimes three at a time, had thickened my sinews. I once stumbled into the gym changing rooms where some six-foot lads were weight-lifting, they goaded me into having a go, I lifted it easy. They were getting all giddy about the fact that I'd lifted way over my body weight. I didn't get it, a bar, some weights, what's the fuss? They tried to persuade me to get into weight-lifting. 'Erm no. Why would I do that?'

I was elsewhere, other-dimensioning, all the way to The Adelphi, through lovely, slimy streets, dirt marbling the buildings, water racing down glass and spot-ringing from the centre of black puddles. The covered market stalls like caiques sheltering in a harbour. To keep the rain off perfect hair, my coat was held above my head like a hang-glider – cruising just above the ground I soared through the space. Tonight I was an elemental force, part of everything, balanced and attuned to forces, more sparking with life than lightning crashing against steel. Entering the pub I could see flashing lights upstairs, and hear the dull-thud back beat of Adelphi music. 'Cool, it's open.' I was relishing the thought of sitting on my own and drifting to the music in the empty room, no need to talk, just fly. There was no one on the door, but the DJ with a groomed *David Live* look came down and took my money. There was no one working the bar so I went downstairs and got myself a double vodka and orange. The almost open-plan pub was friendly, friendly, friendly. I glided back up the stairs, dabbing my wet puppy-dog nose with my coat.

Rounding the corner into the main room, it was empty – empty except for the table full of skinheads, leaning back in chairs, legs akimbo, crotches thrust into the air. Maybe where they lived that was the perfect courting display. That was OK, I didn't know them so I could still float around the room awhile, uninterrupted. I sat a few tables away sucking the vodka through my teeth, felt it warm through my throat and down into my chest. I wish they'd stop staring at me, I want to close my eyes, watch the lights and the slow-gliding, few-cell organisms that live behind my lids. They started saying things at me in slightly raised voices, it was just an incoherent, low buzz, pure noise. This was my space, I was comfortable.

Cigarette butts started to float through the air, there was no gravity, one lit and quicker than the others, due to its flicked take-off, spun towards my shoulder, I dipped from the waist just before impact, hardly any movement, and it hurtled off into space. This dodge seemed to really piss them off. An ashtray was just about to hit the bridge of my nose. I plucked it from the air, about an inch from my face and placed it on the table by my side. Couldn't these people see that I was in tune with the universe? It was as plain as the moon in the sky. Fortunately, the objects were moving in slow motion so I could play with the lads all night. It was becoming obvious that they weren't going to play for long. They were beginning to boil. The scary thing was that I had no fear. Y'see fear is useful, it works like a condom, protecting you from unwanted consequences. Why don't you put your hand in a fire, or try to stop a train with your face? Because you're a scaredy cat, scaredy cat, daren't even wear a hat and have a healthy, normal fear to protect you from fire, trains, heights, toddlers with golf clubs etc.

No matter how I tried to work it out in my head, the layout and maths didn't work, no chair nor table would help. Retreat or get battered, simple. Fear was starting to kick in, which was good. The place was empty, if there had been more people in I could have gone coward kamikaze, safe in the knowledge that it would get broken up before I got seriously battered. But here and now the skins would have time and space to fully express themselves on my young, ever so pretty face and take the beating to its unconscious conclusion. I had no chance, none whatsoever. Unless I moved, and quickly, I was more likely to shag Tutankhamen than leave the establishment without the assistance of two people and a stretcher.

I didn't read very much in my teenage years, but happened at the time to be halfway through *The Lord Of The Rings,* I'd rationed myself to twenty pages a night to be able to savour every page. I read slowly and sipped at Cuppa Soup with the newly introduced and ever so continental croutons. Those little fellas had faced hordes of Orcs and I was seriously considering hiding around the corner from a handful of skinheads, sad fuck. There were huge themes going on here. Freedom, a battle between good and evil, the power of the individual, Mordor to conquer. I couldn't fail at the first test – how bizarre; I was on my way to a Frodo Baggins-inspired kicking.

'Mick it's not real, it's a fiction.'

'Tell that to the walking trees and whispering grass.'

'Mick I'm telling you, it's not real, it's a fiction.'

'Ah, but I must tread the path of righteousness, sword of justice in my hand.'

'Mick, you haven't got a sword. You've got an eyeliner, no sword. There are six skinheads who are getting more and more pissed off and bold. You need to move around the corner, away from them.'

'I am a free man and I cannot hide from oppression wherever I find it.'

'Shut the fuck up, tit, and get round the corner.'

'Mmmmm.'

'Mick, think telephone box with polar bear in it, yes, you have a right to use the phone but do you really need to make the call?'

'Polar bear, tsss, you mean The Great Albino Badger, obviously.'

'Mick, you're missing the point.'

'Point, point, point, you've always got a bloody point.'

As time was slow and I was completely in tune with the hum at the core of the world, this whole episode lasted, in your agreed earth time, about 45 to 70 seconds. Like a librarian trying to decide whether to recommend Dickens or Austen and getting distracted by Orwell, there were just too many factors to facilitate a quick decision. In reality I kept slipping off into psilocybin thought-dreams.

Out of the corner of my eye speed burst through my bubble and into action, faster than fast. The real world suddenly ripped through my trip in an explosion of high-tempo, real-time violence, no fake slow motion in reality. There was a skinhead shielding his nose with blood oozing through his fingers, while the next to rise was being helped back to his seat by an anvil strapped to a rocket of a right hand. A third was on his way to fly down the stairs, I liked the flying downstairs dream and hoped he'd enjoy it. The DJ returned to their table and gracefully swept out his arms, like a matador who'd just finished a bull. The skins at the table stood as one, floated in the air as their feet went round and round, and, Tom 'n' Jerry speed, ran to the stairs. The DJ didn't look up, just altered his hair and minced back to the decks. Who was that man? I didn't have chance to thank him. I didn't even know his name. Well actually I did, he hadn't changed it or anything; strangely. I raised my eyebrows, or rather they raised themselves, and thought, 'God! There was no need for that, I had it covered.' Mushrooms well and truly back in control, I slowly sucked on my vodka and orange, still in command of everything around me.

The girl with no name didn't often go to The Adelphi, she went a couple of times but didn't really know anyone there and found it a bit intimidating. It was a very posy place, she preferred The Staging Post where she knew a lot more people and it was much more of a mixed bag. I didn't really 'go out' with people, I liked to be independent while I was out so I could flit, more freedom to pull or just mess and fool around. Anyway she used to walk to and from The Staging Post, at least a mile and a half each way – me, I'd get the bus. I'd spend time with her in The Staging Post but she was like me and liked to flit around, not perch on a seat.

The world was changing, 'disappearing behind the keyhole' girl was moving to London. She'd been accepted onto a theatre course at Mountview and was going to share a flat with her sensible, parent-approved boyfriend who already lived there. After writing a couple of hundred letters she even got a bit of a grant. For me it was the end of an era, life was different, a bit less pleasant. She was dragging me, kicking and screaming, by my hair, out of my field of butterflies.

'She can't leave me, we're best friends.'

In reality she had to. She loved me, of that I was sure, but even if I'd said, 'Forget college, let's get married and have kids,' she'd have replied, 'Get to fuck, you only want me when you don't think you can have me. I have a career to shape. I'm going to work in theatre, I love it.'

'Yes but you shouldn't grow up, that's disrespectful. Come on forget it, let's play Monopoly.'

'Alright, but I'm still moving to London.'

'No you're not.'

'Yes I am.'

'No you're not.'

'Yes I am.'

'No you're not.'
'Yes I am.'
'Yes you are.'
'Yes I am.'
'Orrr, you were supposed to say, "No I'm not".'
'Mick I'm eighteen, I don't fall for that old routine.'
'Yes you do.'
'No I don't.'
'Yes you do.'
'Can we play Othello? I'm getting a bit bored of Monopoly.'
'WILL YOU PLEASE STOP GROWING UP!'
Unfortunately, we were growing up – there was no point denying it.

26

While I was studying, I did a dissertation on Bowies lyrics, arguing that they didn't fit into the pre-defined, early '70s, white-music genres of 'cock rock', with objectified women who are evil or simply sexy, who done their man no good and are just bad, satanic women. Or the 'puppy love' yearning after a woman they could never have, who is perfect and clean and wholesome. The essay was theoretically flawed, bullshit, but it did lead me to a point of view on a question I'd sometimes asked myself in the less productive moments of life. Was *Young Americans* a bit of an Elvis nicking and playing black music to a white audience because the black artists were excluded from white audiences?

I dug out books on the history of black music and tried to find any references to *Young Americans* – OK, so I'm sad. I didn't expect to find anything as David is white, but he was playing a black musical form so I dug. I found one that was quite contemporary, and was surprised to find a small section on it saying it was largely well received by black-music critics. That was hardly surprising as David had luckily managed to get top soul/funk session players who wouldn't have even looked at it had any other work been available for those weeks. It then surprised me by saying that, following so close to Glam Rock, Bowie's Plastic Soul stuff had returned a white music audience to black music, which was an option that I hadn't even considered.

Here's where I get really ridiculous, where the illness of obsession takes over, where the proper Tony Parsons-ish music experts/critics would lay me out on a rack, pierce my stomach with hooks, while whispering, 'Repent, just say you didn't mean it. No one is listening.' Where I say the unsayable, piss on the whole love, structure, history, achievements of Popular Music, that I love so much, going back to New Orleans, Dublin, Berlin and before. Right I'm saying it, sorry, I'm just going to say it, or perhaps I should just ask it. Yes, I'll ask it, questions are always safer than statements and I wouldn't ever want to appear like I've got unpopular, ignorant opinions, would I? No, even radiators need love. First of all, here is a statement of fact, not an opinion, here is **The 4th Fact What I Know,** and this is a biggy, this one really will shake your world down to ground zero, make you reassess all that you thought you knew about anything. Maybe I shouldn't do it – some things are best left unsaid. If you are content and happy with your life, move on to the next paragraph lest I rip your reality apart, shake your world by the bell bottoms, call into question all that you are. If you're still here, here we go, **The 4th Fact What I Know: Bowie's vocals on _Young Americans_ are his best.** David sings better on _Young Americans_ than he does on any other album. I know, perhaps you should sit, clear your head and just think of something else for a second while the gravity of the statement works through your subconscious. Listen, don't tell me that it's not a fact but an opinion, it isn't, it is in fact **The 4th Fact What I Know,** nobody on Earth knows David's stuff, excluding a couple of eighties things, like I do. As the twenty-odd albums are known best in the world by me, it's a fact. **Bowie's vocals on _Young Americans_ are his best.** Not opinion but **The 4th Fact What I Know.**

Now here is where I get really, really ridiculous, where the illness of obsession takes over, this is where the proper Tony Parsons-ish music experts/critics would petition doctors to commit my sorry soul to the purgatory of padded cells and straps. This is where I say the unsayable, piss on the whole emotional attachment, structure, history and achievements of Popular Music that I love so much, going back to New Orleans, Leeds, Lisbon, Sao Paolo, Madrid and before. I'll do it as a question? Could you tell me a soul album with better vocals, lead and backing? Could you please tell me of a better 'soul' album than _Young Americans_, ever made? Honestly I'd like to know. What are the classic Aretha Franklin, Al Green, Sam Cooke albums? I understand that it is a purely subjective thing, unlike **The 4th Fact What I Know,** there is no right or wrong and what a ridiculous thought, Bowie producing a 'classic' soul album, a top-five soul album. I've listened to _What's Going On_, Marvin Gaye, and I know which album I'd prefer to hear. Having said that, I should listen to the Marvin again a few times before I commit to an opinion, it was a long time ago and, although I expected to love it, I didn't give it enough time. Obviously, on a pure level, anyone singing up for social justice has to get the vote. Bowie is part mimic, magpie, pinching shiny, shiny things, but on _Young Americans_ I think he found himself or found his 'natural' vocal expression. The flat-back reverb bringing the vocals up-front for all to judge and the irony of it being one of the few times the reverb was used after the early Elvis recordings. The album is sometimes described as 'plastic', as in 'Plastic Soul'. Not by me, either because I misunderstand the term or disagree.

With new Bowie albums you always got a shock, a surprise, you couldn't rely on an obvious relationship with the previous album. In retrospect, and with an obsessive knowledge of David's work, I can see subtle through-lines, but you'd struggle. If anybody asks about David and you're floundering but want to feign knowledge, just for the sake of your cultural capital, two things you need to know about *Young Americans*:

1. His vocal peak was on *Young Americans*, fact. It was released in 1975 and contains his best vocals.
2. It is his most sophisticated album.

That album in my hands, 1975, was *the* most sophisticated thing I'd ever touched. The sleeve, the photo, the layout, were simply sophisticated. The music, song structures, vocal interplays, question and answering, arrangements, are sophisticated, that is what they are. Got it? *Young Americans* is a very sophisticated album, popular music's most sophisticated album, containing Bowie's best vocal performance. Should someone challenge you, try to get you to justify it, just reply, 'It's a fact, Mick told me, he knows and that's all you need to know.' If you'd also give them a quick rabbit punch to the liver, I'd appreciate it. Thanks.

This is not a story, it has no beginning, no ending, just a stop that is close. No narrative or plot, just a cross-section of time, a segment of experience, an opinion or lack, and a partial view of Leeds, Yorkshire, England during the 1970s.

It isn't reality, just an impression that relies on the moment of reading, the moment of writing, different day, different reality. Is it the great 'I am' or frank and honest? How much personal detail did I leave out? How much absent colour did I add? Who says that your red and my red have anything other than an abstract relationship? Our mind's eye looking at totally different colours. Yes we'll point at an object and say red but does the object even have colour, or is it a combination of light, wiring, learning, decision and imagination?

This is the authored version of happenings, choice of words nailing nuance to the actuality tree. The accounts are given a level of authority by the fact that they are written down – 'this is what happened'. These are often single-angle snapshots. What if people involved came back and said 'I don't remember it like that' – would I alter it to fit their memory, look for middle ground or a consensus? Stick to my preferred memory or opt for the version that is the most interesting, dramatic or tidy? As soon as an incident happens our brain will arrange it in a way that causes us the least distress, the maximum pride or comfort.

Everything we know or believe has been translated and moulded, worked upon by lifetimes of multiple experiences, it feels almost random.

We negotiate, barter, acquiesce, are taught, simply accept, are conditioned, agree or just try to be awkward. Shift from situation to situation. Conclude from positions that may or may not be linked. Do we look for commonality? Do we look for aberrance? Are we ruled, in everything, by pay-off? Or is it possible to be altruistic? **The 19th Fact What I Know: We perceive differently, (even to ourselves).**

How I appear to you is different from how I appear to him, her, or me. I am a different person to each of my children, play a different role with a 15 year old, to a ten year old or a two year old. I don't need to wipe the arse of the two year old.

We all play roles that fluctuate. Different places, different situations, different me, different you. I don't walk around a school playground in just a T-shirt with my tackle hanging out. I bark at cold callers while being polite to my bin men. I swear more with mates than I do with my mother. I become more Leeds when I've worked with builders for a few days.

My eyes apparently change colour according to my mood and a certain coat makes me look like a gangster while another makes me look like a wrinkled, sad, would-be teenager.

To my two year old I am crucial, to my sixteen year old I am becoming peripheral.

It is easy to see my coming out as the trivial, self-centred narcissism of a pretty, over-confident teenager, because that's what it was but it was also more than that. My favourite art teacher, Mr Barnes, lived in my area and saw me out and about in my full glory. He was a man who I had a lot of time for, he was certainly top-three teacher with Sister Catherine and a geography teacher called 'Miss'. 'Miss' would not discourage me from performing, for the class, a couple of gay characters with a lad called Mark Brighton. Today it would probably be seen as a tad homophobic, at the time it was cutting-edge gay rights.

One day at school, Mr Barnes had seen Bowie perform 'Boys Keep Swinging' on *Top Of The Pops* the evening before and was telling me how much he'd enjoyed it. He was talking to me about my dress code and make-up and asked, 'Doesn't it make you self-centred? Spending all that time on you, on your look?'

'No, I forget about it as soon as I get out. I may adjust my make-up later, if my lipstick has smudged or my eye-liner run. But only when I go to the toilet. I'm usually too excited, having too much fun to waste much time on my make-up.'

'But doing it must make you a bit vain?'

'Is that how you feel when you've finished a picture? It's the process, the combination of clothes and make-up and jewellery. It's not really me. I'm a clothes-horse. The enjoyment is pulling it all together, doing a nice blend on the blusher or a perfect line around my lipstick. Seeing that the dangly earrings go just as well as you thought they would with the look.'

'Yeh, I can see that, but surely there is an element of vanity, there has to be.'

'Maybe. Sometimes, when it goes really well, there's an element of pride, it's a bit like carrying around a nice sketch that everyone can see. It's not "Look at me, I'm gorgeous", which would be silly, stating the obvious like that, but it's "Look how nice my hair is, my make-up, d'y' like my jet necklace?" But usually, once I've finished, I almost forget about it. '

197

Mr Barnes later gave me a canvas of David that he'd painted, *Diamond Dogs* era but live, *David Live* time. It was a stunning picture, he really captured something in David that I never quite did. There was a beautiful flow and looseness to the picture. I treasured it. Much later in life I lost all my belongings, everything. I never really kept keepsakes, just memories. There were two things that I was really upset to lose, even to this day. My mint copy of 'Ragazzo Solo, Ragazza Sola,' Philips '69, to be honest mainly for it's monetary value, and the painting; that was it, everything else was just tat, just bric-a-brac.

I've thought of one other thing that I prized. I had a collection of Bowie bootlegs and one, maybe *Santa Monica*, contained the definitive version of 'My Death', Bowie and an acoustic guitar. 'Yeh, really, that's all.'

That version of the song stirred my soul like nothing else I have ever heard and I need to find a copy before my funeral. I've hopefully got a little while yet to look. I'm not making any huge efforts, if it's meant to be it'll come to me. 'Appen the memory of the song will be superior to the reality, though I doubt it, and I can't share my memory with a room full of people, especially when I'm lying cold and still.

And a fourth thing that I missed when I lost everything, my little Bowie jacket that I'd had since I was eight and painted as I was coming out. Sorry, I'm not really materialistic, honest.

I'd lost everything and the four things that I missed were all connected to Mr David Bowie. Like an Elvis impersonator in a working men's club, I'm still slightly obsessed with the work and tattle of Mr David Bowie.

The devil is in the detail, or rather the devil is in the people, or maybe the detail is in the people. The people are where it's at; they are what put the soul in life and they are what made that period of life magical.

I hold close friends very dear, always have done and I have lost touch with too many over the years. That's life and time and destiny and shit, but they are still my friends. I would not lay down my life for them or anything, I'm just not that kinda guy, but I hold them dear. Sometimes I ended up spending more time with acquaintances than friends, but the time with the friends was more intense and vibrant. They all had their own gifts and specialities, and I love them for those.

I had good friends, people I could rely on, and sometimes I needed them. Gary Numan was dominating the charts, I'd been aware of him for a while but had dismissed the albums without giving them a chance, although I had picked out 'Are Friends Electric?' as the pop classic that it went on to be. It was too pale an imitation for me. You could hardly be more Bowie-influenced than Gary Numan and he appeared to be disrespecting David by not citing him as an influence. Without fully realising or admitting it, like an alky in denial, I was jealous. 'Sound and Vision', 'Heroes', 'Boys Keep Swinging', 'D.J.' didn't top the charts and here was a Johnny Come Lately where everything he put out went to number one. Bowie has had surprisingly few number ones in his whole career, at that time he'd only had one solo, UK No.1. Was David being usurped by a less interesting doppelganger? I felt frustrated and angry in an illogical way. Maybe as I'd tied myself so tightly to David I felt that my time was coming to an end, although I knew that Dave was beyond the vagaries of pop music.

By this time I only occasionally went to the youthy to see mates, before moving on to The Adelphi. 'Are Friends Electric?' blasted out from the P.A. and right next to me, as if challenging me, a Gary Numan fan started miming. I'm sorry, MIMING to Gary Numan, cheeky twat, you mime to Bowie and you may just get away with it to Kate Bush as she had doffed her cap at David, but definitely not Gary fucking Numan. I stared at him; he gave me a look, almost cocky, 'What the FUCK? How dare he?' He was roughly my age group, bigger than me, ergo I am allowed to punch his fucking lights out. Enraged, I moved a little closer, recognising his fear, nerves and confusion – you asked for it y'twat.

'Mick! What y'doing?'

'What?'

'What the fuck are you doing?'

It was a friend, a real friend; the words shook my head. Yes, what the fuck was I thinking? I looked at my friend like someone coming round from drunken unconsciousness, head spinning. 'Thank you.' The Numan fan was watching me like a hawk, I raised the palm of my hand and mouthed, 'Sorry, mate,' shaking my head and moving away – I don't even think he was being cocky, just nervous.

I found the lad later and apologised, he was gracious and said all the right things to ease my conscience. Every time I saw him after that I tried to treat him with warmth and respect and he reciprocated it, but I had ruined any possible friendship: to him, no matter what I did, I was always a possible threat. I could not retract my appalling behaviour and had lost a potential mate.

Without the support of a true friend, someone who would do the right thing, even if it jeopardised our relationship, it could have been so much worse. As much as anything I would have betrayed my soul, everything I stood for, ripped out and spat on my essence. I would have struggled leaving the house, sharing it instead with Jekyll and Hyde, with Hyde being a leper. I would certainly never have been able to hold up my head, high and proud. Every time I looked in the mirror, which was often, I would have shook my head and sighed, like some drunkard realising that they really had done the undoable. No choice but to fully and rightly align myself with the oppressors, a broken boy. I was saved from a lifetime of shame and regret by a true friend. FRIEND, I SALUTE YOU.

It's a minor irritation that the London-based cultural shapers and chroniclers completely overlooked us. A vibrant, working-class youth culture was neglected; to everyone but the participants we never existed. A few years later they were creating youth movements that didn't really exist by tenuously linking bands and pretending that they were part of a 'scene' that they would label sitting at their desks. This cultural invisibility and historical ignorance concerning our late '70s still festers slightly in me. The cultural historians have been shoddy and lazy, burying factual accuracy below their prejudices and patronising indifference.

I'll say again, had someone located the roots of jazz in 1950s Doncaster there would be uproar, yet the masters of 'the authentic' present history with a cultural distortion as simple fact. The only evidence of the Leeds Dandies seems to be oral history and people's private photo albums, and anyone looking at the private photos would simply locate them a few years into the artefacts' future.

Does it really matter that the Leeds Dandies, Yorkshire Dandies and possible counterparts outside London were ignored? Is it important? Well yes, to me it is. That was my youth culture, they were my friends and they had balls like baboons. They were brave and noble. I'd like to posit that the Leeds Dandies were certainly members of a top-three, 'most dangerous to be a member of' youth movement of all time, probably just below 'The Association of Young Capitalists' circa 1919, Russia. Just above 'The Children Of Landed Gentry' 18th century France.

Maybe I'm too close to it, too involved. Maybe I'm missing something, perhaps it wasn't a youth movement but then again, what was it? Perhaps a group hallucination that lasted five years – we did do a lot of substance. Was it the lack of cultural artefacts/production that led to it being ignored?

Here's the last Fact What I Know, **The 13th Fact What I Know: What You Wear Affects Who You Are.** It affects how people perceive you and how you are within and without yourself. If you wear a suit and tie around town for a week, you behave differently than if you wear punky clothes; as soon as you spike your hair you assume the walk. Dress tidily and you are more careful with your clothes, become a bit more prissy and inactive, avoid changing tyres. Dress in old messy clothes and you wipe tomato sauce on your T-shirt and fart in lifts.

We conduct by experience and prejudice; we associate certain clothes with certain behaviours, certain character traits. If a dirty, unshaven man, in very scraggy clothes, coat tied around the waist with string, walks towards you, you prepare the 'Fuck off, before I punch y' fucking lights out, y' scrounging cunt' growl, obviously — we all do. Whereas if you are approached by an immaculately dressed, middle-aged woman, you prepare your manners. (Prejudice is universal.)

We also pre-empt people's reactions to our dress code via their dress codes and our prejudices. When walking past skinheads, I'd be more unapproachable, have a smidgeon more harshness in my face, be a bit more open and confident in my body language, look like I knew people by counting them out on my fingers, aloud, 'Degger, Fegger, Begger and Hard Cunt.' When walking past punks I would expect no hassle and my gait would reflect this.

The least judgemental people, outside my age group, appeared to be middle-aged and above women, starting at the age of about 18 and going to 103 year olds, (not older, they can't see owt when they're older); also older men (kinda 55 up), once they'd recovered and found a seat, were often cool with it.

I slowly realised that people were regularly shocked and confused by my dress code, there wasn't a pre-arranged box for it, it was hard to pre-judge. They didn't know if I was a middle-aged woman or a tramp, a punk or a transvestite, passive or aggressive, friendly or aloof, tense or relaxed. I'd have to say, 'It's OK you can talk to me, I won't bite or be offended,' but would elect instead to talk about the weather. Once they'd got through the confusion they were usually fine. It's impossible to measure, but I'd like to suggest that I had more

201

conversations with strangers than I would have done had I not come out.

Having mentioned that not all people outside our age range were appalled by the girly clothes and make-up, some were intrigued, amused, some were excited by it. When I was fairly newly out, 14 or 15, I was approached in the Wimpy Bar by an old woman, she was probably 25 maybe even 35, anyway, really old. She said that she was a fashion designer, could have been bullshitting, but I absolutely 100% believed her. She sat there gushing about individuality, the expressiveness of the clothes, the balance of shape, the mixture of the masculine and the feminine, the relationship between the accessories, clothes and make-up, the humour (the bitch), the balls. Then she asked if I minded if she took some notes and did a couple of sketches – I didn't. She got me to describe other parts of my wardrobe – it was awful, talking about me and my clothes for twenty minutes, I really struggled. Her sketches didn't contain enough detail for me, more like instructions or a plan, but they were really good and really quick.

We certainly carried around sticks to poke people's homophobia, when homophobia was visible, dominant, acceptable behaviour. We asked questions of preconceptions, prejudices, boys didn't have to be boyish and girls didn't have to be girly. Just because someone dressed like a queen didn't mean that he couldn't kick like a mule. A girl might have short-cropped hair and monkey boots but that didn't mean she wasn't female. If a boy wore make-up and 'effeminate' clothing he may still be able to service all the young women lusting after him. A punk or a freak could be the first there helping the old man who'd fallen over or defending a youngster getting bullied. Querying the connotations.

Snogging hard-looking, male punks, with tongues, in the youthy, just because we could.

I suppose it is easy to think that the punks and especially the dandies were transitory, leaving no real trail. But we opened up our world, broadened attitudes. The social effects upon understanding, tolerance, personal freedom and empowerment are impossible to measure but I think it is at least double what you think it is. You cannot remove the aftershock, it may diminish but it moves on, expanding circles through time. Who knows? In a couple of hundred years' time some kid may read this, or see 'The Book With No Name' and be influenced as I was influenced by my imaginings of Temple Newsam.

Adding a bit of verve and colour into our surroundings, a bit of fun, we were apart from, did not mirror them but pointed at otherness. Turned heads and minds, making other people's idiosyncrasies seem more acceptable, less extreme. More personal things or traits were possible, more tolerable. Opening paths, easing transitions and access. We usually stood our ground; if there was no insurmountable, acute threat we always stood our ground, some stood their ground no matter what the odds.

We were hedonists but, in a strange way, apart from capitalism. Obviously we consumed but mass-produced fashion was something we would never have gone near unless it was to deform, fuck with the index, the association. As long as we could party, we didn't much care about other things, other consumables. All we needed was access to the means of musical/cultural reproduction, distortion or creation and we were happy.

It was about personal power, pushing out boundaries. It was about the moment, that moment. About not sitting back and passively watching the world evolve around you. Yes, I can see a teenager with an over-inflated ego, and perhaps I did think I was the centre of somewhere, maybe I was. But which teenager, if life allows, doesn't think the world revolves around them? Their world does. That's where they are, at the centre of the world ready to try to move and shape it, alter the future. I, and people like me, did change the world, maybe a minuscule shift but a shift nonetheless. Society is completely different now and part of that change was down to us, the punks, the queers and the freaks.

Was it one of the many small developments in 'the individual' that evolved through the twentieth century and will appear to dominate the twenty-first? Were we the youthful, 1970s face of social capitalism, even though we all thought we were socialists?

In line with all adults, no matter how I try, I cannot understand current youth culture, because it is not my culture. Youth culture doesn't seem to contain 'the individual' now. Is that the capitalist con of appearing to be giving us a thousand choices whilst dictating which ones we will make? As I was growing up in Leeds, Yorkshire, England, getting to the jumble sale early and seeing how you could adapt the old ladies hat were Queen, now conformity and prescribed consumerism seem King. I'm not saying it's good or bad, it just *is*.

A million opportunities and I definitely didn't take some important ones but I'm still here breathing and I'm still happy. I've certainly been profligate but what matters in life?

Yes there's a mould for life but you can chip away at the stone. And yes you may feel trapped but don't forget Cool Hand Luke, he may have got killed but he ate a lot of eggs on the way.

You have to grab your life while you can, there is no destiny.

I had good friends and a sex life that your average teenager couldn't even imagine. I seemed to gain the respect of people who I would have wanted it from. I had a lot of fun, a lot of laughs and dollops of euphoria.

In some situations you stood out and did not gain acceptance but it was usually from people whose acceptance counted for shit. Football is about many things but one of them is belonging. In the late '70s and early '80s that camaraderie wasn't quite there for me at football matches, just a crowd with a gap in which I'd stand. Me and my girly clothes, smudged make-up from the night before. I used to love the fucked up look of last nights make-up and having gone home with a stranger the night before gave me the excuse that I hadn't been home and changed. I had as much right to be there as anyone else, nobody's passion for Leeds United was more intense than mine, just as mine was no more intense than many others.

The lads I'd go with were very brave and sometimes answered me from five feet behind, just in case I shouted any louder and drew attention to myself. That was a weird place, the bear pit, which is what it was, really rough, really, really worst side of male. It was like they had built a big pile of 'ists' that they'd piss on while trying to hit the lines-man with a coin. The Kop at Elland Rd at that time was the 'wild north' but wilder and with an absence of anyone as effeminate as John Wayne, except for me. Strangely, I remember a lot of weird looks but not a single comment, my commitment to the badge seemed enough excuse. Had they seen me out Saturday night in town, and not recognised me from the football, there would have been a scene.

We brought a few more people on and put the fear in a whole lot more.

We could not hide, we did not want to hide, our reference points were obscure, people did not understand, could not contextualise. We ran counter to the dominant cultures, to accepted modes of behaviour, to our surroundings. We didn't often move around in groups, we arrived at places in which we congregated but that implies a journey, we had to get there, frequently, alone. I had it fairly easy: some people, every time they stepped out of their front door were deep in red-neck territory and had to negotiate their way to safety through the enemy lines. Arriving unscathed through hostile terrain was, for all of us, often a relief and an achievement.

Our humour was not to be underestimated – I lost count of the number of times that I agreed with aggressive bullies, employing the first rule of jousting, surprise: 'I know I look like a cunt, what a bummer, queer bastard, not a proper bloke.' Often knowing that I'd have had sex with more women in the last fortnight then they would in their entire lifetime. Not many women wanted to shag red-necks. At that time, they wanted to shag pretty, young boys in make-up called Mick. These self-put-downs left them nowhere to go except confusion central, and by the time they came to terms with the fact that I wasn't arguing or seemingly scared, I was usually past the danger.

The second option was the cocky-taunt routine. The big, 40-year-old bull elephants whose idea of a good night out was a skinful of beer and a fight, often couldn't resist shouting, 'Queer cunt.' The last thing they expected was for the nancy boy to shout back, 'Shut up, you fat bastard!' This manoeuvre required space to run and taunt and run, 'What? You think y' c'n catch me y' fat fuck? Look at y', y' c'n 'ardly walk. Ay, fatty, keep chasing mi and when y' coughing y' guts up in the gutter I'll sneak up behind you and batter y', y'whale.'

What did they see, the bullies, young and old? An effeminate, gentle, girly puff, mincing through their streets, posh and soft. Their expectation loaded another weapon that came in handy. The 'lay the Leeds accent on thick as mud and turn, growling and spitting aggression' routine. It was the last thing they expected and usually left them shaking with shock, brain screaming, 'Fuck! What is this?' Their three brain cells all trying manically to decipher and make sense of the information but arguing instead. I always had an escape route if it was dangerous, the aggression was just an act; buy time, suss the situation, and prepare to run. But I often walked away from people I felt I could handle with comments like, 'Just get on with it. Stop talking about it, do it, because I'm walking.'

Not dominated by the vagaries of fashion, we looked and lived how we believed we should and not how we were instructed by the music press/media/fashion industry. I've only been inside my head, so I can't speak for a whole movement but for me, the whole coming out in complete isolation was such a socially dangerous thing to do that it gave me unexpected freedom. Nothing else that I might do could come anywhere near the risk that was coming out on my own. I was emancipated from the need to be 'cool', I could look or behave any way I chose without it impacting on my street cred.

There was no doubt that what I had done was seen, within the majority of my peer group, as brave and genuine, I was the antithesis of a shallow poser, I meant it and my sincerity or motivation was almost unquestionable. As a consequence it was simply accepted if, sandwiched in-between 'The Clash' and 'The Damned' written on my white beetle crushers, was 'The Dooleys'. You couldn't get anymore girly mainstream than 'The Dooleys'. They had produced one poptastic single, 'We Are The Chosen Few', I liked one song. It was amusing to put them alongside growling youth culture that I loved, it made people smile and furrow their brow. I was laughing at myself and our youth culture.

It was also a clear challenge to anyone stupid enough to question my 'authenticity', a snare waiting to snag some dumb, elitist animal.

On a subtler level, I was questioning these strongly held and socially agreed 'authentic' signs, the elitism of people aligning themselves with the street cool or obscure and using it as a way to look down on other people, as not real, not authentic, simply posers. I was being a snadge aberrant, 'I'm not really street cool, just a stiff who got lucky – no cultural capital here.'

Everyone has got soul, and my soul is no deeper than yours just as yours is no deeper than mine.

I was the first 'coming out' that I knew of, though there were obviously people out, just not in my area, and for credibility, longevity counted. Paradoxically, someone could have been a punk or a dandy for two minutes and yet be more the essence of that movement, that attitude, than someone who had seen and classified themselves as such for years.

28

Even the gods can fall and graze their knees; Bowie didn't fall, I tripped him.

Before I start I need to say, I am David Bowie and he is me. My influence on David Bowie was not that big but it was definite and poignant, making him face up to some fundamental things about himself and the nature of his universe. I had the man, the big guy, in my sights, like an alky pouring vodka down a sink.... Sorry, I need to rewind.

A small sweaty venue in Leeds, The Town and Country Club, mid '90s. These gigs had not been publicised, it was mainly word of mouth, but David was returning to his roots, connecting with the real, the loyal fans. I cannot remember how much people were offering for tickets outside but it was a lot. The numbers were stripped of meaning, no one would sell a ticket for such a personal audience with David, he was stepping into our front room. As we entered the room, I kissed my wife, it was her shrewdness that had got us the tickets. The place was buzzing. Dale (remember? The scourge of the red-neck bullies?) was there, with a woman in a wheelchair. It was lovely to see him, and Shep. Giddy excitement hung in the air, long-lost friends embracing. The increase in electricity in the ether meant that David was close to the stage and it transformed into a magnet, ending conversations and dragging the people to it.

I had a plan, I was calm and focused, my wife said, 'Come on Mick, we need to move or we won't be able to see anything.'

'Vicky, this is the most important gig of our lives, do you think I would blow it? Trust me, I've got it sussed.'

'But they're ten deep at the front already, we need to get in there or we'll be stuck right at the back; you're not tall Mick.'

'Vicky, the bar is clear, get another drink, the time is not yet upon us.'

'But Mick—'

'Do you trust me?'

'Yes, but–'

'Do you really trust me?'

'Yes but look, they're fifteen deep at the front now.'

'So, unless you trust me we will have a crap view at the most important gig of our lives. The timing has got to be perfect.' After a few minutes I said, 'Come on Vic, this is it.'

There was a large cab (speaker) in the middle of the room, on a platform, pushed up against a railing. The sound man was about 40 feet away, he was about to 'do' David Bowie. David Bowie, y'know, like proper Rock 'n' Roll royalty. In the Rock 'n' Roll hierarchy, you could put Bowie next to anyone – how good would this look on the sound man's CV? I whistled over to him and waved but he was panicking over buttons, dials and sliders that were perfectly positioned, checking and double checking. A bloke next to him was looking over, I looked at him, pointed at the sound guy and nodded, he pointed at the sound guy, raised his eyebrows, and I nodded. He prodded the sound guy and pointed. I had to get this right, I held our drinks high in the air, clearly placing them somewhere safe and climbed up on top of the cab and then shrugged, nodded my head in a persuasive manner and gave him the thumbs up. He nodded in a 'Yeh, whatever, can't you see I'm busy?' kind of way and I pulled Vicky up.

My God, it was better then I thought, we were six feet above the crowd, 25 feet away from the stage. As the lights went down Vicky looked at me and grinned with 'You little rascal, I knew there was a reason I loved you' dancing in her eyes.

He opened with 'Quicksand' (*Hunky Dory*, '71) – just him and a guitar; phew wee…what a song, what a performance. We were way above the crowd, in complete comfort, right in David's eye-line. He was constantly looking and smiling at us, so close that I could have gobbed on him; after a few minutes' deliberation I decided not to. I was fighting a Dooleys moment and only just winning. Sometimes I have an overbearing urge to be inappropriate. To me, there was the ultimate cultural untouchable standing before me, the coolest man on earth, doing what he does best, hanging slap-bang in his element. My defining youth-culture icon, my soul. All around me people just like me were rejoicing, he was in complete control, the audience held in his mesmeric aura – I could resist no longer.

Using my girliest, high-pitched voice with a definite comic undertone, slowly letting it trail off, break and deepen at the end as if I was on the verge of tears, I shouted,

'David……I love – yoooou.'

I could not believe what happened next – he lost it. Staring into my eyes, he'd gone, words forgotten, grasping at reality, more than 30 years of legendary stage-craft lost, looking at band members for his location in the universe. For a moment I'd brought Bowie down into the realms of the mortal. Then dreaded realisation slivered across his face, battering any chance of him recovering the situation – 'It used to be gorgeous young women offering themselves and now it's fat, forty-year-old men, with crap eighties haircuts. What has happened to me? When did that happen? Fuck, have I lost it?'

David, sorry, you did lose it, for those moments you were naked and alone with only the image of my fat, smiling face and your mortality for company, reassessing your role and place in the cosmos. Like the rest of us you will die and it's awful, but as compensation know this: when I die I'll have had at least as much fun as you. Do you feel better? Also, if you die first I'll be very sad for a long time. David, I'd like to thank you for stirring my soul and sometimes reminding me that I'm alive.

He composed himself, and didn't look in my direction for the rest of the gig, which was an achievement as I was right in his eye-line. I'd blown the smiling approval of the one I love, of David Bowie. I could have died having received the smiling approval of David Bowie, but that's OK, I didn't expect that we'd get on anyway, who likes uncontrollable giddiness? That gig was *the* gig of a lifetime, a 'waking for the milk-round when it's not your day' happening. He was so there, so relaxed, warm and radiant, genuine and soulful. I was honoured and grateful.

My influence on David Bowie was not that big but it was definite and poignant, making him face up to some fundamental things about himself and the nature of his universe, his mortal soul.

One of the shocking things about the gig was that, in between songs, he was telling long, humorous stories, like a stand-up comedian. Damn it, he *was* a stand-up comedian. He was really funny, belting timing syncopating bizarre monologues. He loved it, he was really enjoying himself. One story he started with, 'I have performed this song in so many different ways but you will never guess which song it is....' Surely he knew that you should never challenge Vicky like that – she immediately shouted '"Stay".' His shoulders dropped, his face screwed up and he sighed long and deep, his favourite story, the funniest routine lay slaughtered before him, he smiled graciously and mumbled, 'Yeh, "Stay".'

Totally deflated, he looked over at Earl Slick, raised his eyes and shrugged; Earl hit the riff and his special moment was gone forever.

He loved us, Bowie – me and Vicky – you could tell; kept inviting us round for tea.

What about 'disappearing behind a door' girl? We slowly drifted apart, she moved to London, a town a couple of hundred miles south of Leeds. Lived with various friends and boyfriends – we kept in touch as best we could but life takes over. She always came to gigs I was doing in London and got in touch when she returned to Leeds to visit her mother and we'd meet up.

She came back one Christmas, contacted me and we went for a night out. In the past our messing had been sporadic, fumbled, slightly nervous affairs. This evening we were both excited to see each other, we were relaxed and babbled endlessly. The thought hadn't entered my head that she was going to take me like a woman. She'd seen more of life. For the first time, with me, she was confident and forward, a powerful young woman who knew what she wanted and was going to get it. She had fully discovered her sexuality and was extremely comfortable with it. It shone out of her, she glowed and wanted to light me up. It was a lifetime moment, a 'waking for the milk-round when it's not your day' moment. She was the sexiest woman I had ever experienced. Years of repressed emotional and sexual tension flew through our fingertips, it was a glorious union, rarely experienced in a lifetime.

We were honoured and grateful. Afterwards we smugly giggled and went again. We couldn't experience this euphoria another time as she was returning to London the following morning and I was just about to embark on a 'serious' relationship. But with 'slotting a key into a lock' girl it was a marvellous moment, a matching odd socks kinda moment, a finding a wild flower grasping at tarmac in the middle of a busy car park kinda moment.

So in my time of stalking some of the mean streets of Leeds, dressed like a freak, in an aggressive time, I wasn't beaten senseless once. I had hairy incidents, threats and taunts, but nobody stepped up to the mark in reaction to my appearance. 'Appen I didn't realise how generous the Yorkshire spirit was. Were people more accepting than I'd given them credit for or just slightly wary of the unknown, the different, the freak? I know that there were people who could have easily beaten me to shit but chose not to. Perhaps the first Teddy Boy in west Sheffield, twenty-odd years earlier, didn't get beaten shitless either.

There's nowt s'strange as folk.

This was just a bit of a journey really, no great departures or arrivals, no huge happenings. A series of short stories or incidents. The plot didn't twist and turn or even thicken, but rarely does a life. Most lives don't really have a plot, they just meander through time and space, picking through the small happenings of a small life. We think lives are supposed to be exciting but that's because us normal folk get battered by the exceptional, incredible happenings, the exciting lives of the successful or interesting. Lives have events, but rarely do these combine to create a thrilling plot, just times of empathy, sympathy, excitement, despair, ecstasy, shame, humour, depression, surprise or predictability.

I've shared with you small incidents and a slow movement through a strange period of an ordinary life, lived to the full for those seven summers, autumns, eight winters and springs. Autumn is my favourite time of year so 'appen I'll enjoy my maturity but hopefully I can, on occasion, touch that teenager, still me.

Coming down off a trip, on a wet lawn, listening to the water seep into ground, run down bark and drip through cracks. Look at the leaves start to stretch in appreciation, the grass pricking up. Witnessing the water's magical powers, refreshing the world. Rain dropping from my nose into my open mouth, moistening the back of my throat and reminding me of essence. Feeling the slow throb of the world tight with the liquid beat of my blood.

I can smell the chemical reaction of water and earth. The pungent odour of nutrients leaching from soil to root. Ground layering the tree with its hard casing and sprouting delicately from its extremities. I can feel my roots sucking in the nutrients of Leeds, Yorkshire, England, and the strengths of the people of Leeds, Yorkshire, England, whom I love.

The sun is skimming the top of the school roof, exploding through windows that focus its intensity. I hold a calmness that I treasure. Time is still. I am conscious that I should log this moment (this artistic streak spoils everything). The heat penetrates my skin and warms my bones, freeing chemicals that sweep back and glow up through pores, precipitation soaking my being in goodness, in the certainty of blind faith. I bask in these five minutes of life when I am ecstatic. I am not ecstatic because I have just had the best shag of my life. I am not ecstatic because Leeds have won the title. I am not ecstatic because I've just passed the twenty-minutes-after-fungus mark. I am simply ecstatic. My mind is so clear and focused that it

211

heats and powers my soul. Tomorrow belongs to me. I love my world, I love my future.

Now to get on with the rest of my life – I hope it's as colourful as the first quarter.

The wind is blasting through my face and hair, blowing away the irrelevant, leaving only the essence of life. The beast sweats below me, thundering through the periphery. This is familiar, this is family. The everyday routine of recognised rock faces, shrubs, plants and plumes of dust. My excitement is growing as I get closer to the people I love. My children are so close that I can smell their skin. I am hot and cold, full of joy, twenty seconds from the open arms of my world, the full contented belly, full of love. Just around this jutting outcrop is my life.

'Mick.'

'No.'

'Mick.'

'Ssh, Go away.'

'Mick.'

The world is about to change.

'MIIII-I-I-CK.'

I love my life.

'MIIII-I-I-CK.'

But I have to leave it now.

'WHAT?'

Shit, I'm not really returning to the ones I love, my friends and family in the woods. I am in fact tripping in The Warehouse with my face in the huge fan.

'Have you seen Billy?'

'What?'

'Have you seen Billy?'

'What?'

'HAVE YOU SEEN BILLY?'

'Have you really just deprived me of a wife and children, a mother, a father – no wait a minute he wasn't there – just to ask me that?'

'What?'

'Nothing. Billy? Have I seen Billy? How would I have seen Billy riding across the North American plains? What would he be doing there?'

'What are you talking about, the North American plains? You've just had your face in the blower for the last ten minutes.'

'So how the fuck am I going to have seen Billy?'

'Have you seen him?'

'Kim, I love you, but fuck off.'

'Get lost y'stupid get, there's no need to be rude.'

'OK, OK, no sorry, I haven't seen Billy. I haven't seen Billy because I've just been horse riding with my face in a huge fan for the last hour, now please, don't take offence, can we lose the whereabouts of Billy?'

'So you haven't seen him?'

'NO. NO. NO. I haven't seen Billy.'

'Alright, there's no need to be like that, y'grumpy twassock. When did you last see him?'

'About two days ago, he was rapping all night about a suicide, how he's going to kick it in the head when he's twenty-five but I think that's just speed jive. I don't want to stay alive when I'm twenty-five. And I haven't, definitely have not, seen Lucy.'

'Who the fuck is Lucy?'

'Y'don't know Lucy? She's been stealing clothes from unlocked cars.'

'Has she? Well people shouldn't leave their cars open, should they? What does she look like?'

'Who?'

'Lucy.'

'Don't know, never met her.'

'You're off y'fucking trough you are.'

49 – 60 – 114

213

Song Lyrics:

If you borrowed this book off a mate and enjoyed it, buy your own – y'cheating get. I'm not fucking Madonna or Richard Branson. The copy you buy will mean I can spend an extra 20 minutes writing instead of labouring for a builder. I prefer writing. Think of yourself as my patron.

Also available from Armley Press:

**Hot Knife –
Love bullets and revenge
in Leeds, Yorkshire, England
By John Lake
ISBN: 978-0955469916**

Lightning Source UK Ltd.
Milton Keynes UK
UKHW040958300819
348826UK00001B/94/P